BASIC LETTER & MEMO WRITING

H

Susie H. VanHuss, Ph.D.
Executive Director, University Foundations
and Distinguished Professor Emeritus
University of South Carolina
Columbia, South Carolina

THOMSON
★
SOUTH-WESTERN

Australia · Canada · Mexico · Singapore · Spain · United Kingdom · United States

THOMSON

SOUTH-WESTERN

Basic Letter & Memo Writing, 5th Edition

Susie H. VanHuss, Ph.D.

VP/Editorial Director:
Jack W. Calhoun

VP/Editor-in-Chief:
Dave Shaut

Senior Publisher:
Karen Schmohe

Acquisitions Editor:
Jane Phelan

Project Manager:
Dr. Inell Bolls

Consulting Editor:
Elaine Langlois

VP/Director of Marketing:
Carol Volz

Marketing Manager:
Lori Pegg

Marketing Coordinator:
Georgianna Wright

Editor:
Kim Kusnerak

Production Manager:
Tricia Matthews Boies

Sr. Print Buyer:
Charlene Taylor

Production House:
GGS Information Services

Printer:
Edwards Brothers
Ann Arbor, Michigan

Sr. Designer:
Mike Stratton

Cover/Internal Designer:
Mike Stratton

Cover Images:
Digital Vision

Permissions Editor:
Linda Ellis

Photo Researcher:
Deanna Ettinger

Microsoft and PowerPoint are registered trademarks of Microsoft Corporation in the United States and/or other countries.

The names of all products mentioned herein are used for identification purposes only and may be trademarks or registered trademarks of their respective owners. South-Western disclaims any affiliation, association, connection with, sponsorship, or endorsement by such owners.

CONTENTS

Basic Letter & Memo Writing

Keyboarding & Formatting Essentials

VanHuss/Forde/Woo (0-538-72757-8, 0-538-72774-8)

This brand new series introduces the keyboarding and formatting skills most important for career success. The *Essentials Series* uses proven learning techniques and skillbuilding applications to guide users from the basics of new-key learning to mastery of advanced formatting using the functions of Word 2002 or Word 2003.

Basic English Review

Schachter/Schneiter (0-538-72720-9)

The eighth edition of this popular text takes a unique and time-proven approach to understanding the fundamentals of English. This user-friendly text and CD package motivates learners with activities focused on grammar, punctuation, spelling, vocabulary, and writing skills.

Business Applications with Microsoft Word

VanHuss/Forde/Woo (0-538-72549-4, 0-538-72756-X *hard cover*)

A simulated company serves as the overall structure for this one-of-a-kind text. Realistic workplace challenges integrate business vocabulary, critical-thinking strategies, and Web research skills into the instruction of document processing. The project-based applications reinforce the full range of word processing features and provide over 150 assignments.

Integrated Business Projects

Olinzock/Arney/Skean (0-538-72761-6)

All Core and many Expert level Microsoft Office competencies are incorporated into this revision. Project-based applications reinforce computer applications, document formats, and workforce skills within a business setting. New topics include multimedia, Web-page development, computer concepts, and skillbuilding drills.

Join us on the Internet at www.swlearning.com

THOMSON
SOUTH-WESTERN

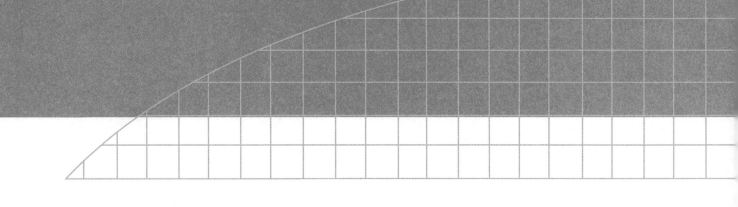

THE FOCUS IS CLEAR

COMMUNICATION – A FRESH APPROACH

The Fifth Edition of *Basic Letter & Memo Writing* has a brand-new look and new features to grab your attention and help you become the effective writer you want to be.

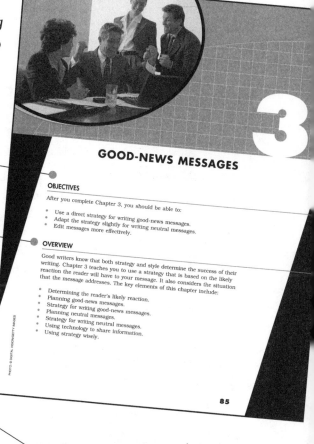

GOOD-NEWS MESSAGES

OBJECTIVES

After you complete Chapter 3, you should be able to:

- Use a direct strategy for writing good-news messages.
- Adapt the strategy slightly for writing neutral messages.
- Edit messages more effectively.

OVERVIEW

Good writers know that both strategy and style determine the success of their writing. Chapter 3 teaches you to use a strategy that is based on the likely reaction the reader will have to your message. It also considers the situation that the message addresses. The key elements of this chapter include:

- Determining the reader's likely reaction.
- Planning good-news messages.
- Strategy for writing good-news messages.
- Planning neutral messages.
- Strategy for writing neutral messages.
- Using technology to share information.
- Using strategy wisely.

PHOTO: © DIGITAL VISION/GETTY IMAGES

85

OBJECTIVES—allow you to look ahead to what you will be learning and to pace your work.

OVERVIEW—gives you a clear perspective on the elements you will be studying in the chapter.

"Business Talk"

Communicating effectively requires you to understand and use appropriate vocabulary in a business setting. Look for the following terms in this chapter. Review the terms and their definitions. Remember, some words have more than one meaning.

Brainstorming—a freewheeling approach to generating as many ideas as possible. Critical evaluation of the ideas does not occur until after the brainstorming process.

Coherence—the quality of being linked logically to each other. Related ideas, for example, can have coherence.

Empathy—placing yourself mentally in the reader's position.

Guide—a recommended or suggested way of writing. It is not an inflexible rule that can never be violated.

Jargon—terms used in a particular industry but not generally known by outsiders.

BUSINESS TALK—introduces you to terms that are commonly used in business so you will understand and use them correctly.

These are not the only sources of jobs, however. In fact, employment specialists estimate that only about one-third of all jobs are advertised in the newspaper or posted with agencies. Two-thirds of jobs may be in what is often called the hidden job market. The higher the level and pay for a job, the more likely it is to be part of the hidden job market.

Success Tip
Networking to discover jobs in the hidden job market may be the best career skill to learn.

Two of the best ways to find out about jobs in the hidden job market are to talk to knowledgeable individuals and to read specialized publications. Well-informed people in a field are most likely to know about jobs that are available in that field.

Many people have no idea how to go about **networking** for job information. You can start by listing people you know who might be able to provide you with information about jobs. The more names you list, the better your chances of getting a contact. Friends, relatives, parents' friends, instructors, business associates (such as bankers, lawyers, doctors, and association members), and any other contacts you can think of are all potential sources of job information. A friendly letter or telephone call letting these people know you are in the job market and telling them you value their advice may be all you need for someone to suggest that you contact a particular company.

Specialized publications are journals, brochures, newsletters, and other communications that are read by people in certain fields. For example, publications are designed for bankers, insurance agents, computer programmers, and other occupations. You can obtain these publications from a local library, the Internet, or local employees who work in those occupations.

If you search only advertised sources or agencies, you may miss out on the best opportunities. If you are willing to devote the time and energy necessary to search for the best possible job, you are much more likely to find it.

TECHNOLOGY AND EMPLOYMENT

Both employers and individuals seeking jobs can use technology to great advantage in the employment process. Job seekers must understand the technology that companies use to ensure that their applications are considered.

Technology Connections
Input Technologies
Many options exist today for entering text and data for messages. While the keyboard and mouse remain the dominant input technologies, other digital tools are also used. Tablet PCs, personal digital assistants (PDAs), wireless telephones, scanners, pagers, digital cameras, and speech recognition all provide ways to enter text and data. Regardless of the input tools, proofreading and editing are still critical skills needed to produce high-quality messages.

CRISP AND EASY TO FOLLOW

Strong examples, concrete suggestions, and easy-to-follow instructions will help you learn the basics first and then apply what you have learned to solve a problem and communicate that information effectively.

TECHNOLOGY CONNECTIONS—emphasize the impact technology has on both the quality of communications and the manner in which they are distributed. You will understand and use technology to create, process, and produce communications.

SUCCESS TIPS—provide pointers to help you be successful in your career.

GLOBAL CONNECTIONS—acquaint you with issues confronting companies that market their goods and services internationally and strive to work with people from diverse backgrounds.

...y phrases	Efficient words
...resent time	currently or now
...he fact that	because
...appropriate manner	appropriately
...mount of	for
...near future	soon

...y Essential Modifiers
...are words, phrases, or clauses that describe, limit, or qualify another ...group of words. Modifiers should be used when they add variety or con-... the message in other ways. Some words, however, should not be quali-... stand alone. Examples of words that should not be qualified follow:

...ords that stand alone	Inappropriate modifiers
...ooperate	cooperate together
...novation	new innovation
...aximum	maximum possible
...merge	merge together
...repeat	repeat again
...vert	revert back

...mize the Use of Descriptive Words
...riptive words should be used when they clarify information. Some descriptive ...s contribute nothing of value to the sentence. They should be eliminated to ...ce message length and wordiness. For example, when writing about New York, ...nguishing between the city and the state is important. Therefore, it may be ...ntial to say the state of New York to distinguish the state from the city of New ...s. However, saying the city of New Orleans wastes space and adds nothing of ...ae. Note the following examples of unnecessary descriptive words:

Use	Wasted descriptive words
. . . box is square	. . . box is square in shape
. . . in Ohio	. . . in the state of Ohio
. . . 10 pounds	. . . 10 pounds in weight
. . . 40 pages	. . . 40 pages in length

Sentences containing extra descriptive words are correct. The words simply are ...wasted because the meaning is clear without them. Some additional words may be ...used to add variety. Overuse of descriptive words creates wordy communications.

Clear examples teach you the difference between weak and strong writing.

Points to Remember summarize the key strategies you have learned in the chapter.

Global Connections
Ethics
Do ethics differ from culture to culture? That is a very difficult question to answer. Rules for conducting business vary from one culture to another. What is legal in one country may not be legal in another country. Child labor laws and human rights issues are two examples. While companies and their employees have to be flexible and sensitive to cultural differences, employees should not have to compromise their integrity or morals. Sincerity and honesty are important regardless of cultural differences. If a severe ethical conflict exists, then the whole issue of doing business in that particular culture needs to be examined.

that led to the problem is provided. Background information is particularly useful when the reader is not familiar with the reasons for studying the problem. Care must be taken not to repeat information the reader already knows.

Methods
Methods consist of a brief statement indicating where and how you obtained the information used to solve the problem.

Data Analysis
The data analysis consist...

...sed to solve the ...an interpretation of ...**ualitative** (judgment) ...sed to analyze data. ...tative data might be

...lysis
...ting using the ...scale from 1 ...est and 1 as.

...n? ___
...ive? ___

! Points to Remember

About Employment Communications

☑ Having a good employment strategy is essential. A well-planned, thorough job search is much more likely to produce good results than a disorganized, half-hearted effort.

☑ As a job seeker, you should determine your interests, strengths, and weaknesses; what you want to do; the types of jobs you are qualified for; the kind of work environment you prefer; and where and how you will find a job.

☑ Networking is one of the best ways to find out about jobs on the hidden job market.

☑ Understand and use technology effectively in your job search.

☑ The Internet has extensive information about the employment process. Use it especially to research companies before applying for a job.

☑ A résumé is a summary of your education, qualifications, and work experience.

☑ Many companies scan résumés. Therefore, you should learn how to prepare a scannable résumé.

☑ A chronological résumé works best for individuals who have a record of successful work experience over a number of years.

☑ A functional résumé works best for individuals who have limited work experience or who are changing careers.

☑ The information you choose to present in a résumé and the way you organize it should be designed to showcase your strengths.

☑ The goal of an application letter is to persuade the employer to interview you.

☑ A good strategy for writing an application letter is to establish a point of contact, specify the type of job you seek, highlight your major qualifications and strengths and show how they match job requirements, refer to your résumé, and request an interview.

☑ Always write a thank-you letter after an interview. Use it to reinforce your strengths and show how they match the job requirements.

☑ Select references who will give you a good recommendation, and request their permission before providing their names.

☑ Use the good-news strategy to accept job offers. Use the bad-news strategy to decline job offers, and do so gracefully.

PROVEN, PRACTICAL, AND REALISTIC ACTIVITIES

End-of-chapter activities provide extensive practice in language arts, communication, and editing principles.

CASE STUDY—provides a scenario that allows you to utilize your decision-making skills in a "what if" situation to solve a problem.

TEAM AND INTERNET ACTIVITIES—provide practice in skills required in the workplace.

MASTERY CHECK—a list of questions to check your knowledge of the chapter.

EDITING AND LANGUAGE ARTS—reinforces writing principles to ensure messages are error-free.

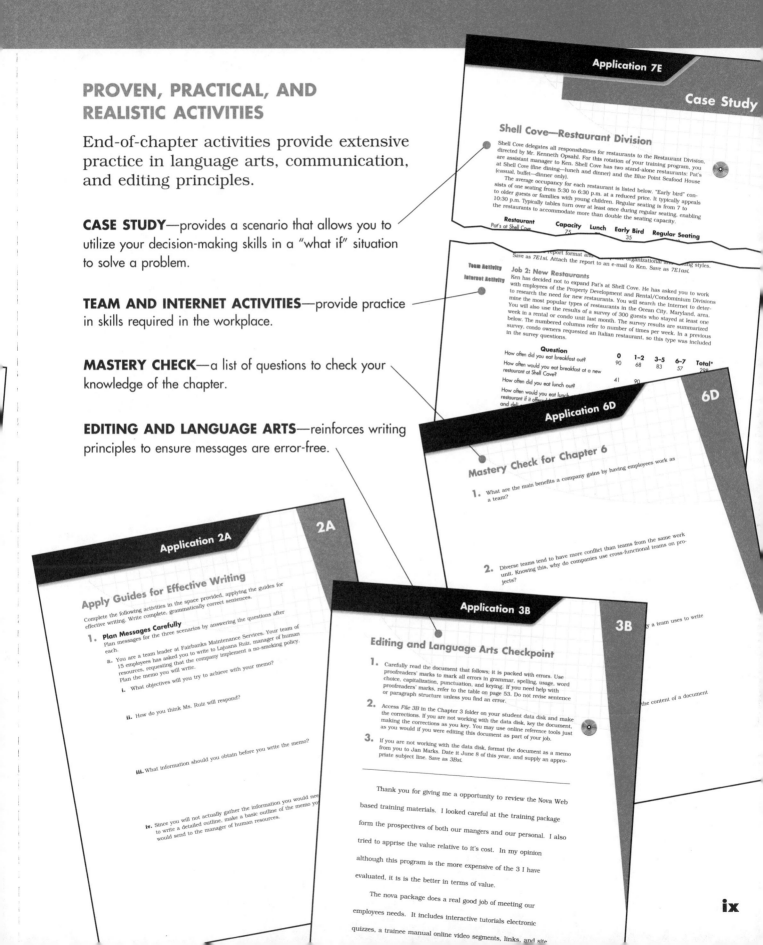

Application 7E
Case Study

Shell Cove—Restaurant Division

Shell Cove delegates all responsibilities for restaurants to the Restaurant Division, directed by Mr. Kenneth Opsahl. For this rotation of your training program, you are assistant manager to Ken. Shell Cove has two stand-alone restaurants: Pat's at Shell Cove (fine dining—lunch and dinner) and the Blue Point Seafood House (casual, buffet—dinner only).

The average occupancy for each restaurant is listed below. "Early bird" consists of one seating from 5:30 to 6:30 p.m. at a reduced price. It typically appeals to older guests or families with young children. Regular seating is from 7 to 10:30 p.m. Typically tables turn over at least once during regular seating, enabling the restaurants to accommodate more than double the seating capacity.

Restaurant	Capacity	Lunch	Early Bird	Regular Seating
Pat's at Shell Cove	75		35	

...report format and... the organizational and... ing styles.
Save as 7E1sl. Attach the report to an e-mail to Ken. Save as 7E1asi.

Team Activity
Internet Activity

Job 2: New Restaurants
Ken has decided not to expand Pat's at Shell Cove. He has asked you to work with employees of the Property Development and Rental/Condominium Divisions to research the need for new restaurants. You will search the Internet to determine the most popular types of restaurants in the Ocean City, Maryland, area. You will also use the results of a survey of 300 guests who stayed at least one week in a rental or condo unit last month. The survey results are summarized below. The numbered columns refer to number of times per week. In a previous survey, condo owners requested an Italian restaurant, so this type was included in the survey questions.

Question	0	1–2	3–5	6–7	Total*
How often did you eat breakfast out?	90	68	83	57	298
How often would you eat breakfast at a new restaurant at Shell Cove?					
How often did you eat lunch out?	41	90			
How often would you eat lunch... restaurant if it offered... and del...					

Application 6D
6D

Mastery Check for Chapter 6

1. What are the main benefits a company gains by having employees work as a team?

2. Diverse teams tend to have more conflict than teams from the same work unit. Knowing this, why do companies use cross-functional teams on projects?

...y a team uses to write

Application 2A
2A

Apply Guides for Effective Writing

Complete the following activities in the space provided, applying the guides for effective writing. Write complete, grammatically correct sentences.

1. **Plan Messages Carefully**
   Plan messages for the three scenarios by answering the questions after each.
   a. You are a team leader at Fairbanks Maintenance Services. Your team of 15 employees has asked you to write to Lajuana Ruiz, manager of human resources, requesting that the company implement a no-smoking policy. Plan the memo you will write.

   i. What objectives will you try to achieve with your memo?

   ii. How do you think Ms. Ruiz will respond?

   iii. What information should you obtain before you write the memo?

   iv. Since you will not actually gather the information you would nee... to write a detailed outline, make a basic outline of the memo yo... would send to the manager of human resources.

Application 3B
3B

Editing and Language Arts Checkpoint

1. Carefully read the document that follows; it is packed with errors. Use proofreaders' marks to mark all errors in grammar, spelling, usage, word choice, capitalization, punctuation, and keying. If you need help with proofreaders' marks, refer to the table on page 53. Do not revise sentence or paragraph structure unless you find an error.

2. Access *File 3B* in the Chapter 3 folder on your student data disk and make the corrections. If you are not working with the data disk, key the document, making the corrections as you key. You may use online reference tools just as you would if you were editing this document as part of your job.

3. If you are not working with the data disk, format the document as a memo from you to Jan Marks. Date it June 8 of this year, and supply an appropriate subject line. Save as 3Bsi.

...the content of a document

Thank you for giving me a opportunity to review the Nova Web based training materials. I looked careful at the training package form the prospectives of both our mangers and our personal. I also tried to apprise the value relative to it's cost. In my opinion although this program is the more expensive of the 3 I have evaluated, it is is the better in terms of value.

The nova package does a real good job of meeting our employees needs. It includes interactive tutorials electronic quizzes, a trainee manual online video segments, links, and site...

Success in virtually every career requires the ability to write effectively. The same can be said of success in education—if you have the ability to write well, you are very likely to be successful. *Basic Letter & Memo Writing, 5th edition*, will help you become a more effective writer. Not only are effective writing skills marketable, they are transferable; that is, the skills you develop in this course can be transferred to your first or your next position and to each new position as you progress in your career.

Learn to Write Effectively

Effective writing incorporates many subskills, such as planning, organizing, analyzing, evaluating, and decision making. In addition, organizations expect you to use correct grammar, spelling, and punctuation. With *Basic Letter & Memo Writing*, you will learn to:

- Communicate ideas clearly, accurately, and concisely using appropriate language.
- Improve your writing style and adapt it to meet the needs of the reader.
- Vary the approach you use based on the expected reader reaction and the situation.
- Employ creative strategies for solving business problems.
- Use effective editing and proofreading techniques to ensure your messages are error-free.
- Enhance the image of your documents with appropriate formatting.
- Collaborate and write as a team member.
- Use technology to create, process, and transmit documents.
- Be effective in communicating globally.

Master Writing Principles

Basic Letter & Memo Writing combines a problem-solving and a writing strategy to make it easy to learn the process of planning and writing high-quality business messages. You begin by mastering basic principles and then applying them to simple documents before progressing to more complex business documents. You will master the basic principles in the first two chapters. Then, in the remaining seven chapters, you will learn to apply them to specific writing situations.

Chapter 1—Effective Communication: Introduces ways that individuals and organizations communicate and examines factors that influence the effectiveness of communication. This chapter and the chapters that follow focus on excellence in communication.

Chapter 2—Ten Guides for Effective Writing: Presents, illustrates, and applies these ten basic writing guides: plan messages carefully; write for the reader; present ideas positively; write in a clear, readable style; check for completeness; use an efficient, action-oriented style; use concrete language; use effective sentence and paragraph structure; format documents effectively; and edit and proofread carefully.

Chapter 3—Good-News Messages: Stresses that both strategy and style determine the success of a message. This chapter presents the planning process and strategies for writing good-news and neutral messages.

Chapter 4—Bad-News Messages: Focuses on planning the best way to respond to bad-news situations. Presents both indirect and direct strategies for writing bad-news messages and a strategy for messages with both good and bad news.

Chapter 5—Persuasive Messages: Introduces ways to build credibility and strategies that use both logical and psychological appeals for writing persuasive messages. Stresses the importance of ethics in persuasion.

Chapter 6—Team Writing: Emphasizes the importance of working effectively as a team and presents strategies for team writing that will result in consistent, high-quality documents that read as if they have been written by one person.

Chapter 7—Letter and Memo Reports: Presents strategies for planning, organizing, and writing messages used for decision making and documentation.

Chapter 8—Goodwill Messages: Presents messages designed purely to build professional relationships and goodwill. Includes strategies for writing congratulatory, thank-you, and special occasion messages.

Chapter 9—Employment Communications: Views employment communications from the perspective of both the employer trying to hire effective employees and the individual seeking employment in a suitable position. Focuses on writing employment communications including chronological and functional résumés, application letters, and follow-up letters.

Produce High-Quality Results

The "learn and apply" approach used in *Basic Letter & Memo Writing* helps you develop confidence in both your ability to write effectively and your ability to solve problems. In business writing, you achieve high-quality results by solving a problem and communicating that information effectively to the reader. Both problem-solving and writing skills require you to learn the basics first and then to apply what you have learned in a creative way.

Each chapter is designed and organized to present small segments of new material followed by extensive application. This simple-to-complex approach makes learning easier and helps ensure that you will achieve good results.

Chapter Content

Each chapter includes the following items:

- Objectives—the competencies that you will develop by studying the materials carefully and completing the applications.

- Overview—a preview of the contents of the chapter.

- Business Talk—a section devoted to helping you understand and use appropriate vocabulary in a business setting.

- Chapter content—discussion of the topics in each chapter with full-page illustrations of formatting and document content.
- Global Connections—a feature on global issues as they relate to business communication.
- Technology Connections—a feature that will help you understand and use technology to produce effective business messages.
- Success Tips—pointers to help you be successful in your career.
- Points to Remember—a quick summary/reinforcement of the key points.

Chapter Applications

The applications for the first two chapters vary slightly from those in the remaining chapters. This is because these two chapters focus on basic principles, whereas the remaining chapters focus on applying the principles to specific messages.

Chapter 1 includes the following applications:

- Select the most appropriate media.
- Mastery check for the chapter.
- Shell Cove—an exciting and fun case study that is introduced in this chapter and continues with applications in every chapter.

Chapter 2 includes the following applications:

- Apply guides for effective writing.
- Editing and language arts checkpoint.
- Mastery check for the chapter.
- Shell Cove.

Chapters 3–9 include the following applications:

- Review guides for effective writing.
- Editing and language arts checkpoint.
- Write messages that apply the chapter content.
- Mastery check for the chapter.
- Shell Cove.

An evaluation guide is provided with Chapters 3–9 that both you and your instructor can use for evaluating the messages you write.

E-Book

Basic Letter & Memo Writing is also available in e-book format. Now you can access this text in a dynamic new way and take learning to a new level.

Appreciation

The author and publisher express their appreciation to the instructors who used the previous editions of this text and provided suggestions for improving the 5th edition. We especially thank the following instructors for reviewing the manuscript for this edition:

Sarah Durham
Instructor, Business Systems Technology
Tennessee Technology Center
Dickson, Tennessee

Melody Marlay
Business Instructor
Vatterott College
Springfield, Missouri

Susie H. VanHuss

EFFECTIVE COMMUNICATION

OBJECTIVES

After you complete Chapter 1, you should be able to:

- Select the best way to communicate.
- Assess styles of writing.
- Understand influences on writing.
- Use technology effectively.
- Develop a plan to improve your writing.

OVERVIEW

Chapter 1 introduces ways that individuals and organizations communicate and examines factors that influence the effectiveness of communication. This chapter and the chapters that follow focus on excellence in communication. The key elements of this chapter include:

- Viewing communication from the perspectives of the organization, the employee, and the reader.
- Determining the most effective way to communicate in a given situation.
- Understanding the impact of technology on communications.
- Recognizing factors that contribute to the cost and quality of communications.
- Understanding style and adapting your writing style to the reader's style.
- Understanding the process of writing and improving your writing skill.

"Business Talk"

Communicating effectively requires you to understand and use appropriate vocabulary in a business setting. Look for the following terms in this chapter. Review the terms and their definitions. Remember, some words have more than one meaning.

Medium (singular form; *media*, plural)—the way in which a message is communicated.

Organization—a structure, body, or group. Examples of organizations include businesses, clubs, government agencies, professional firms, and nonprofit groups.

Perspective—a point of view.

Recipient—the person who receives a communication.

Style—a pattern of behavior or characteristics.

Thesaurus—a reference tool that provides a list of words with similar definitions so that writers can select the best word to convey the meaning intended.

COMMUNICATION AT WORK

Effective communication is essential to the success of any **organization** and its employees. When things are going well, most people take effective communication for granted. However, when things go wrong, lack of communication or poor communication is often a major cause of the problem.

- From the **perspective** of the organization, effective communication achieves the company's goals. It presents the company to the public in a favorable way. It answers the needs of current customers and brings in new ones. It ensures that people within the organization have the information they need to do their jobs properly.

- From the perspective of the **recipient**, effective communication satisfies a need. Often, it is the need for information. Even if a need cannot be met, an effective communication will help the recipient understand why. Sometimes, effective communication may even persuade the recipient to do something the writer is suggesting.

- From the perspective of the employee (you), effective communication gives you the information you need to do your job to the best of your ability. It helps build good relationships with supervisors, customers, and fellow workers. It will serve you well in any position and will help you advance in your career. The ability to communicate effectively is essential to your success.

Effective communication does not just happen. It results from:

- Having a strong desire to communicate effectively.
- Being persistent in an effort to communicate effectively.
- Making wise choices about how and when to communicate.
- Having the knowledge needed to be effective.
- Executing the communication plan masterfully.

CHOOSING A MEDIUM

People at work communicate through different **media**: sometimes orally, sometimes in writing, and sometimes nonverbally—with facial expressions or body language. When you need to communicate with someone, one of the most important decisions that you must make is selecting the best medium to use.

Although this textbook focuses on written messages, sometimes a better approach may be to use other media or a combination of media. For example, you might talk briefly about a new project with your supervisor and then follow up with a memo that provides details.

You should base your decision on which medium to use on a number of factors. Here are some good questions to ask yourself as you think about selecting the best medium:

- **How do you think the recipient will respond to the medium you are using?**
  If the recipient does not like the way you chose to communicate, you are not likely to achieve your objective. For example, some people prefer to communicate through e-mail. Others dislike e-mail and prefer a telephone conversation.

  People sometimes choose the wrong medium for the situation. Consider these two examples. Suppose your company is celebrating its 50th anniversary, and executives of other companies are being invited to attend the event. Now, suppose you are celebrating your birthday and want to invite friends to attend the party. Is e-mail the best medium for both invitations?

  Your friends would probably respond favorably to an invitation sent by e-mail. You would be likely to achieve your goal of having them attend the party. But because e-mail is an informal means of communicating, executives might conclude that the company event was not very important. The company might not achieve its goal of having them attend the event.

- **How sensitive is the situation?**
  If your message contains bad news or personal information, the way you choose to convey it is especially important. For example, a doctor who has learned that a patient has a serious medical problem should inform the patient in person or by telephone. A written message would be too impersonal. Privacy is also a concern. E-mail would not be a very secure way to send the information.

- **How quickly does the recipient need the information?**
  The best way to convey information quickly is usually by telephone, in a personal conversation, by e-mail, or by fax (scanning a paper document to create an electronic version that can be transmitted over phone lines).

- **How complex is the information you need to convey?**
  Information that is difficult to understand may best be conveyed by a combination of media. Having a well-written document that can be analyzed carefully and read several times may be more effective than trying to communicate the information verbally. On the other hand, a personal meeting or phone call allows the recipient to ask questions after reading the information.

- **Do you or does the recipient need a written record of the message?**
  Businesses often require their employees to communicate in writing. Putting things in writing provides a permanent record of the business's operations and transactions.

- **Is the recipient a fellow employee?**
  Most firms tend to be less formal with internal messages and more formal with external messages.

- **Is the person easy to reach by all media?**
  If the recipient doesn't check e-mail regularly, a memo may be the best choice.

- **What will this communication cost?**
  Travel is a big expense for business. A personal visit may be more effective in a given situation, but if the person lives far away, it may not be possible because of the costs.

  You might have to compromise in making your final decision. For example, a sensitive situation may be best handled in person, but if the cost is too great, a telephone call may be the option you select. If a phone call would be ideal but the person cannot be reached by telephone, you may have to use e-mail.

Application 1A:

Select the Most Appropriate Media. Turn to page 15 and complete the application.

TYPE AND VOLUME OF COMMUNICATIONS

A major portion of every employee's day is spent communicating. The product of that time and effort is a huge volume of communications. Some organizations require many more written communications than others. However, nearly every organization has a pressing need to put its ideas in writing, to share those ideas with others, and to maintain a record of them. Some of these ideas remain within an organization, while others are shared outside of it.

Success Tip

Learn about other cultures and be sensitive to differences among cultures to make your communications more effective.

- Internal communications stay within an organization. Examples include forms, memos, reports, newsletters, and e-mail.

- External communications go to clients, customers, suppliers, and a host of other individuals and businesses. Documents that go outside an organization include letters, reports, newsletters, proposals, forms, e-mail, and many other documents.

Global Connections

Communicating Across Cultures

More and more companies are marketing their goods and services internationally. They are also marketing to people and hiring people with diverse backgrounds. To succeed in many jobs, you will need the ability to communicate across cultures.

Communicating effectively with people in other countries and cultures can be a challenge. Careful planning is required to ensure that messages are consistent and accurate for groups with cultural differences. Language translation is a major problem. Companies have found that statements such as the product "adds life" might be translated as the product "brings back the dead" and that "diet foods" imply illness.

What personal qualities would be helpful in trying to communicate across cultures? What steps could a company take to prevent errors in communication?

You have probably noticed that many of the same types of documents can be used for both internal and external communications. Two exceptions are letters, which are used to communicate with people outside an organization, and memos, which are used for internal communications.

Often one business transaction triggers many communications. A business applying for a loan to erect a new office building may create hundreds of documents. Internal documents may focus on the needs of work groups, approvals from managers, specifications for facilities, and other factors. External communications may focus on obtaining cost information from a variety of sources to determine the amount of money to be borrowed, finding sources of funding, and comparing options. The financial institution that receives the loan application may, in turn, generate 50 or more internal and external communications to process the loan.

TECHNOLOGY

Technology impacts virtually every aspect of communication. Not only has it blurred the distinction between internal and external communications, it has also changed who prepares documents, how you prepare them, how you obtain information for documents, how you edit them, how you distribute them, and even how you share information.

The traditional way of producing written business documents separated the person who wrote the document from the support staff who typed it. Today, documents are written and produced by the same person, different people, or even a team of writers. The approach used to produce a document often determines the way it is distributed.

E-Mail

E-mail has evolved from a very informal, internal means of sending messages to perhaps the most frequently used—and misused—type of communication. E-mail provides an easy and quick way to transmit information. Many documents that a few years ago were mailed or faxed are now sent by e-mail. Billions of e-mails reach companies each day. The typical business user may receive 30 or more e-mails per day.

Many companies have serious concerns about the use of e-mail for company documents. These concerns include lack of security for company information, the ease with which messages can be forwarded to unintended recipients, communications being too casual, poor quality of messages, and inappropriateness of the medium for certain types of messages.

Software Applications

Today, most documents are produced using personal computers and a suite of software applications such as Microsoft® Office. They typically include word processing, spreadsheet, database, and presentation software. You will use word processing software most of the time. However, an increasing number of jobs require some familiarity with the other types of software. For example, you may need to pull information from a database into a word-processed report or insert a spreadsheet chart in a presentation. Software applications in suites are designed to work similarly and easily together.

Word processing software offers many features that help you create, format, and edit documents quickly and easily. These include the online reference tools: spell-check, grammar-check, and **thesaurus**. Although these tools do not eliminate

Technology Connections

E-Mail Policies

Many companies allow limited personal use of e-mail, but they hold employees responsible for the content of the e-mail they write and receive. They do not tolerate e-mails that contain chain letters, solicitations, obscene language, pornographic images, or political, religious, or sexual content. Disciplinary action may be as severe as losing your job. The best approach is not to use your company's e-mail system for personal use.

the need for editing and proofreading, they do assist the writer in editing and proofreading more efficiently. Word processing software also contains tools to help people write in teams.

The ability to store files in a shared location or in a database often eliminates the need for many internal documents. In the case of the loan application for an office building described earlier, much of the information could be posted in a shared location or in a company database. Then it could be accessed by anyone needing it. Once employees know where to find the information, they can access it on an as-needed basis.

Internet and Intranets

Many companies have a Web site for customers and other people outside the company who are interested in it. For communicating and sharing information within the organization, and with selected suppliers and special customers, companies often set up intranets. Intranets are proprietary or company-owned computer networks. The company determines what should appear on an intranet and who can access it. Because intranets are owned and controlled by the company, employers feel they are more secure.

People use the Internet in their jobs in a variety of ways. The most common is to research topics and gather information. A real estate agent might use the Internet to find comparable prices for houses. A financial analyst might use it to gather data on the economy. A writer might use it to research a story.

Your work will likely require you to use the Internet in some way. When you do, you must take special care to ensure that the information you obtain is reliable. You will learn some ways to do this later in the text.

COST AND QUALITY ISSUES

Companies spend large amounts of money on written communications. Most companies think of communication in terms of an investment rather than a cost. The cost of communicating effectively may be very high—but not nearly as high as the cost of not communicating effectively. The average cost of a single letter or memo is estimated to be more than $20. One letter or memo, however, may cost hundreds of dollars while another may cost only a few cents. Many factors influence the cost.

Writer Costs

Most of the costs associated with document preparation stem from paying employees for the time it takes to plan, write, and edit the document. Documents written by highly paid employees, such as senior executives, cost far more than those written by lower-paid employees, such as clerks. Documents that require input from a team of employees often cost more than those written by one person. However, teams often produce higher-quality documents because they include the perspectives of a variety of people and departments.

Production Costs

The cost of keying documents is very minor compared to the cost of the writer's time. Today's technology has reduced the cost of producing a document. However, the cost savings is often offset by the high volume of documents produced. More is not always better. E-mail is an excellent example of this concept. The cost of producing an e-mail can be very low, but spam (unwanted junk e-mail) costs companies billions of dollars every year.

Distribution Costs

The cost of distributing documents is also very minor compared to the cost of the writer's time. When the Internet and e-mail are used wisely, their cost compared to mail, fax, and overnight mail services can be very low. The ability to send a document from your desktop saves both time and money.

Quality of Communications

The same factors that impact costs often impact quality. Companies tend to be very cost-conscious, but they place quality before costs. They simply are unwilling to sacrifice quality to obtain cost savings.

WRITING SKILLS

The ability to communicate effectively in writing is one of the skills needed for success in every career. Lifetime employability requires, among other things, the ability to write well. If you develop this ability, you will have a very marketable skill that will facilitate your career growth. This skill will also transfer to other jobs and other companies.

Basic Writing Skills

Effective writing requires many basic skills that are emphasized in this textbook. You must communicate ideas clearly, accurately, and concisely using appropriate language. Companies expect you to use correct grammar, spelling, and punctuation.

Advanced Skills

In addition to basic writing skills, you need a variety of more advanced skills to prepare effective documents. Some of these skills include critical thinking, analytical skills, reading skills, interpersonal skills, research skills, and information management skills.

Different types of situations and documents require different skills and approaches. In many cases, a variety of skills have to be used together to solve a complex problem. Often the purpose of a document determines the skills required to produce that document. Consider the skills you need to write effective documents for the following situations:

Success Tip

Good writing skills are required for success in virtually every career. When you change jobs, your writing skills can be transferred to any job you may hold. Time spent developing your writing skills is an investment in your career that will pay big dividends.

- A document intended to convey information requires you to obtain the information, evaluate it, organize it, and interpret it before you can communicate it effectively.

- A document intended to solve a problem requires you to use a different set of skills that focuses on creative thinking, decision making, and problem solving.

- A document intended to persuade individuals to do something that they would not normally do requires you to use both logical and emotional appeals.

- A document containing complex information may require you to use graphs, charts, and illustrations to help the reader understand it.

STYLE

Each person has a unique or preferred **style**—a pattern of observable behaviors or characteristics. Your style is reflected in the way you dress, the way you wear your hair, the way you interact with people, the way you speak, the way you write, and a variety of other ways.

Style in dress and style in writing have many similarities. Examine the picture on this page very carefully. Note the style of clothing worn by each individual. Then think about the following points:

- Most people feel more comfortable with some styles than with other styles.
- Different degrees of formality exist.
- Cost does not really determine the level of formality.
- Different styles may not be compatible.
- Style is not just about preference; style must be appropriate for the situation.

Compare Styles

Communication always involves more than one person. The preferred style of a writer (or speaker) may not match the preferred style of the reader (or listener). In fact, the preferred styles may not even be compatible. Also, a style you prefer may not be appropriate for a particular situation. For example, would you use the same style to write a congratulatory note to a fellow employee who received a promotion as you would to write a sympathy note to a fellow employee who lost a family member?

The degree of formality of a situation influences the style that is appropriate. Think about the picture you have just examined. You would probably be very uncomfortable if you attended a formal banquet in shorts or a sweat suit! Your shorts or sweat suit may be very stylish and of the best quality. It may have cost more than the formal attire worn by others. Still, you would not be dressed appropriately for the occasion. Likewise, you would probably not be comfortable if you attended a picnic in formal or business attire.

This analogy also applies to writing. Think about the types of messages you would write inviting people to attend a formal banquet and to attend a picnic. The same style would not be appropriate for both situations.

Adapt Your Style

The key to using style effectively is to adapt your style to meet the needs of the reader and the situation. Writers tend to write from their perspective rather than from that of the recipient. As a writer, you know and understand the information you are trying to convey to the reader. The reader does not have that same information. Therefore, anything you can do to help the reader understand the information you are conveying helps you to achieve your goal.

Adapting your style to the needs of the reader implies that you know about the reader's style. Perhaps you know the reader personally. Or, if you have a written message from the person, you can analyze the style used in writing to you. If the writer used a very formal style, it probably would not be appropriate to respond in a very casual way. If the individual used technical and complex language, it probably would not be wise to respond in a simple, nontechnical manner.

> **Success Tip**
>
> Business information belongs to your organization. Employees are expected to protect company information and keep it confidential. Failure to do so could jeopardize your career.

Evaluate Styles

The following pages contain a letter that Ms. Maria Martinez, executive director of Rosewood Development, Inc., wrote to Mr. Seth Rosen, president of Rosen Construction, and three responses that illustrate different styles Mr. Rosen might use to answer the letter.

Read the letter from Ms. Martinez carefully. Think about the style of writing she used. Then read all three responses. Compare the styles before you complete the questions following each response.

Letter From Ms. Martinez

Dear Mr. Rosen

You made many contributions to the development of our community as a member and former president of the Midlands Builders Association. You helped to organize the volunteers who worked on many of the projects in our community that we can now point to with great pride. On the Midlands Youth Recreation Complex, you served as coordinator and project overseer. That project today is a model for what can be done when caring citizens work together to improve the community for all our citizens.

As you probably read in the newspaper, the Rosewood Neighborhood Master Plan has been approved by all the parties involved and is ready to become a reality. The Rosewood Development Corporation is now assembling an advisory board to coordinate the individual building projects in the plan. The Rosewood Neighborhood Advisory Board will review bid specifications, evaluate all bids that are received, select the winning bid, and provide oversight during development to ensure that all projects adhere strictly to the Master Plan. We invite you to serve as a member of the Rosewood Neighborhood Advisory Board and to help ensure the successful completion of the project.

Please let me know within the next two weeks whether you will be able to assist us in this important endeavor. We truly need your guidance.

Sincerely

Maria Martinez

Why is it important to analyze the style of a message you receive?

_____

_____

_____

_____

_____

Reply From Mr. Rosen: Style 1

Dear Ms. Martinez

Thank you for your most kind and generous letter with a gracious invitation to serve on the Rosewood Neighborhood Advisory Board. Nothing would please me more than to be able to serve our wonderful community once again as it moves forward with its extremely ambitious and exciting plans to develop the Rosewood Neighborhood. However, I am unable to do so at this time.

Our business has increased significantly, and I have made major commitments of my time to building projects scheduled over the next two years. Therefore, I would be unable to devote either the quality or the quantity of time that this most worthy project deserves. In fact, one of the projects we have on the drawing board may potentially be a candidate for a site in the Rosewood Neighborhood.

Again, thank you for the most complimentary remarks about my community service activities and your confidence in my ability to serve on this prestigious advisory board. Please call on me again sometime in the future if I can be of service. You may be assured that I will give future requests from you serious consideration with the expectation that I will be in a position to reply affirmatively.

Sincerely

Seth Rosen

How did you react to this style? ❑ Favorable ❑ Unfavorable ❑ Neutral

What did you like about the style? Why?

_____

_____

What did you dislike about the style? Why?

_____

_____

Reply From Mr. Rosen: Style 2

Dear Ms. Martinez

Thank you for your kind letter inviting me to serve on the Rosewood Neighborhood Advisory Board. The Rosewood Neighborhood Master Plan is an excellent plan for our community, and I was delighted to learn that it had been approved.

The Rosewood Neighborhood project offers many exciting challenges, and I wish I could be a part of guiding the program to a successful conclusion; however, I am unable to serve on the advisory board at this time. Our business has increased significantly, and I have already made commitments to several new projects. Hopefully, one of the projects will be a potential candidate for a site in the Rosewood Neighborhood.

Best wishes with the Rosewood Neighborhood development. I am confident it will be successful.

Sincerely

Seth Rosen

How did you react to this style? ❑ Favorable ❑ Unfavorable ❑ Neutral

What did you like about the style? Why?

_____

_____

What did you dislike about the style? Why?

_____

_____

Reply From Mr. Rosen: Style 3

Dear Maria

Thanks for a neat letter. Sure wish I could help you by serving on the Rosewood Neighborhood Advisory Board, but I can't.

Our business is zipping, and I can barely keep it on course with all the activities that are going on now.

Good luck with the project. Hope it is a huge success.

Sincerely

Seth

How did you react to this style? ❑ Favorable ❑ Unfavorable ❑ Neutral

What did you like about the style? Why?

_____

_____

What did you dislike about the style? Why?

_____

_____

The content of the three responses is basically the same; however, the style is very different. Typical reactions to the letters from Mr. Rosen are noted below. If you disagree, explain why.

Reply From Mr. Rosen, Style 1: Style is wordy and self-centered.

Reply From Mr. Rosen, Style 2: Style seems to be sincere and appropriate for the situation.

Reply From Mr. Rosen, Style 3: Style seems to be insincere and too casual.

_____

_____

THE PROCESS OF WRITING

People generally think of writing only as a product and devote relatively little thought to the process of developing that product. In their minds, a message is either effective or not effective. Thinking of writing as a process is important because any process can be learned.

Good writers tend to have several qualities in common. First, they have a strong desire to write well. Second, they recognize that many subskills—such as the ability to think logically, to apply basic principles, and to use language appropriately—are involved in writing. Third, they realize that effective writing is generally not achieved in the first attempt. Good writing is usually the product of revising and editing to achieve the desired results. Fourth, good writers work hard at improving their writing skills. They develop the skills needed, and they revise and edit documents until the final product is effective.

Fortunately, the more that writers work at improving their writing skills, the easier writing becomes. Once writers have mastered the basic skills and have gained experience in the process of writing and revising, they are able to produce high-quality documents in less time and with less effort. The actual process, or the way in which people write, varies widely.

Using a Free-Form Approach

Some writers like to put their thoughts down on paper quickly as those thoughts occur. Afterwards, they go back and organize their thoughts and add substance to produce a first draft. Then they revise, edit, and proofread the draft to produce the desired result.

Using a Structured Approach

Other writers prefer to use a more structured approach. Usually they follow a very systematic procedure of planning a message, collecting and organizing the information needed to write it, preparing a detailed outline, writing a draft, reviewing it to determine its effectiveness, and then revising, editing, and proofreading the document.

Using a Combined Approach

Many writers use an approach that combines or modifies features of the two approaches described above. Usually this approach consists of planning the document, having at least a mental outline, preparing the draft, revising the draft, and editing and proofreading to ensure that the message is effective.

Application 1B:

Mastery Check for Chapter 1. Turn to page 17 and complete the application.

Selecting an Approach

The process that will work best for you depends on the basic skills that you bring to the task, the amount of experience you have in writing, and the way that you are most comfortable writing. The key is to select a process that focuses on writing in a way that is natural and easy for you. You may want to start by using a very structured approach. As your writing skills improve and as you gain more experience, you can combine and eliminate some of the steps in the process.

! Points to Remember

About Effective Communication

- ☑ One of the most important decisions you must make when communicating with someone is selecting the best medium to use.

- ☑ E-mail is one of the most frequently used and abused methods of communicating.

- ☑ The cost of communicating is high, but the cost of not communicating is much higher. The primary cost is the time of the writer.

- ☑ Basic writing skills are key to effective writing. In addition, you need a variety of more advanced skills to prepare effective documents.

- ☑ The key to using style effectively is to adapt your style to meet the needs of the reader and the situation.

- ☑ Writing is a process that can be learned. The process that will work best for you depends on the basic skills that you bring to the task, your experience writing, and the way you are most comfortable writing.

Select the Most Appropriate Media

- For each of the following situations, select the one medium that would be the most appropriate to convey the information. Place a check mark in the blank before it.

- For the other media listed, consider whether each medium would be acceptable or unacceptable to use in the situation. Check the appropriate box.

- Use the space after each question to explain your choices.

1. An employee with a good performance record has been spending excessive time on personal telephone calls and e-mails during the past month. You must call the situation to the attention of the employee.

    ____ E-mail   ❑ Acceptable   ❑ Unacceptable

    ____ Memo   ❑ Acceptable   ❑ Unacceptable

    ____ Telephone call   ❑ Acceptable   ❑ Unacceptable

    ____ Personal visit   ❑ Acceptable   ❑ Unacceptable

2. You want to congratulate a fellow employee who just received an advanced college degree and a major leadership award.

    ____ E-mail   ❑ Acceptable   ❑ Unacceptable

    ____ Memo   ❑ Acceptable   ❑ Unacceptable

    ____ Telephone call   ❑ Acceptable   ❑ Unacceptable

    ____ Personal visit   ❑ Acceptable   ❑ Unacceptable

3. You wish to express your sympathy to an out-of-state customer whose spouse died recently. You have a business, not a personal, relationship with the customer and have never met the spouse.

_____ Sympathy card   ❏ Acceptable   ❏ Unacceptable

_____ Personal letter   ❏ Acceptable   ❏ Unacceptable

_____ Telephone call   ❏ Acceptable   ❏ Unacceptable

_____ E-mail   ❏ Acceptable   ❏ Unacceptable

4. A customer is considering installing new garage doors that your company sells. The customer has requested specifications for the doors and has indicated that the information is needed urgently. You need to send printed information with drawings.

_____ E-mail   ❏ Acceptable   ❏ Unacceptable

_____ Letter   ❏ Acceptable   ❏ Unacceptable

_____ Telephone call   ❏ Acceptable   ❏ Unacceptable

_____ Fax   ❏ Acceptable   ❏ Unacceptable

5. A customer has requested a credit limit increase from $5,000 to $10,000. The customer has a bad credit rating, and you cannot grant the increase.

_____ Letter   ❏ Acceptable   ❏ Unacceptable

_____ Telephone call   ❏ Acceptable   ❏ Unacceptable

_____ Personal visit   ❏ Acceptable   ❏ Unacceptable

_____ E-mail   ❏ Acceptable   ❏ Unacceptable

Mastery Check for Chapter 1

1. List several factors that influence the decision to use one communication medium rather than another.

2. Describe the key factors that influence the cost of communications.

3. Explain what is meant by style and how it affects communications.

4. Describe how technology affects the creation and distribution of documents.

5. Explain how developing the ability to write effective communications can positively impact your career.

6. For each of the terms shown below, write a complete, correct sentence using the term.

Medium

Perspective

Recipient

Style

Shell Cove—Corporate Headquarters

Shell Cove Enterprises, Inc., has offered you a position as a management trainee, and you have accepted this position. You will now report to corporate headquarters for your orientation and begin the management training program.

Shell Cove Enterprises, Inc. Shell Cove Enterprises is an exciting new company that specializes in oceanfront resort living and entertainment. Shell Cove Enterprises was incorporated three years ago to develop a series of businesses on Shell Cove in Ocean City, Maryland. The company has seven divisions in addition to the corporate headquarters:

- Entertainment Division
- Property Development Division
- Rental/Condominium Division
- Conference Center Division
- Hotel Management Division
- Restaurant Division
- Golf/Tennis Division

The president and the senior vice presidents of development, finance, human resources, legal services, and marketing are the major officers in corporate headquarters. These executives work with all the divisions. Each division has a director and a number of managers, technical staff, and support staff.

Shell Cove has eight businesses in full operation. Five additional businesses are under construction.

- Tidewater Golf Course
- Inn at Shell Cove
- Coastal Stampede
- Showtime at Shell Cove
- Pat's at Shell Cove
- Shell Cove Water Park
- Village at Shell Cove
- Blue Point Seafood House
- Captain's Watch (Condos)
- Crescent at Shell Cove
- Shell Cove Conference Center
- Shell Cove Comedy House
- Shell Cove Beach & Racquet Club

Shell Cove Management Training Program. Shell Cove selects and hires employees who have excellent technical skills (specific skills required to perform the job), interpersonal skills, and communication skills. All employees hired at the management level participate in an 18-week Management Training Program that is designed to help them develop conceptual (big-picture) skills. Shell Cove wants all of its managers to understand the general operations of each division and to observe how the divisions work together to make the entire operation successful.

To gain this understanding, management trainees begin in corporate headquarters as an assistant to one of the senior executives. They then rotate to each division and serve as the assistant manager of the division. After they have completed the rotation to all seven divisions, trainees return to corporate headquarters. Each rotation lasts for two weeks. At the conclusion of the 18 weeks, trainees have the opportunity to request assignment to a permanent position in corporate headquarters or in one of the divisions.

Training program requirements. You were hired because of your excellent communication skills. Your primary responsibility will be to assist the executives to whom you report in writing documents. Save all documents in a folder named Shell Cove. You will use some of these documents to develop a portfolio at the end of your training program when you request assignment to a permanent position at Shell Cove.

Contact database. Shell Cove maintains a database with contact information for its employees, customers, and vendors. The database appears in Appendix B. It is also in the Shell Cove folder on the student data disk for those students who are using it. Consult this database for addresses for all documents you prepare as you work for Shell Cove. The e-mail address for Shell Cove employees consists of the first name(period)last name@shellcove.com (example: Charles.Austin @shellcove.com).

Shell Cove letterhead and memo head are also provided on the student data disk. Note that all divisions use the same basic letterhead or memo head with the division name added to it. If you do not have the student data disk, prepare your letters and memos on plain paper. Shell Cove's address is 12500 Coastal Highway, Ocean City, MD 21842-4711.

Job 1: Orientation

For your rotation in corporate headquarters, you report to Ms. Jane Cargile, senior vice president of human resources. She has asked you to review the material provided on these two pages very carefully and to respond to the following questions. She is designing an orientation program for new customer service employees and values the perspective you bring to Shell Cove. Your answers to these five questions will help her develop the new training program.

a. Describe your first impression of Shell Cove Enterprises, Inc.
b. What do you like most about the way the Management Training Program is organized and structured?
c. What do you like least about the way it is organized and structured?
d. Describe your strengths that will enable you to perform well in this program.
e. Describe the areas in which you hope to improve your skills during the training.

Key your responses to these questions, name the file *1C1si* (*si* stands for *student's initials;* substitute your initials for *si*), and save it in your Shell Cove folder.

Team Activity

Job 2: Team Project

Select two members of your class and either ask them personally or send them an e-mail asking each to be on your team. The three members of the team should review the answers each of you prepared and saved in the first activity. Note the things that are similar and those that are different in your responses. The team's task is to combine the individual responses to the five questions and prepare one document that represents the views of all team members. Save the document as *1C2tp-si* in the Shell Cove folder (on team projects, you will use *tp* and the initials of one team member). Include your names in the document.

TEN GUIDES FOR EFFECTIVE WRITING

OBJECTIVES

After you complete Chapter 2, you should be able to:

* Apply the guides for effective writing.
* Format letters, memos, and e-mail using a consistent style.
* Edit messages more effectively.

OVERVIEW

You can learn to be an effective writer. The first step in the process is to learn and apply basic guides for effective writing. A writer with limited experience should follow the guides closely. More experienced writers can take a little more latitude in adapting basic guides to accomplish the objectives of a message.

Chapter 2 contains ten sections. One basic guide for effective writing is presented and explained in each section. The ten guides are:

* Plan Messages Carefully.
* Write for the Reader.
* Present Ideas Positively.
* Write in a Clear, Readable Style.
* Check for Completeness.
* Use an Efficient, Action-Oriented Style.
* Use Concrete Language.
* Use Effective Sentence and Paragraph Structure.
* Format Documents Effectively.
* Edit and Proofread Carefully.

"Business Talk"

Communicating effectively requires you to understand and use appropriate vocabulary in a business setting. Look for the following terms in this chapter. Review the terms and their definitions. Remember, some words have more than one meaning.

Brainstorming—a freewheeling approach to generating as many ideas as possible. Critical evaluation of the ideas does not occur until after the brainstorming process.

Coherence—the quality of being linked logically to each other. Related ideas, for example, can have coherence.

Empathy—placing yourself mentally in the reader's position.

Guide—a recommended or suggested way of writing. It is not an inflexible rule that can never be violated.

Jargon—terms used in a particular industry but not generally known by outsiders.

GUIDE 1—PLAN MESSAGES CAREFULLY

Planning is the most critical step in writing a message. Think about why you are writing. You do not write just for the sake of writing. You write to accomplish a specific purpose. The purposes of communications vary widely. They might be to:

- Provide information.
- Seek information.
- Solve a problem.
- Build good relationships.
- Persuade a reader to do something.
- Force action.

Your message must be designed to accomplish the purpose for writing it.

Focus on Achieving Objectives

Careful planning is the key to ensuring that a message accomplishes its intended purpose. Planning sounds very simple, and the need for careful planning seems to be obvious. Many writers, however, skip the planning process. They start writing, dictating, or keying the message and try to plan as they write. Writers who skip the planning process run the risk of creating a message that does not achieve its objective.

Writers who plan as they write also run another risk—that of creating a stereotyped message. Stereotyped messages all sound alike. When writers plan while they write, they tend to use the same opening and closing statements. For example, when they answer letters, they may always begin with a statement such as *Thank you for your letter of (insert date)*. They may always end with a statement such as *If I can be of further service, please let me know*. These statements may be good for certain situations. However, in other instances, they may not be appropriate at all.

Think Through the Entire Scenario

Planning is a mental, or thinking, process. It requires that you think through a scenario, or situation, carefully and determine the best way to handle it. Effective planning focuses on meeting the objectives of both the reader and the writer.

Think about this scenario. Put yourself into the position of a sales representative for an Oriental rug dealer who has just received an inquiry about a large, high-quality Oriental rug. The letter requests information about

- Price range.
- Availability of 14′ × 20′ or larger rugs.
- Availability of one-of-a-kind and museum-quality pieces.
- Literature on available Oriental rugs.

Think carefully about this situation in order to plan the best possible approach for answering this letter.

Use questions to facilitate thinking. The best way to begin a thinking exercise is to brainstorm. **Brainstorming** involves generating as many ideas as possible and waiting to evaluate the ideas until after the brainstorming process. Brainstorming can be an individual or team activity. In this example, you will brainstorm by yourself first. Then you will work with team members. Teams usually produce better results because groups tend to come up with a greater number and variety of ideas than a single person. A new idea from a team member may lead you to think about an idea that otherwise would not have occurred to you.

Asking questions is an excellent way to begin the brainstorming process. Think of as many questions as you can about the writer, the purpose for writing, and the entire situation. The following list of questions provides a good start for the process of thinking through this particular situation. As you think about the questions, jot down possible answers.

At this point, do not worry about whether your questions or answers are good. You can evaluate them later. An important thing to learn is that often people who have very little technical knowledge about a topic can ask very important questions or come up with excellent ideas. They can also ask questions that do not apply or come up with bad ideas. You may not know much about Oriental rugs, which is why this topic was selected. However, if you were a sales representative for an Oriental rug dealer, you would probably be very knowledgeable about the topic.

1. Why did the individual request the information?

2. Do you think the individual contacted other rug dealers?

3. What do you know about the individual who requested the information?

4. Do you think the individual knows much about the quality and prices of Oriental rugs?

5. Does the information requested give you any clues about the lifestyle of the individual?

6. Does the information requested give you any clues about the financial status of the individual?

7. What mental image do you have of the individual?

8. How do you think your competitors would respond to the request for information?

9. What do you have to gain from this situation?

Add your own questions here:

10. _____

_____

11. _____

_____

12. _____

_____

Team Activity **Team analysis.** Form a team with two or three other members of your class. Compare the answers each team member jotted down. As you compare answers, add ideas from team members to what you have written or additional ideas that occur as you compare responses. Also, try to add more questions.

The important point here is that thinking through the situation usually begins with analyzing the reader, but it eventually leads you to consider both the reader's objectives and your own.

© V.C.L./TAXI/GETTY IMAGES

You are more likely to hit the target if it is clearly identified.

Plan Messages Systematically

The planning process recommended in this text consists of five steps:

Determine objectives. The key questions to ask are, *What do I expect to accomplish by writing this message?* and *What does the reader expect to accomplish with my message?* Effective planning requires careful consideration of the objectives of both the writer and the reader.

Most writers have a general idea of why they are writing a message. A general idea is a good beginning, but it is not adequate to ensure an effective message. Specific ideas need to be identified. Unless you know exactly what you are trying to communicate, you are not likely to be successful in getting the message across.

Analyze the reader. Two key questions to ask are, *What information do I have about the reader that will help me understand the reader's needs?* and *Can I visualize the person?*

Knowledge about a reader's occupation or understanding of a topic is important. An engineer could use engineering terms in communicating with another person who understands those terms. Other people, however, would not be likely to understand them. Terms that are used by people in a particular industry are known as **jargon**. Jargon is appropriate only for people who are likely to understand it.

Other factors that could affect the style of a message and, therefore, should be considered include culture, approximate age, rank or position, and the importance of the topic to the individual.

Make decisions. A key question is, *What decisions must be communicated in the message?* All decisions should be made before writing the message. In the business world, both information that will be received positively and information that will be received negatively must be communicated. The same writing style is not appropriate for both types of messages. You will learn about different writing styles and when to use them in the next few chapters.

Collect information. Two key questions are, *What information is needed to write this message effectively?* and *Is the information available?* Once you have determined the information that you need, you should assemble that information before you start writing. Knowing what you are going to include in a message enables you to organize the material and arrange it in the order that will be most effective in communicating the points you want to make.

Develop a plan. A key question is, *Do I have a written outline or at least a mental plan for the entire message?* The entire message should be planned before you begin to write. The beginning and end of the message deserve particular attention.

Writing a message is simple once you have planned it. The only thing left to do then is to ensure that you implement your plan effectively. Start the writing process using a detailed outline until you become more comfortable writing. Then move to a very brief outline, and finally, move to a mental plan.

> **Application 2A-1:**
>
> Plan Messages Carefully. Turn to page 55 and complete the application.

GUIDE 2—WRITE FOR THE READER

Always remember that you are writing to communicate to the reader. A good message meets the needs of both the reader and the writer. Most readers expect a message to be logical, helpful, sincere, and courteous. Even messages that contain negative information can meet these expectations.

Use Empathy

Using **empathy** is the best way to adapt a message to meet the needs of the reader. Think of yourself in the position of the reader. If you were the reader, how would you react in the same situation? Would you view the message as logical, helpful, and sincere? The person who receives a message often views it differently than the person who sends that message. A person writing a message may want the reader to do something. The reader, on the other hand, is likely to view the message with a "What's in it for me?" attitude.

Messages written from an empathetic, considerate point of view are likely to be the most effective. Writing from the viewpoint of the reader is sometimes called the *you attitude*. The you attitude is often misinterpreted to mean that the pronoun *you* should be used frequently and the pronoun *I* should rarely be used. Both pronouns are appropriate and can be used effectively. However, good writers usually try to avoid beginning an entire message and the majority of paragraphs within the message with *I*.

Overuse of the pronoun *I* makes the writer appear to be self-centered. A common and very obvious overuse of the pronoun *I* is to begin every paragraph with it. The pronoun *you* can also be misused.

The you attitude is appropriate only when it is used in a sincere and honest manner. The idea is to show respect and a genuine concern for the reader. The attitude is far more important than the pronoun choice.

Compare the following sentences that illustrate writing from the perspective of the writer and that of the reader. The message is essentially the same in each example, but the tone is very different. Which of these messages would you prefer to receive?

Writer's perspective
- I reviewed your report, and I think it is excellent.
- I need copies of the photographs to include in the report, and I want you to have them printed today.
- I will be out of town and cannot attend the zoning hearing Wednesday at 2:30 p.m. I want you to represent me at the hearing unless you have something scheduled that cannot be canceled.

Reader's perspective
- Your report is excellent.
- If possible, would you please have copies of the photographs to include in the report printed today?
- If your schedule permits, would you please represent me at the zoning hearing on Wednesday at 2:30 p.m., while I am out of town?

Use a Courteous Tone

Being courteous means being polite, kind, and considerate of others. *Please* and *thank you* are words most often associated with courtesy. Most people appreciate requests that are prefaced with *please*. They also appreciate being thanked *after* they have done something for someone else. Note the timing of the words—*please* is appropriate before something has been done and *thank you* is appropriate only after something has been done.

Some writers with good intentions make the mistake of thanking people before they grant a request. *Thank you in advance* assumes that the person will do what you are asking, and most people do not like to be taken for granted. It also implies that you do not plan to thank them after they have done something. Rather than thank a person in advance, show gratitude in another way, using comments such as *I would appreciate*.

Courtesy implies more than just saying please and thank you. Courtesy also includes the tone or manner in which something is said. Sarcasm, lectures, condescending statements, derogatory comments, and crude language offend most readers. Write in a way that respects rather than offends readers.

Offensive tone
- Report to my office for a short meeting at 2:00 today.
- Since you are so late with your report, fax it to me as soon as you finish it.
- If you had mailed your July payment on time, your account would have been credited correctly.

Courteous tone
- Please come to my office for a short meeting at 2:00 today.
- Please fax your report to me just as soon as you finish it.
- Your July payment arrived after your statement was prepared; therefore, the credit does not appear on your August statement.

Write in a Fair and Unbiased Manner

Good writers present their ideas using a nondiscriminatory style. Using a fair and unbiased style avoids the possibility of offending the reader. Discrimination in writing occurs in several ways:

- Using sexist or racist words.
- Using masculine pronouns to refer to both men and women.
- Using words that stereotype women and minorities.
- Using words that reduce the status of individuals.

Often writers use discriminatory language without intending to be discriminatory; they simply do not realize that a problem exists. Good writers also try to avoid awkward phrases such as *he/she.*

Application 2A-2:

Write for the Reader. Turn to page 59 and complete the application.

Discriminatory or awkward style
- The girls won more medals at the Olympics than the men did.
- If a manager does his job well, he will be promoted.
- Did the black judge question the tactics used by the salesman?
- If a customer wants to pick up his or her clothes the same day, he or she must bring them in by 8:30 a.m.

Fair and unbiased style
- The women won more medals at the Olympics than the men did *or* the girls won more medals at the Junior Olympics than the boys did.
- Managers who do their jobs well will be promoted.
- Did the judge question the tactics used by the sales representative?
- Customers who wish to pick up their clothes the same day must bring them in by 8:30 a.m.

GUIDE 3—PRESENT IDEAS POSITIVELY

Positive thinking is powerful. You can accomplish far more with a positive attitude than with a negative attitude. In business, conditions often require you to convey both positive and negative information. Most writers find it easy to convey positive information and difficult to convey negative information. Rarely is receiving negative news a pleasant experience. However, you can make the situation less painful for the reader by using an honest—but positive—writing style.

Two people can look at the same situation and view it from different perspectives. For example, one person may look at a half glass of water and describe it as half full, while another may look at the same glass and describe it as half empty. The difference is simply a matter of attitude.

Disagree, But Do Not Be Disagreeable

Disagreeing is often necessary and is perfectly acceptable. But being disagreeable is neither necessary nor acceptable. The ability to disagree without being disagreeable is an art. You may not always agree with an individual to whom you must write, but you do not have to be disagreeable just because you see things from a different perspective. Good writers present their views without offending the reader.

Disagreeable
- The payment plan you proposed is totally ridiculous.
- You sold us a worthless piece of junk that you called a printer. Bring us a real printer or refund our money.

Disagree without being disagreeable
- The following payment plan builds on your proposed plan and makes it a workable solution.
- The printer you sold us continues to malfunction; please replace it with a printer that functions properly.

Use Positive Ideas and Focus on What Can Be Done

Writers with good intentions often use negative statements to present positive ideas. One of the most frequently used sentences to close business letters is *If I can be of further service, please do not hesitate to let me know.* Note that the negative form is used. Why should the reader hesitate to ask you for additional service if it is needed? The intention is good, but the result is not as good. A more effective closing would be *Please let me know if I can be of further service.*

Good writers tell readers what they can do rather than what they cannot do. Focusing on the negative frequently accomplishes only half the job. It tells you what cannot be done, but it leaves out what can be done. A sign saying "No parking in this area" only indicates what cannot be done. Drivers are not told where they may park if they desire to do so. A sign saying "Visitors may park in Lot 1 only" would be more effective.

Negative
- Don't forget to mail this letter today.
- Why don't you call your doctor for an appointment?
- Don't smoke in the office.

Positive
- Please remember to mail this letter today.
- Perhaps you should call your doctor for an appointment.
- Smoking is permitted only on the outside terrace at the west entrance.

Limit the Use of Negative Words

Many words have negative meanings. Use negative words sparingly. Although it may be necessary to convey a negative message, you should select words that are not too strong. The best approach is to focus on the solution rather than the problem. Writing negative messages is discussed in more detail in Chapter 4.

Application 2A-3:

Present Ideas Positively. Turn to page 61 and complete the application.

GUIDE 4—WRITE IN A CLEAR, READABLE STYLE

Clarity means being clear. A message with clarity is written so clearly that it cannot be misinterpreted. Clarity involves more than writing a message that the reader can easily understand. You achieve clarity when the reader interprets the message exactly the way you intended. Clarity is more important in written than oral communications because immediate feedback is not available. In a conversation, a listener who does not understand your message can ask questions. That option is not available in a written message.

Most people use different language in written messages than they do in conversations. Conversations tend to be more informal. Written messages are often stiff, stilted, and self-important.

Stilted language
- The above-referenced matter was acted upon in an expeditious manner at the Executive Committee meeting yesterday with an affirmative response.
- Pursuant to our discussion on Thursday, I evaluated the inventory levels and ascertained that they are being maintained according to prescribed guidelines.

Conversational language
- The Executive Committee considered and approved your proposal at its meeting yesterday.
- After we talked on Thursday, I checked our inventory levels and found them to be in line with the guides we established.

Factors Influencing Clarity

The purpose for writing a message is to communicate ideas to the reader. You should do everything possible to ensure that the reader will understand and interpret the ideas in the way you intended. Good writers write to express an idea clearly. They rarely write with the purpose of impressing the reader. Therefore, good writers tend to simplify their writing as much as possible. A number of factors influence the clarity and readability of a message.

Vocabulary. Word selection is a very important factor that influences clarity. The difficulty of the vocabulary depends on the reader and can be viewed from several different perspectives. The length of words and the number of syllables influence difficulty. Generally, longer words with many syllables are more difficult than shorter words, but this is not always the case. Words such as *agricultural* and *satisfactorily* are long and have many syllables, but the average reader would not have difficulty with these words. *Albeit* (meaning "although") is a short word with three syllables, but the average reader would find it relatively difficult. Familiarity is the difference in those two examples. Most readers are familiar with *agricultural* and *satisfactorily*, but not with *albeit*.

Jargon, foreign expressions, and acronyms affect the clarity of messages. Jargon is language that is common within an industry but not generally known by outsiders. Foreign expressions, such as *pro forma* (meaning "as a matter of form") and *antebellum* (meaning "before the war") can be a problem to readers who are not familiar with the terms. So can acronyms, such as *ASAP* (meaning "as soon as possible"), when readers do not know what they stand for.

Difficult vocabulary
- The recalcitrant, obstreperous students commenced with an interminable dissertation about the eccentricities of the professor.
- Distractor analysis performed on the questionable item on the SQT and appropriate decision criteria provided a basis for determining if the response on the answer key was incorrect.
- We must scrutinize alternative solutions, strategize, and develop an appropriate implementation plan.

Easier vocabulary
- The defiant, noisy students began a long discussion about the teacher's odd behavior.
- The answer choices on the questionable item on the Skills Qualification Test were analyzed to determine if the answer was wrong.
- We must analyze possible solutions, determine the best strategy, and develop an action plan.

Sentence length and structure. Sentence length and structure influence clarity. Short, direct sentences are easier to understand than long, involved sentences. Often a long, involved sentence must be read more than once to grasp its meaning.

Long, involved sentences
- During her tenure of 25 years with the agency, Mary's manager said that she had been absent only a total of 10 days.
- If by some fortuitous opportunity you should discover my umbrella, which I appear to have abandoned in your office facility, please give me the courtesy of a telephone call.

Short, direct sentences
- Mary's manager said that Mary had worked with the agency 25 years and had been absent only 10 days.
- I think I left my umbrella in your office. Please call me if you find it.

Note how easily the first long sentence could be misinterpreted. Did Mary or Mary's manager have a tenure of 25 years with the agency? Was Mary or her manager absent 10 days?

The sentence is the foundation of all writing. Developing effective sentences is critical to achieving the objectives of a message. Guide 8 provides additional information about structuring sentences effectively.

Paragraph length and structure. The length and structure of paragraphs influence clarity. Long paragraphs are difficult to read and often have to be read more than once to determine the meaning. When a paragraph contains a series of items, listing them on separate lines often makes them easier to read.

Complex paragraph
The content of the training program was based on five recurring themes, which consisted of developing an ownership mentality, giving good customer service, working as a team, communicating openly and effectively, and following up on action promised.

Simplified paragraphs
The content of the training program was based on five recurring themes:
1. Developing an ownership mentality.
2. Giving good customer service.
3. Working as a team.
4. Communicating openly and effectively.
5. Following up on action promised.

Although the information in the complex and simplified paragraphs is the same, the simplified paragraphs are easier to read. Numbering items makes it easier for the person responding to a message because the items can be easily checked off.

You can use graphs, charts, tables, and other illustrations to present complex or statistical information in a simpler way.

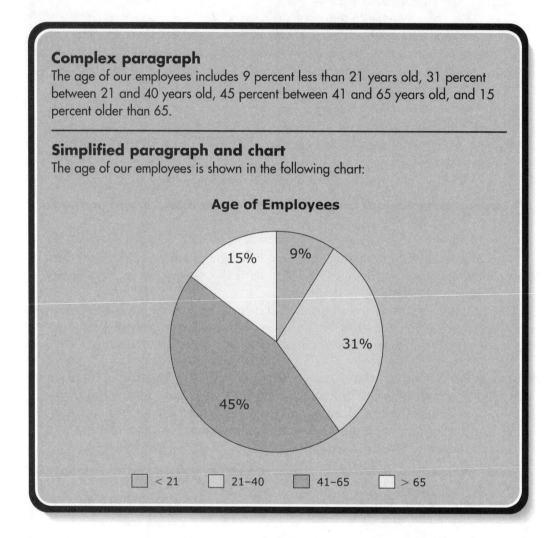

Complex paragraph

The age of our employees includes 9 percent less than 21 years old, 31 percent between 21 and 40 years old, 45 percent between 41 and 65 years old, and 15 percent older than 65.

Simplified paragraph and chart

The age of our employees is shown in the following chart:

Age of Employees

15% — 9% — 31% — 45%

< 21   21–40   41–65   > 65

The chart provides a clear picture of the spread of ages within the company. In many cases, a picture is worth a thousand words. Guide 8 provides additional information on structuring paragraphs effectively.

Technology and Readability

Word processing software provides two tools that help you analyze the difficulty an average person would have in reading a message you write—document properties and readability statistics.

Document properties. The document, or file, properties feature gives general information about a document, such as when it was created, how many changes were made to it, how much time was spent editing the document, and the last time it was accessed. This feature also provides a variety of statistics, including the following:

- Number of pages.
- Number of paragraphs.
- Number of lines.
- Number of words.

Global Connections

Applying the Guides

The following tips from the guides for effective writing will help when you are writing to people in different cultures:

- Use familiar words and a simple, straightforward writing style.
- Use concrete language. Specific writing is more easily understood than general language.
- Use bulleted items and graphs, charts, and other illustrations to clarify and simplify data.
- Americans tend to prefer a concise, direct style of writing. In some cultures, this style is considered rude. Some cultures prefer a writing style that includes more descriptive, colorful material.
- Simple sentences are easier to interpret than complex and compound sentences. Use short sentences and short paragraphs to make documents more readable.

These statistics focus mostly on size. They are very helpful if you have a word or page limit. For example, a job or college application may ask for an essay with a 300-word limit. Document statistics are generally accessed by selecting Properties on the File menu.

Readability statistics. Readability statistics are more valuable in determining how much difficulty the average person would have in reading and understanding a document. The readability feature gives you the following information:

- How many paragraphs and sentences a document contains.

- The average number of sentences per paragraph, words per sentence, and characters per word.

- What percentage of sentences in the passive voice the document contains. Generally, the passive voice is harder to read.

- How easy the text is to read overall and what the grade level is.

Long words, sentences, and paragraphs tend to make reading more difficult. Documents with technical information are usually harder to read than those with general information. If the reader understands the technical information, though, the document will not be difficult.

Most people are comfortable reading well below their grade level. Even if you are in college, reading a document written at the tenth-grade level is easier and more comfortable for you than reading one at the fourteenth-grade level (college sophomore).

Readability statistics generally can be accessed through the spell-check and grammar-check features. Once you have selected the readability option, the statistics for the document display each time spelling and grammar are checked. You can also check readability for specific text, such as a paragraph, by selecting it and running the spell- and grammar-check.

Application 2A-4:

Write in a Clear, Readable Style. Turn to page 63 and complete the application.

GUIDE 5—CHECK FOR COMPLETENESS

A complete message is one that contains all the information necessary to meet the objectives of both the writer and the reader. Messages that have been planned and edited carefully will usually contain all the essential information. Incomplete messages often require a second communication. Therefore, you should ensure that a message has all the essential information to avoid the cost, embarrassment, and lost time that often result from incomplete messages.

Anticipate Questions

In addition to presenting the information needed, you should also anticipate questions that the reader may have and provide answers to those questions. Analyze the following situation to determine the essential information that must be provided and the types of questions that can be anticipated from the reader.

Scenario for analysis

You are coordinating a special expense-paid function for the high-volume independent agents who sell insurance for your company. The event will be held on Saturday, October 7, at Pat's Place, a beach resort near Charleston. It will begin with a two-hour business meeting, to be followed by lunch and an afternoon of recreation, including a choice of golf, tennis, or beach activities. The day will conclude with an appreciation dinner for the agents. Your company will provide hotel accommodations for Saturday night.

Essential information

- Address, telephone number, and directions to the resort.
- Complete schedule of activities.
- List of those invited, including the names of agents' spouses.
- Agenda for the business meeting.
- Descriptions of recreational events.
- Procedure for handling expenses for agents and their guests.

Anticipate questions

- What type of attire is appropriate for the various functions?
- How should "casual dress" be interpreted?
- Can reservations be extended? At whose cost? What is the room rate?
- Are accommodations available for children?
- How are children's expenses handled?
- Which activities include spouses or other guests?

A message that anticipates questions that readers may have and provides answers to those questions is more effective than a message that assumes readers know the information. A complete message keeps the reader from making assumptions that may prove to be incorrect or even embarrassing. It also saves time for both the writer and the reader by making additional inquiries unnecessary. A writer may not always be able to anticipate all questions that a reader may have, but the writer who plans carefully will be able to anticipate as many key questions as possible and provide answers to those questions.

Make Sensible Assumptions

Assumptions deserve special attention. They are similar to walking a tightrope. It is difficult to strike a balance between providing too little and too much information. Making assumptions means making judgments. Determining whether the reader knows or does not know the information is a judgment call. If the reader does not know the information and it is omitted, the message is incomplete. If the reader knows the information and the writer repeats it, the message is likely to be considered wordy.

In the situation just described, two different scenarios might occur. Agents who had been invited previously would probably know the answers to most of the anticipated questions. Agents who had not been invited previously would probably not know the answers. If the same information is to be sent to all the agents, you will have to provide more information than some of the recipients may need.

Assuming too little and providing more information than needed serves as a safety net. This generally is better than assuming too much and omitting needed information.

The best way to ensure that a message is complete is to edit for completeness after the message has been written but before it has been printed or sent. Ask yourself what information should have been included, and then check to see if the message contains that information.

> **Application 2A-5:**
>
> Check for Completeness. Turn to page 65 and complete the application.

GUIDE 6—USE AN EFFICIENT, ACTION-ORIENTED STYLE

Writing in an efficient style means saying everything that needs to be said and nothing more. Most businesspeople are busy and would prefer to read only what is necessary. Conciseness is a virtue in business writing. However, you should not confuse an efficient style with a blunt or curt style. Most people expect courtesies and do not consider them to be wordy. An efficient writer strives to get the message across in a considerate manner and with the fewest words possible. Building goodwill should never be sacrificed in the name of efficiency.

Writing in an action-oriented style means writing in a strong, lively style that gives a sense of movement. An action-oriented style is generally preferred. However, in some situations, this style could be a poor choice. For negative messages, it may be interpreted as too aggressive or strong. A neutral or less lively style may be more appropriate.

Messages written in an action-oriented style use the active voice. In addition to giving a feeling of movement, these messages tend to be shorter than those written in a passive style, using the passive voice. Remember, readability statistics in word processing software include the percentage of passive sentences. Use these statistics to avoid overuse of the passive voice.

Busy people appreciate messages that are condensed. Condensed copy contains all the information needed to achieve the objectives of the message and omits all unnecessary words, phrases, and details.

Writing efficiently generally requires replacing correct, but wordy, elements with shorter elements. Efficient writing is accomplished in several ways. The technique that is most effective depends on the situation and the style preferred by both the reader and the writer. Good writers use a variety of different techniques depending on the situation.

Use a Direct Style

Information presented in a logical, straightforward manner usually results in efficient writing. A direct style of writing normally takes fewer words to accomplish the objectives of a message than an indirect style. A direct style generally works best when you are conveying positive information.

Eliminate Repetitive Material

Efficient writing eliminates material that has already been presented or that the reader already knows. The writer should be wary of assuming that a reader already has information and should try to make sure of this before eliminating it. Some repetition is useful and even necessary. Repetition can be used effectively to emphasize ideas and to show relationships between new material and material that has already been presented. Unless repetition accomplishes a specific purpose, repetitive material should be eliminated.

Avoid Hidden Verbs

Verbs are sometimes hidden in noun form. Using a noun form rather than an active verb tends to weaken a sentence and make it wordy. In the sentence *Pat announced that the tour will start at 10:15 a.m.*, the active verb *announced* is used. In the sentence *Pat made the announcement that the tour will start at 10:15 a.m.*, the verb *announced* is changed to a noun form and another verb is added to the sentence.

Compare the following sentences that use a hidden verb form with those that do not:

Hidden verb form
- Robert sent Leigh an invitation to the Carolina Cup.
- Fred must make a decision on the builder today.
- Please let me know if I can be of assistance to you.
- Please take all factors into consideration before making a decision on the issue.

No hidden verb form
- Robert invited Leigh to the Carolina Cup.
- Fred must decide on the builder today.
- Please let me know if I can assist you.
- Please consider all factors before deciding on the issue.

Note the differences in the length of the sentences that use the hidden verb form and those that do not. Noun forms are correct; they just tend to weaken writing and add words to the sentence. However, using too many short sentences can result in abrupt, choppy writing. This topic is discussed in Guide 8.

Replace Wordy Phrases

Wordy writing often contains phrases that could be replaced by a single word, while still conveying the message adequately. Phrases add variety and should not be eliminated totally. A workable approach consists of substituting a word for the phrase and then evaluating the sentence to see if the change weakened it in any way. The following examples illustrate words that can be used to replace phrases:

Wordy phrases	Efficient words
at the present time	currently *or* now
due to the fact that	because
in an appropriate manner	appropriately
in the amount of	for
in the near future	soon

Use Only Essential Modifiers

Modifiers are words, phrases, or clauses that describe, limit, or qualify another word or group of words. Modifiers should be used when they add variety or contribute to the message in other ways. Some words, however, should not be qualified; they stand alone. Examples of words that should not be qualified follow:

Words that stand alone	Inappropriate modifiers
cooperate	cooperate together
innovation	new innovation
maximum	maximum possible
merge	merge together
repeat	repeat again
revert	revert back

Minimize the Use of Descriptive Words

Descriptive words should be used when they clarify information. Some descriptive words contribute nothing of value to the sentence. They should be eliminated to reduce message length and wordiness. For example, when writing about New York, distinguishing between the city and the state is important. Therefore, it may be essential to say *the state of New York* to distinguish the state from the city of New York. However, saying *the city of New Orleans* wastes space and adds nothing of value. Note the following examples of unnecessary descriptive words:

Use	Wasted descriptive words
. . . box is square	. . . box is square in shape
. . . in Ohio	. . . in the state of Ohio
. . . 10 pounds	. . . 10 pounds in weight
. . . 40 pages	. . . 40 pages in length

Sentences containing extra descriptive words are correct. The words simply are wasted because the meaning is clear without them. Some additional words may be used to add variety. Overuse of descriptive words creates wordy communications.

Use the Active Voice Appropriately

You have learned that the active voice generally is preferred because it condenses copy and influences style, strength, and movement. Sometimes, however, the passive voice is a better choice.

When a verb is in the active voice, the subject performs the action. When a verb is in the passive voice, the subject receives the action. Passive verbs require some form of the verb *to be* (*am, are, is, was, were, be, being,* and *been*) and a past participle, or past form of a verb (*learned, started*). Passive statements usually contain a *by* phrase to identify who or what is acting on the subject (*The lawn was mowed by Terry*).

Knowing when to use the active voice is important. The active voice is used effectively to convey positive information and to show the importance of the subject. The passive voice is used effectively to convey negative information and when the subject does not matter. Compare the sentences that follow:

Passive sentences

The announcement of the Employee of the Year will be made by the President.
Mark was presented with the award by the senior senator.
The baby was saved by Eve Young.
✓   The annual report is mailed to stockholders on March 30.
✓   Your check was mailed today.
✓   The watch was broken when the box was opened.

Active sentences

✓   The President will announce the Employee of the Year.
✓   The senior senator presented the award to Mark.
✓   Eve Young saved the baby.
The corporate secretary mails the annual report to stockholders on March 30.
The accounting clerk mailed your check today.
You broke the watch when you opened the box.

Application 2A-6:

Use an Efficient, Action-Oriented Style. Turn to page 67 and complete the application.

Note the checked ✓ sentences. The first three passive sentences are more effective when they are converted to the active voice. The sentences are stronger and place appropriate emphasis on the subject. The last three passive sentences are more effective in the passive voice. In the fourth and fifth sentences, who mails the annual report or the check does not matter. No one cares who mails it. The last sentence would be far too strong if it were written in the active voice. The active voice places blame and would be considered offensive.

GUIDE 7—USE CONCRETE LANGUAGE

Concrete language is very specific language that conveys precise meaning. Using concrete language is important because readers can usually relate better to specific statements than to general ones. General ideas can often be interpreted in different ways. Specific language takes the guesswork out of reading. Consider the following scenario:

Scenario
- Bill complained that he received a poor raise and was unhappy about it.
- Jim indicated that he received a very nice raise and was pleased.

Analysis of scenario
- In fact, both employees received a 5 percent raise.
- Jim's performance evaluation was better than Bill's.

This situation points out the confusion that can occur when general language is used. What one individual perceives to be very bad, another may perceive to be very good.

Specific language conveys stronger messages than does general language. Specific language calls attention to and adds emphasis to statements. Therefore, it is often preferred. However, general language may be more appropriate for handling sensitive or negative situations.

The expression *ASAP*, which means "as soon as possible," deserves special attention in business. Writers use it when they need something immediately. However, readers often interpret the message to mean "when I can get around to it." How would you respond if your bills came with an ASAP notice? Would you pay them immediately? Most people would delay paying the bills. The expression *at your earliest convenience* is often misunderstood in the same way.

Read the following sentences that contain general language. Then interpret the general language in the space provided. For example, if a person said, "I walked a long way," how far would you estimate the person walked? Answers might range from a few blocks to miles.

Application 2A-7:

Use Concrete Language. Turn to page 69 and complete the application.

General language
- Jean makes a good salary. (How much?) _____
- Joe bought a substantial number of books. (How many?) _____
- Please send me the material as soon as possible. (When?) _____
- I need a good supply of forms. (How many?) _____
- Pat wears expensive suits. (How much do they cost?) _____

Specific language
- Jean makes $90,000 annually.
- Joe bought 12 books.
- Please send me the material by May 1.
- I need 750 forms.
- Pat wears $3,000 suits.

GUIDE 8—USE EFFECTIVE SENTENCE AND PARAGRAPH STRUCTURE

Good writers pay careful attention to sentence structure and to the way paragraphs are organized. Effective sentences and paragraphs provide the foundation for effective messages. Sentence structure can be used to add variety to writing and to make a message interesting. Effective sentences must be organized appropriately to form effective paragraphs. Messages that are carefully organized are easier to read and understand. Paragraphs divide material into manageable units of thought.

Sentence and Paragraph Length

The length of sentences and paragraphs directly affects readability. Good sentence length averages about 17 to 20 words, and good paragraph length averages about 4 to 8 lines. The length of individual sentences and paragraphs should vary. You do not need to count words and lines. Remember, however, that if you are using word processing software, you can select a sentence or paragraph and get readability statistics on it quickly. A good option is to develop a feel for the amount of copy that is appropriate for a sentence or paragraph. If either seems too long, restructure it.

Use Sentence Structure Strategically

The three basic types of sentences—simple, compound, and complex—should be used strategically to accomplish objectives.

Simple sentences. A simple sentence, which has a subject and a verb, presents an idea clearly and emphatically. Thus, to emphasize an idea, use a simple sentence. Conversely, to de-emphasize an idea, use a complex sentence. Too many short, simple sentences result in choppy, dull writing. Use complex and compound sentences to add variety and to break the monotony of simple sentences.

Compare the following paragraphs about a stock prospectus (a booklet providing investment information). The first paragraph contains only simple sentences. The second contains a variety of sentences.

Simple sentences
Thank you for sending me the prospectus on the stock. I reviewed it carefully. The investment looks very good. It matches my goals very closely. A significant investment is required. I hope that I will be able to afford it.

Variety of sentences
Thank you for sending me the prospectus on the stock. I reviewed the investment opportunity carefully, and it looks very good. Although a significant investment is required, the program matches my goals very closely. I hope that I will be able to afford it.

Note that the paragraph using a variety of sentences reads better than the one using just simple sentences.

Complex sentences. A complex sentence contains an independent clause and one or more dependent clauses. Complex sentences can be used to present two ideas of unequal importance. The main clause should contain the more important idea, and the dependent clause should contain the less important idea. The two ideas should be related so that the sentence will have unity. Review the following examples of complex sentences that contain ideas of unequal importance:

> **Complex sentences**
> - Although the atmosphere was very informal, **the food was elegant**.
> - **The food was well worth the cost,** even though it was expensive.
> - When we are in town, **we will come back to this restaurant**.
> - If we hurry, **we may be able to make the next movie**.

Note that the writer placed the most important idea in the independent clause (shown in bold) in each sentence.

Compound sentences. A compound sentence contains two or more independent clauses joined by a conjunction or a conjunctive adverb, such as *moreover* or *nevertheless*. When you want to present ideas of equal importance, use compound sentence structure. Place each idea in an independent clause. The two ideas should be related so that the sentence will have unity. Review the following examples of compound sentences that contain ideas of equal importance:

> **Compound sentences**
> - The service was delightful, and the prices were reasonable.
> - Terry bought the brown coat, and Pat bought the black one.
> - The drive was long, but the beautiful scenery made it worthwhile.
> - We were strangers, but she welcomed us warmly.
> - The environment was pleasant, and we were in a happy mood.

Note that the compound sentences indicate the writer considered both ideas in each sentence of equal importance.

Structure Sentences Carefully

Sentences with good structure provide the foundation and building blocks for an effective message. Using sentences strategically is important, but it is also important that sentences be clear and grammatically correct. Several sentence structure errors that occur frequently are reviewed in this section.

Position words carefully. The position of words in a sentence can change the meaning. Keep related words as close together as possible to ensure clarity. Note how position affects clarity in the following sentences:

Position confuses
- Leslie talked about interviewing for a job with her ten-year-old brother.
- Lynn thought about the meeting that she had to attend while walking her dog.
- Beth described her vacation in the employees' lounge.

Position clarifies
- Leslie talked with her ten-year-old brother about interviewing for a job.
- While walking her dog, Lynn thought about the meeting that she had to attend.
- In the employees' lounge, Beth described her vacation.

Avoid dangling modifiers. Dangling modifiers are a common sentence structure error. A dangling modifier is a modifier that is incorrectly placed; that is, it modifies the wrong word or words. Sometimes, the word or words that a modifier is supposed to modify are not stated clearly in the sentence. Compare the following sentences with dangling modifiers to those that have improved structure:

Dangling modifiers
- If your nose is packed during surgery, it will be removed in three days.
- At maturity, I will pay the note.
- At the age of three, Lee taught his son to play the piano.

Improved structure
- If your nose is packed during surgery, the packing will be removed in three days.
- When the note matures, I will pay it.
- Lee taught his three-year-old son to play the piano.

Use parallel structure. Equal, or coordinate, ideas (ideas connected by *and*, *but*, *or*, or *nor*) should be expressed in the same form. If one coordinate idea is in an infinitive form, then all coordinate ideas should be in an infinitive form. This is known as parallel structure. Lists of items should also have parallel structure. Compare the following examples that have parallel structure with those that do not:

Structure not parallel
- We like to eat, go swimming, and take a hike.
- Our goals include quality products, meeting deadlines, and customer satisfaction.
- To use this program:
  1. Insert the disk in Drive A and press Enter.
  2. You should then key your password.
  3. When the title screen appears, the user presses the Escape key.

Parallel structure
- We like to eat, to swim, and to hike.
- Our goals include providing quality products, meeting deadlines, and satisfying customers.
- To use this program:
  1. Insert the disk in Drive A and press Enter.
  2. Key your password.
  3. Press the Escape key when the title screen appears.

Avoid overusing expletives. Expletives are unneeded words. They take up space and contribute nothing to the message. Examples of expletives include *it is, there is, there are, it was,* and similar words used to begin sentences. Compare the following sentences that contain expletives and the sentences without the expletives:

Expletives
- There is a meeting scheduled at 10:30 a.m. on Monday.
- It is important to be at the meeting on time.
- There are six reports listed on the agenda.

Revised to eliminate expletives
- A meeting is scheduled at 10:30 a.m. on Monday.
- Being at the meeting on time is important.
- Six reports are listed on the agenda.

Structure Paragraphs Carefully

Paragraph structure often makes writing interesting or dull. Unity, **coherence**, and emphasis are the key concepts that must be considered in developing effective paragraphs.

Unity. A paragraph has unity when all sentences in it relate to one topic. Limiting the number of sentences in a paragraph helps to ensure unity. The longer the paragraph, the more likely it is that sentences will stray from the main topic. Including a topic sentence helps to build unity. The topic sentence expresses the main idea of the paragraph. All other sentences should develop and support the main idea expressed in the topic sentence.

Although topic sentences are not required, most good paragraphs do have them. The placement of topic sentences varies depending on the objective of the paragraph. Normally, topic sentences begin or end paragraphs. Occasionally, a writer will choose to bury a topic sentence in the middle of a paragraph. Rarely is a buried topic sentence effective unless it is used to tone down a negative situation.

The following paragraphs illustrate topic sentences (shown in italics) positioned at the beginning, at the end, and in the middle of a paragraph:

Topic sentence at the beginning of a paragraph

Small businesses provide excellent career opportunities for new workers. Often, small businesses cannot afford to hire many people. <u>Thus</u>, those they hire must be able to carry out a variety of duties. By handling a wide range of tasks, employees of small businesses gain more experience in a year than workers in large businesses gain in several years.

Topic sentence at the end of a paragraph

Visuals aids are not required for a successful presentation. <u>However</u>, they can add interest and help emphasize important points. <u>In addition</u>, an audience can grasp complex concepts much more quickly and easily when visual support is provided. <u>Consequently</u>, time spent preparing visuals is usually invested wisely. *Effective visuals make a good presentation even better.*

Topic sentence in the middle of a paragraph

We have received your request to increase your credit limit to $5,000. When we extended credit to you six months ago, a $3,000 limit was set based on your level of income. Your request indicates that your income is still the same. <u>Moreover</u>, our records show that your payments have been late for three of the past six months. <u>*Therefore*</u>, *we are unable to extend your credit limit at this time.* We will be happy to consider an increase in your credit limit after you have maintained your account properly for one year.

You can determine if a paragraph has unity by identifying the topic sentence and then checking to see if the other sentences relate to it.

Coherence. A coherent paragraph contains ideas that are linked logically to each other. The transition from one idea to the next should be smooth and flowing. The best way to ensure coherence is by limiting the ideas in a paragraph to those that logically relate to each other. Coherence can also be gained by using carefully selected transitional words to link ideas. Examples of transitional words include *thus, consequently, however, subsequently, for example, in addition, therefore, moreover, likewise,* and *also.* Repetition is another way to link ideas.

Review the three paragraphs above that illustrate topic sentences. In these paragraphs, coherence is achieved in two ways. First, all the sentences are logically linked to the topic sentence. Second, the underlined transitional words help to link ideas.

Emphasis. Using emphasis appropriately means stressing important ideas and de-emphasizing less important ideas. A variety of techniques can be used to emphasize ideas:

- **Mechanical techniques.** These include capital letters, bold print, large font sizes, underlining, color, and clip art.

- **Space.** The amount of space devoted to developing an idea indicates the amount of emphasis given to that idea. An idea that takes several paragraphs to develop receives more emphasis than an idea developed in a single paragraph.

- **Isolation.** The empty, or white, space around an idea can be used for emphasis. A one-sentence paragraph can be very emphatic because the space around the paragraph makes it stand out. One-sentence paragraphs should be used sparingly and should be reserved for ideas meriting special attention. A postscript (P.S.) at the bottom of a letter or memo is an example of a one-sentence paragraph. A postscript should be reserved for ideas that require special emphasis. It should never be used for something left out of a message.

- **Sentence structure.** Simple sentences are direct and give emphasis to ideas. Complex and compound sentences provide less emphasis than simple sentences. In complex sentences, the idea in the main clause receives more emphasis than the idea in the dependent clause. In compound sentences, the ideas are given equal emphasis.

- **Language.** Specific language gives more emphasis to what is said than general language. Ideas that you wish to stress should be stated very specifically. General language is more appropriate for ideas that need to be de-emphasized. It is often used in sensitive situations.

- **Position.** The first and last sentences are the key emphasis positions in a paragraph. To emphasize important ideas, position them as the first or last sentence of a paragraph. To de-emphasize negative information, bury it in the middle of a paragraph.

Deciding which ideas to emphasize is a matter of judgment. Always consider the reader and the situation before determining which ideas to emphasize. A good rule of thumb is to emphasize positive ideas that will be received well by the reader and to de-emphasize negative or sensitive ideas that are not likely to be received well.

> **Application 2A-8:**
>
> Use Effective Sentence and Paragraph Structure. Turn to page 71 and complete the application.

GUIDE 9—FORMAT DOCUMENTS EFFECTIVELY

An effective format does more than make a document look pleasing. It helps the writer communicate the message by making it easier to read and understand. Good formatting accomplishes a number of objectives. For example, it:

- Creates a good first impression.
- Supports the document content.
- Adds organizational structure.
- Provides a consistent image.
- Gives a sense of formality.
- Improves readability.
- Emphasizes important points.

Many companies use a standard format and design for all their documents. Standard formats present a consistent image and make document production more efficient. Companies research document design carefully, and most focus a lot of attention on their logo and trademarks. Visual design is a key element in corporate identity and image.

Most organizations create a variety of internal and external documents ranging from letters, memos, and e-mail to forms and reports. This text emphasizes preparing letters, memos, and e-mail, so these are the formats illustrated here. Carefully review the formats illustrated in Figures 2-1 through 2-5 on pages 47–50. Read the letters and e-mail for additional formatting information.

Application 2A-9:

Format Documents Effectively. Turn to page 73 and complete the application.

GUIDE 10—EDIT AND PROOFREAD CAREFULLY

Often the difference between high-quality and mediocre messages is in how carefully they are edited and proofread. In many cases, the same individual composes and keys documents in final form. In other cases, one individual may compose a document, and another may key the document and produce it in final form. Both individuals should share responsibility for the quality of the document.

Each document produced should be edited and proofread carefully. Editing and proofreading are separate activities done at separate times that require different sets of skills.

Editing

Editing focuses on both content and mechanical correctness. From a content perspective, editing ensures that the objectives of the message were achieved and that the guides for effective writing were applied appropriately. Editing generally occurs after a document has been drafted and before producing it in final format.

Editing is a mental process that involves checking to see that the document meets certain standards. If it does not meet standards, you should revise it as part of the editing process. Editing usually is more successful if you take one step at a time.

- **Edit for content accuracy.** Determine what needs to be included in the message. Check that the message contains the information and that all information is accurate.

- **Edit for organization.** Ensure that you presented ideas logically and used appropriate sentence and paragraph structure. Check to see that the material flows smoothly.

- **Edit for writing style.** Ensure that the message is crisp, concise, and written at the appropriate level for the reader. Clarify vague statements.

- **Edit for mechanical correctness.** Check for errors in grammar, spelling, punctuation, capitalization, number usage, and word usage.

The writer is most often responsible for editing, although sometimes another person or a team edits the writer's work. Most writers like to edit their own writing to find and correct any problems. For many people, editing on the computer is quicker and easier than working on paper. Some writers, though, prefer to edit a printed copy.

Figure 2-1: Block Format Letter With Open Punctuation

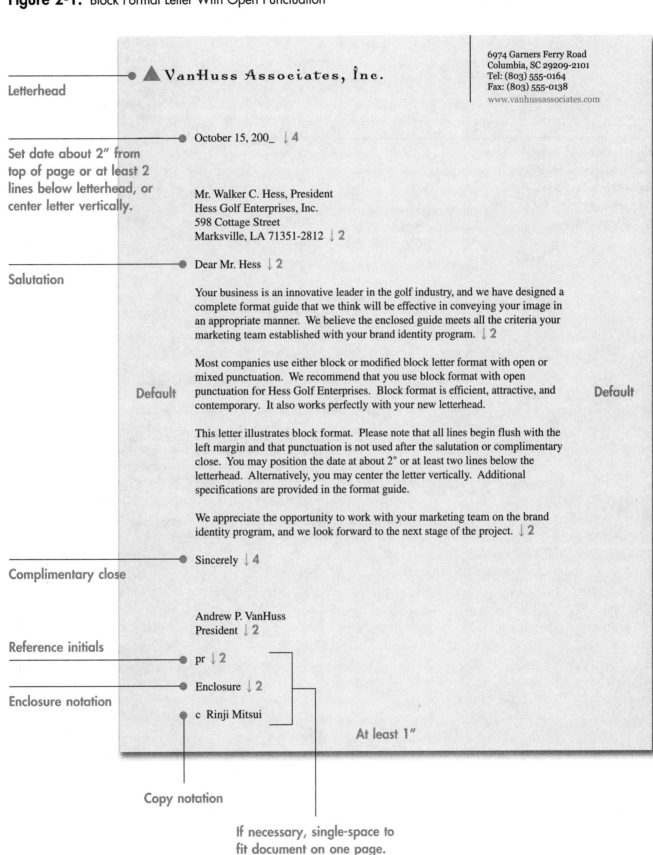

Letterhead

6974 Garners Ferry Road
Columbia, SC 29209-2101
Tel: (803) 555-0164
Fax: (803) 555-0138
www.vanhussassociates.com

 **VanHuss Associates, Inc.**

October 15, 200_ ↓ 4

Set date about 2" from
top of page or at least 2
lines below letterhead, or
center letter vertically.

Mr. Walker C. Hess, President
Hess Golf Enterprises, Inc.
598 Cottage Street
Marksville, LA 71351-2812 ↓ 2

Salutation

Dear Mr. Hess ↓ 2

Your business is an innovative leader in the golf industry, and we have designed a complete format guide that we think will be effective in conveying your image in an appropriate manner. We believe the enclosed guide meets all the criteria your marketing team established with your brand identity program. ↓ 2

Default

Most companies use either block or modified block letter format with open or mixed punctuation. We recommend that you use block format with open punctuation for Hess Golf Enterprises. Block format is efficient, attractive, and contemporary. It also works perfectly with your new letterhead.

Default

This letter illustrates block format. Please note that all lines begin flush with the left margin and that punctuation is not used after the salutation or complimentary close. You may position the date at about 2" or at least two lines below the letterhead. Alternatively, you may center the letter vertically. Additional specifications are provided in the format guide.

We appreciate the opportunity to work with your marketing team on the brand identity program, and we look forward to the next stage of the project. ↓ 2

Complimentary close

Sincerely ↓ 4

Andrew P. VanHuss
President ↓ 2

Reference initials

pr ↓ 2

Enclosure notation

Enclosure ↓ 2

c Rinji Mitsui

At least 1"

Copy notation

If necessary, single-space to
fit document on one page.

Figure 2-2: Modified Block Format Letter With Mixed Punctuation

VanHuss Associates, Inc.

6974 Garners Ferry Road
Columbia, SC 29209-2101
Tel: (803) 555-0164
Fax: (803) 555-0138
www.vanhussassociates.com

October 15, 200_ ↓ 4

Set date about 2" from top of page or at least 2 lines below letterhead, or center letter vertically. Key date at center.

Ms. Brianna A. Tallon, President
Central Medical Services, Inc.
2265 Main Street
Birmingham, AL 35210-4377 ↓ 2

Dear Ms. Tallon: ↓ 2

Your business has been a tradition in Birmingham for many years and has a very fine reputation for providing outstanding service. We have designed a complete format guide that we believe will be effective in conveying your image in an appropriate manner. We believe the enclosed guide meets all the criteria your marketing team established with your brand identity program. ↓ 2

Default

We recommend that you use modified block letter format with mixed punctuation for Central Medical Services. Modified block format is efficient, attractive, and traditional. It also works perfectly with your new letterhead.

Default

This letter illustrates modified block format. Please note that the date and closing lines are positioned at the center. A colon is used after the salutation, and a comma is used after the complimentary close. Paragraphs may be blocked, as this letter illustrates, or the first line may be indented 0.5" from the left margin. Additional specifications are provided in the format guide.

We appreciate the opportunity to work with your marketing team on the brand identity program, and we look forward to the next stage of the project. ↓ 2

Sincerely yours, ↓ 4

Key closing lines at center.

Andrew P. VanHuss
President ↓ 2

pr ↓ 2

Enclosure

At least 1"

Figure 2-3: Memorandum Format

▲VanHuss Associates, Inc.

2"

Strike Tab once or twice after *TO, FROM*, etc., to align the following text.

TO: Public Relations and Marketing Team ↓ 2

FROM: Andy VanHuss ↓ 2

DATE: October 29, 200_ ↓ 2

SUBJECT: Contract Extension ↓ 2

Thanks to all of you for a great job on the Hess Golf Enterprises, Inc., project. Walker Hess and his entire team were extremely pleased with the work we did on the first phase of the brand identity project and with the format guide we prepared for them. ↓ 2

Default

As a result, Hess Golf Enterprises has extended our contract. We will work with the company on the next phase of the brand identity project. In addition, Hess representatives are talking with us about a new project. A copy of the preliminary project description is attached.

Default

My assistant will call you to set up a meeting next week so that we can review our responsibilities for the next phase of the project. We will also talk about the new project that Hess is proposing. ↓ 2

pr ↓ 2

Attachment

Reference initials (the initials of the person who keyed the memo) are used when someone other than the writer keyed it.

At least 1"

Figure 2-4: E-Mail Format

Multiple addresses may be entered.

Always include a short subject line.

Files may be attached to an e-mail.

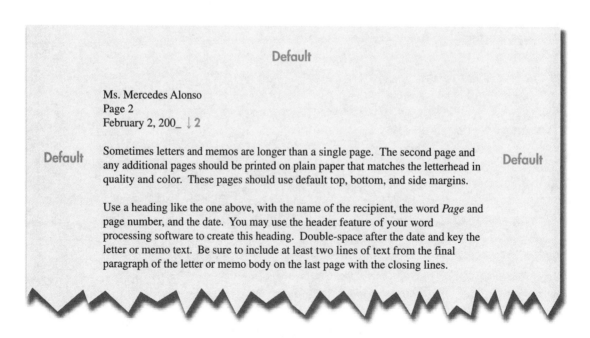

New Message	Send	Address	Attach	Options	Spelling	Print	Save	File	Edit	Format	Insert	Tools	View	Help

To: @ Walker.Hess@hessgolf.com
Cc: @ Lois.Clark@hessgolf.com, Jane.Marcotte@hessgolf.com
Subject: Format Guide
Attachments: Format Guide

An e-mail is formatted in the same way that a memorandum is formatted. It is simply distributed electronically. The header of an e-mail is prepared by filling in appropriate boxes designated for the person(s) to whom the e-mail is being sent and those who will receive copies. The current date and the sender's name are included automatically.

Some writers prefer to include the receiver's name at the beginning of the e-mail to personalize it. They then double-space and begin the body of the message. Writers may also add their name at the bottom of the e-mail, two lines below the last line of body text.

Including a short subject line is very important. It helps the recipient to sort out junk mail from business mail. Document files may be attached to an e-mail.

The design and appearance of an e-mail depends on the software used. However, all e-mail systems provide locations for entering the information shown on this e-mail.

Figure 2-5: Second-Page Heading Format

Default

Ms. Mercedes Alonso
Page 2
February 2, 200_ ↓ 2

Default

Sometimes letters and memos are longer than a single page. The second page and any additional pages should be printed on plain paper that matches the letterhead in quality and color. These pages should use default top, bottom, and side margins.

Default

Use a heading like the one above, with the name of the recipient, the word *Page* and page number, and the date. You may use the header feature of your word processing software to create this heading. Double-space after the date and key the letter or memo text. Be sure to include at least two lines of text from the final paragraph of the letter or memo body on the last page with the closing lines.

Proofreading

Proofreading focuses on the accuracy of the final document. It includes such activities as ensuring that the proper stationery was used, that appropriate mailing notations were used, and that the document does not contain any mistakes. Proofreading generally occurs after a document has been produced in final format. At this point, most errors should already have been found and corrected. Proofreading is the final check to ensure that the document is error-free.

Just before proofreading, run the spell-check and grammar-check features. Then read through the document on the computer. Use the print preview feature to see how the printed document will look. Most people proofread hard copy better than copy on a computer screen. Therefore, print out the document and proofread the printed copy.

- **Check the overall appearance of the document.** Check for appropriate stationery, attractive placement, and correct and consistent format.

- **Check for content accuracy.** Check for accuracy and completeness.

- **Check for mechanical correctness.** Check for keying errors and mistakes in grammar, spelling, punctuation, capitalization, word usage, and number usage.

You may find a guide helpful when proofreading paper copy. Get a letter-size envelope, a ruler, or a folded piece of paper. Move it down line by line as you read. This helps you focus on individual lines. If you make a lot of corrections, run the spelling feature again afterwards. A set of proofreaders' marks that are commonly used for marking corrections appears on page 53.

Proofreaders sometimes have to check a final document against an earlier version. A good method is to place the two documents side by side and to use guides to compare them. For lists of figures and other technical material, having one person read the text to another is a useful way to detect errors.

Office support staff should and usually do proofread documents carefully. However, when writers are producing their own documents, it is their responsibility to proofread them.

Technology Connections

E-Mail Quality

Many organizations use a standard style for letters and memos to ensure a consistent, high-quality corporate image. Yet, their e-mails often violate this standard. Frequently, writers send e-mails that have not been proofread or edited carefully. Creating a positive image is just as important with e-mail as it is with paper-based documents.

Technology for Editing and Proofreading

Word processing software contains several electronic reference tools that writers should use extensively. These tools aid writers in the editing and proofreading processes. They do not, however, replace careful editing and proofreading.

Spell-check. The spell-check feature scans a document and compares all words in the document to its dictionary. The feature identifies misspelled words and suggests alternative spellings. The spell-check tool can be very useful, but it has limitations. Some words that the feature identifies are not necessarily incorrect. They simply are not contained in its dictionary. Technical words and proper nouns are common examples of words that may not be in the software dictionary.

On the other hand, just because words in a document match words in the dictionary does not mean that the words were used properly. For example, if the word *form* is substituted for *from* and *principal* is substituted for *principle*, the spell-check tool would not identify them as spelling errors. The spell-check tool will not detect errors in word usage, number usage, spelling of proper nouns, punctuation, and capitalization. However, the grammar-check feature can identify many of these errors.

Grammar-check. The grammar-check tool scans a document to determine if basic rules of grammar have been applied correctly. Options for setting grammar rules and style choices are available. The same limitations that apply to checking spelling apply to checking grammar and style. Some writing problems identified are not errors, and some problems are not identified. The user can select an option so that readability statistics are displayed after grammar checks, to indicate the difficulty of the writing.

Application 2A-10:

Edit and Proofread Carefully. Turn to page 75 and complete the application.

Thesaurus. An electronic thesaurus provides online access to a dictionary of synonyms. Many times, a writer cannot think of a word that accurately fits the situation being described. The thesaurus provides a list of words meaning approximately the same thing, so that the writer can select the best word to convey the meaning intended. An electronic thesaurus can be very helpful in determining appropriate substitutes when particular words are overused.

Proofreaders' Marks

The proofreaders' marks shown on the next page are generally accepted symbols used to mark changes or revisions in a paper copy of a document. Review the proofreaders' marks carefully. You will use them in this and all the remaining chapters.

Proofreaders' Marks

SYMBOL	MEANING	USE THE SYMBOL	RESULTS
∿∿∿	Bold	Illustrate the bold symbol	Illustrate the **bold** symbol
≡	Capitalize	capitalize a letter or word	Capitalize a letter or WORD
/	Lowercase	Løwercase a letter or WORD	Lowercase a letter or word
◠	Close up space	Close up space	Close up space
✄	Delete	Delete this this word	Delete this word
∧	Insert	Insert a word	Insert a word
⌃	Insert a comma	Insert a comma then	Insert a comma, then
#	Insert a space	Insert aspace	Insert a space
∨	Insert an apostrophe	Insert an apostrophe in Pats title	Insert an apostrophe in Pat's title
—M	Insert an em dash	Insert an em dash then	Insert an em dash—then
—N	Insert an en dash	Insert an en dash in page range 6,10 N	Insert an en dash in page range 6–10
⬭→	Move	To move text to another position in a document, use this symbol	Use this symbol to move text to another position in a document
⎵	Move down	Move this text down	Move this text down
⊏	Move left	Move this text left to block the paragraph	Move this text left to block the paragraph
⊐	Move right	Move this text right to align the copy properly	Move this text right to align the copy properly
⎴	Move up	Move this text up	Move this text up
⬭ sp	Spell out	5 boxes	Five boxes
⎵⎴	Transpose	To properly align text	To align text properly
___ und	Underline	Use underline und	Use underline
___ ital	Use italics	Use italics ital	Use italics
⬭ wf	Wrong font	Next week	Next week

! Points to Remember

About the Ten Guides for Effective Writing

☑ The most critical step in writing a message is planning. Planning involves determining objectives, analyzing the reader, making decisions, collecting information, and developing a plan.

☑ A message must meet the needs of the reader. Readers expect messages to be logical, helpful, sincere, and courteous.

☑ You can accomplish more by presenting your ideas positively. Even if you have to disagree with the reader, you do not have to be disagreeable.

☑ A message should be written so clearly that it cannot be misinterpreted. Use appropriate vocabulary, sentence structure, and paragraph structure.

☑ A complete message is one that contains all the information needed to meet your objectives and those of the reader.

☑ An efficient, action-oriented style means saying everything that needs to be said and nothing more. It also means using a strong, lively style that gives a sense of movement.

☑ Concrete or specific language calls attention to and adds emphasis to statements. In most situations, it is a better choice than general language. Concrete language also conveys a precise meaning, so the reader does not have to interpret it.

☑ Effective sentences and paragraphs provide the foundation for effective messages. Sentences should be carefully arranged, clear, and grammatically correct. Paragraphs should have unity, coherence, and emphasis where appropriate.

☑ Effective formatting gives a document a pleasing appearance. It also makes the message easier to read and understand.

☑ Careful editing and proofreading produce high-quality documents.

Apply Guides for Effective Writing

Complete the following activities in the space provided, applying the guides for effective writing. Write complete, grammatically correct sentences.

1. **Plan Messages Carefully**

Plan messages for the three scenarios by answering the questions after each.

a. You are a team leader at Fairbanks Maintenance Services. Your team of 15 employees has asked you to write to Lajuana Ruiz, manager of human resources, requesting that the company implement a no-smoking policy. Plan the memo you will write.

i. What objectives will you try to achieve with your memo?

ii. How do you think Ms. Ruiz will respond?

iii. What information should you obtain before you write the memo?

iv. Since you will not actually gather the information you would need to write a detailed outline, make a basic outline of the memo you would send to the manager of human resources.

b. As manager of group services for the Roan Mountain Resort, you have received a request from Mr. Sean Roberts to book ten double rooms for one week beginning July 1. He and his wife are giving their three children and their families a vacation. Mr. Roberts has indicated a preference for three cabins with three bedrooms and two baths per cabin and one cabin with one bedroom. He has also inquired about planned activities, baby-sitting services, and other information about the area. Plan the letter that you will write.

    i. What do you expect to accomplish by writing the letter?

    ii. What do you think Mr. Roberts's objectives are?

    iii. How do you visualize Mr. Roberts?

    iv. What types of information should you send him?

    v. What other information must you have before you write the letter?

vi. Make a basic outline of the letter you would send to Mr. Roberts.

c. You are employed by Jackson Paving Company. You have received an inquiry from Evan Maxwell, manager of a small gated community called Crown Lake Estates, requesting a price quotation for developing a private road one mile long to the homes in the development.

i. What objectives will you try to achieve with your letter?

ii. What do you think Mr. Maxwell's objectives are?

iii. Do you think Mr. Maxwell sent the inquiry to your competitors?

iv. What information must you have before you provide a price quotation?

v. What information should you send Mr. Maxwell with this letter?

vi. What other information should you obtain before you write the letter?

vii. Make a basic outline of the letter you would send to Mr. Maxwell.

2. Write for the Reader

Rewrite these ten sentences and paragraphs from the perspective of the reader.

a. I like the new product packaging options you prepared for me, and I will send them to the Selection Committee.

b. If you had ordered your supplies earlier, you would have had them when you needed them.

c. What was that man telling the girls who work in the Customer Service Department?

d. Did the lady judge question the black attorney?

e. The Design Committee will consider the new product design at our 10 a.m. meeting on Friday. Before the meeting, read the report I sent you and be prepared to discuss it. Also, show up on time, as we have a lot to cover.

f. Pick up our express package on the way back from your meeting.

g. Fill out the form and bring it to the Asian guy who prints the tags.

h. I told you that you were not smart to spend your money on that stock.

i. Inform each employee that if he/she wants to hear the speech by Jane McKee, the lady attorney from the corporate office, he/she can go to the meeting.

j. Thank you in advance for representing me at the meeting.

3. Present Ideas Positively

Rewrite these sentences, presenting the ideas positively.

a. Never fax a bid without sending a confirmation copy by express mail.

b. Don't schedule a meeting if you don't have important things on the agenda.

c. Tell the customer not to complain about the product he sent back to us; his worker didn't follow the directions for adjusting it properly.

d. Why don't you call the Help Desk if you don't know how to install the new virus checker?

e. Never transmit confidential documents from a workstation that has not been cleared for security.

f. Don't forget to mail the tax form by April 15 so you won't have to pay a penalty.

g. Don't call José Sanchez today because he won't be in the office all week.

h. The cheap tickets you sold us were pathetic. Why didn't you tell us they were so high in the balcony and that we needed to go to the next price level to get a decent seat?

i. Why don't you join me for dinner tonight if you are not busy?

j. Do not use the Bradley team; they do not do high-quality work like the Henley team.

4. Write in a Clear, Readable Style

Rewrite these eight sentences or paragraphs with the following changes:

- Use a conversational tone.

- Strip long, involved, or wordy sentences of unnecessary words.

- Substitute lists or tables for series of items.

- Replace difficult vocabulary with simpler words, using a dictionary or thesaurus if necessary.

a. Mr. Jenkins admonished his youngest offspring about her excessive extravagances, which he speculated would be construed by her friends as conspicuous consumption.

b. Please make sure that all employees in your department are notified that they must participate in one of the software training programs that are scheduled every Friday morning in October and November and that they must inform Jean Nauman, our training coordinator, as to which session they will attend so that a seat can be reserved and appropriate materials made available for them.

c. Pursuant to your request about the above-referenced software training program, I have scheduled you to participate on Friday, September 15.

d. Mayo recapitulated the prevalent opinions of both the opponents and proponents of the controversial proposal at the conclusion of the discussion and promised to provide a written synopsis in a reasonably expeditious manner.

e. The selection process is a complicated one involving screening interviews by recruiters on campus. Then the second step is to have in-company interviews with a manager from the human resources department, and then the manager of the department with the position available interviews the candidates who pass the first two screening hurdles.

f. The new online real estate service lists four homes that may be of interest to you. The first one is at 4937 Maple Street, has 3,950 square feet, and is listed at $269,575. The second one is at 2186 Queen Street, has 4,380 square feet, and is listed at $290,725. The third one is at 6274 Sims Alley, has 5,100 square feet, and is listed at $324,500. The fourth one is at 2864 Oak Street, has 5,264 square feet, and is listed at $340,725.

g. Your design class requires a design ruler, a furniture template, an appliance template, graph paper, an architectural symbol guide, several sharpened pencils, an art eraser, and tracing paper.

h. Will the major ramification of automation of the plant be a permanent displacement of employees, or will the major ramification be a redeployment of employees to other positions here or in other localities?

5. Check for Completeness

For the following situations, indicate the information you must provide and the questions you should anticipate to ensure the message is complete.

a. The regional playoff baseball game scheduled at 1:30 p.m. today has been canceled.

Information you must provide:

b. All senior managers are expected to participate in the off-site Strategic Planning Retreat on March 6.

Information you must provide:

Questions you should anticipate:

c. You are writing a memo to inform all managers that the company will provide an automobile allowance for them to use their own cars rather than furnish them with a company car.

Information you must provide:

Questions you should anticipate:

d. You must send an e-mail to all employees encouraging them to participate in the blood drive on Friday.

Information you must provide:

Questions you should anticipate:

e. You are preparing a memo telling all employees that Shirley Wilcox, the company's chief financial officer, will visit the plant on October 10 to discuss the impact of the budget cuts announced last week.

Information you must provide:

Questions you should anticipate:

f. You are writing a memo to your supervisor to request that your expenses be paid to attend a three-day technical writing seminar in San Francisco.

Information you must provide:

Questions you should anticipate:

6. Use an Efficient, Action-Oriented Style

Rewrite these ten sentences with the following changes:

- Use an efficient, action-oriented style.
- Use the active voice unless it is awkward or inappropriate to do so.

One sentence does not require any changes.

a. Anne is of the opinion that the resolution of the zoning issue may occur in the month of October.

b. Jack was given an invitation to a reception to be held before the football game by the president because of his position as a member of the Foundation Board of Directors.

c. The agreement was read and was approved by the neighborhood association and by the property owners.

d. Lynn made the statement to the two teams that if they did not cooperate together he would seriously take into consideration merging them together and reverting back to the previous organizational structure.

e. Pattie not only was able to find us a house that was nice in her neighborhood but also gave us a lot of help and assistance when we moved to our new home.

f. They packaged four boxes that were square in shape and 20 pounds in weight and sent them to the mayor of the city of Tulsa in the state of Oklahoma.

g. The furniture was scratched either during shipment or during the unpacking process.

h. Please make the announcement that the alternate location of the picnic in the event of rain will be the Field House.

i. The scholarship in the amount of $5,000 was presented by the president of the Civic Club, Dylan Johnson, to the recipient, Julie Morrison.

j. Please make the correction in the invoice so that it will be an accurate reflection of the cost.

7. Use Concrete Language

Read the following sentences and interpret the general language from your perspective. Rewrite the sentences, substituting what you believe to be appropriate specific language. After you complete all ten sentences, compare your revisions with those of your classmates to see if their interpretations were similar to yours.

a. Bert bought a lot of expensive books for his classes this semester.

b. They worked a long time and produced a short paper.

c. Please send me a good supply of brochures as soon as possible.

d. A large percentage of our students work a lot during the week.

e. Michelle makes a lot more money as an investment banker than Brian does as a surgeon.

f. Natalie and Nicholas stayed too long at the party and got home much too late.

g. We made a significant investment in the project, but it brought us a great return.

h. Kevin makes a lot of money each month in addition to what he earns in his regular job.

i. Please pay the invoice for your dental work at your earliest convenience.

j. Susie works very late quite often.

8. Use Effective Sentence and Paragraph Structure

Revise these sentences and paragraphs with the following changes:

- Improve the sentence structure.
- Combine choppy sentences to make them more coherent.
- Make sentences clear and grammatically correct.

a. If your payment on your automobile is late again, it will be repossessed.

b. On our trips, we prefer to shop for good bargains, swimming in the ocean, and not dressing up.

c. There is a meeting the president scheduled at two o'clock this afternoon in the auditorium. Do you plan to go? No agenda was sent out. I think the new product line will be discussed.

d. When cooking the pasta, the salt was left out.

e. There is a reception at six o'clock.

For item f, place parentheses around the topic sentence and underline transitional words.

f. A number of organizations have gotten rid of management positions in the process of downsizing. In addition, more people are seeking management jobs. Managers with excellent communication skills are in the best position to move up the career ladder. Therefore, managers who want to increase their chances for promotion should work hard to develop good communication skills.

g. Write a three- or four-sentence paragraph explaining why you would prefer to live in a small town rather than a large city (or the reverse— why you would prefer a large city to a small town). Put parentheses around the topic sentence and underline transitional words.

h. List the techniques you used for emphasis in the paragraph you just wrote in *g* above.

i. Write a paragraph of at least five sentences explaining why good communication skills are necessary for most jobs. Place parentheses around the topic sentence and underline transitional words.

j. List the techniques you used for emphasis in the paragraph you just wrote in *i* above.

9. Format Documents Effectively

a. Describe the differences between a block letter format and a modified block letter format.

b. Describe the differences between mixed and open punctuation.

c. Write the heading for a memo to all employees in the Marketing Department from you telling them that the new telephone system will be installed next week. Use the current date. Be sure to include a subject line.

d. Give at least five reasons why effective document format is important.

e. The letter on the next page is supposed to be in block format with open punctuation. Mark any changes on the letter that need to be made to correct the format. If necessary, refer to the table of proofreaders' marks on page 53.

METRO MANUFACTURING, INC.

WWW.METROMANUFACTURING.COM

Current date

Mr. Zachary Jacobs
Vice President, Marketing
The Holly Resort
3298 Holly Avenue
Flint, MI 48506-3057
Dear Mr. Jacobs,

Thank you for your order for four customized snowmobiles for The Holly Resort.
We appreciate your business, and we anticipate that the job can be completed in
about two weeks.

In reviewing the specifications you provided, we noted several differences from the
specifications for the order you placed last year. These differences will have a
significant cost impact. Before we begin work on your order, we want to give you
several options to consider. These options would provide approximately the same
results at a substantial cost savings.

Please review the attached design suggestions and itemized cost estimate. As soon
as you authorize the final design and approve the cost, we will begin the work. We
look forward to hearing from you soon.

Sincerely yours

Christian T. Austin, Jr.
Production Manager

Attachments

si

10. Edit and Proofread Carefully

Guide 10 is reviewed in Application 2B of this chapter and in Application B of all the remaining chapters in this textbook. Write the proofreaders' marks you would use to make the following edits:

a. Delete

f. Transpose

b. Capitalize

g. Move right

c. Insert a space

h. Close up space

d. Insert an em dash

i. Bold

e. Use italics

j. Underline

Editing and Language Arts Checkpoint

1. Carefully read the document that follows; it is packed with errors. Use proofreaders' marks to mark all errors in grammar, spelling, usage, word choice, capitalization, punctuation, and keying. If you need help with proofreaders' marks, refer to the table on page 53. Do not revise sentence or paragraph structure unless you find an error.

2. Access *File 2B* in the Chapter 2 folder on your student data disk and make the corrections. If you are not working with the data disk, key the document, making the corrections as you key. You may use online reference tools just as you would if you were editing this document as part of your job.

3. Add a memo heading to the document, which will be sent to department managers from you. Use May 20 of this year as the date, and supply an appropriate subject line. Format the two-page memo correctly, referring to the models on pages 49 and 50. Save the file as *2Bsi* (replace *si* with your initials).

The executive committee plans to meet on june 7 at 2 o'clock in conference room A to develop a strategic plan for implementing technology changes. At it's meeting on March 15th, the comittee discussed our current computer an network systems with Ashley Price a leading Consultant with Central Technology services, who we hired on Gina's recommendation. Ms. Price agreed to apprise our situation, and to report back to us.

2 weeks ago Ms. Price called Rick in our Personal Department and asked whether she could interview 5 Managers and about 20 experienced knowledgeable computer users early next week? Rick

is scheduling 45 minute slots for managers and thirty minute slots

for computer users. The interviews will be held at our new facility

on Highway Ten on the South side of the city. This sight is more

convenient for staff then the building at 1 Main Street.

All managers should do they're best to acommodate requests

form Rick for staff and managerial time. If you are unable to

schedule an interview please call me immediately so i can choose

someone else to participate.

Ms. Prices has prepared a preliminary report which is

attached. As we might of expected, it recomends extensive

changes. To slow and lacking sufficient memory, the report states

that our 486's cannot meet our projected processing and storage

needs. It also points out the that computers cannot run the newer

(8.0) version of our office suite. Ms. Price thinks we should replace

it with Pentium IV computers with 256 MB or RAM, 40-GHz hard

drives, and nineteen″ monitors. She also proposes that we upgrade

our office suite and invest in top of the line Firewall and Virus

Protection Software. In addition Ms. Price suggests switching to

broadband Internet connections.

The report also analyzes our data storage and and file-sharing problems. According to Ms Price an NAS (network attached storage server is the answer. On Page 8 of the report, she says "an NAS server will plug into your network easy. It will appear in users desktops as an extra drive.An NAS server can back up any type file, and can offer you're employees quick easy and secure access to shared files." Ms. Price adds that NAS servers are cost-effective, and can be upgraded easily to meet our data storage and file-sharing needs.

The cost of all these improvements are 27% higher than anticipated. If we except Ms. Price's advise, our Long Range Budget committee will have to determine the affect these expeinditures will have on our budget before we precede.

This upgraded technology will sure save our empoyees a grate deal of time and make them even more productive. We must compliment our investment in hardware and software with a investment in our personal. We have invited 4 companies to submit proposals to provide us with Web based training materials. I will review these materials. And will report on all these developments at the June meeting.

Please review Ms. Prices report; and be prepared to coment on it at the meeting. You are welcome too right or stop by before then to discuss their conclusions and your department's needs. We appreciate the efforts you have made to insure that the technology we choose will work good, grow with us, and be cost-effective.

Attachment

Mastery Check for Chapter 2

1. List the five steps that you should use to plan messages systematically.

2. Provide two examples of statements that are written from the writer's perspective and may offend the reader.

3. What does the statement "Disagree, but do not be disagreeable" mean?

4. What are some of the key factors that determine whether a message is clear and easy to read?

5. What are assumptions and how do they affect the completeness of a message?

6. Explain what is meant by an efficient, action-oriented style of writing.

7. In what types of situations might general language be more appropriate than specific language?

8. Why is a topic sentence positioned at the beginning or end of a paragraph generally more effective than one positioned in the middle of a paragraph?

9. How does editing differ from proofreading?

10. For each of the terms shown below, write a complete, correct sentence using the term.

Brainstorming

Empathy

Jargon

Shell Cove—Entertainment Division

In your second rotation at Shell Cove, you are serving as assistant manager of the Entertainment Division, reporting to Ms. Samantha (Sam) Howard, the director. The Entertainment Division is responsible for creating, marketing, managing, and financing all entertainment *venues* (sites or places for events or activities). Currently, these include Showtime at Shell Cove, Coastal Stampede, Shell Cove Water Park, and Shell Cove Comedy House. A brief description of each venue follows:

Showtime at Shell Cove. This venue features a 12-screen theater that shows current movies, an IMAX theater, a dancing-waters fountain on the cove, a theater for Broadway and off-Broadway shows on tour, and the Beach Music Club. Additional attractions need to be developed.

Coastal Stampede. This venue features a combination of country, western, and vaudeville-style entertainment. The first phase, which has already been developed, consists of an open-air arena with raised, covered seating and a concourse for dancing, dining, and staging dinner shows. Food is a country-type preset menu (barbeque, fried chicken, corn on the cob, baked beans, etc.). The floor of the arena has not yet been developed, but it will be used for shows involving teams of outstanding horses ridden by talented performers in gala costumes who guide their horses through a variety of precise drills as well as for other selected events. Currently, Coastal Stampede is used only in the evenings.

Shell Cove Water Park. This venue features a full-size water park with multiple attractions and different areas designed to appeal primarily to young children and teenagers. Additional features need to be considered to make this venue appeal to families and people of all ages.

Shell Cove Comedy House. This venue attracts college students and other young adults. It features one professional or "semi-professional" comedian each evening. In addition, afternoon auditions are held to select local comedians who wish to learn the trade and build a following. These unpaid entertainers perform as a warm-up to the paid entertainers each evening.

An analysis completed this week shows that all venues have excellent attendance and are now profitable. These results far exceed the original projections.

Job 1: Coastal Stampede Arena

Sam Howard has asked you to write a description of the process for determining the ultimate use of the Coastal Stampede arena. She will include this description in a memo to Chuck Austin, director of the Property Development Division, asking him to proceed with the development of Phase 2.

Originally the open arena floor was going to be used only for evening shows, including the horseback riding events described above, drill troupes, and acrobatic and gymnastic riders. Now the plan is to include daytime activities that would appeal to families and children. Two employees from the Entertainment Division will use the Internet to research competitive sites and activities and to make recommendations for appropriate entertainment. A representative from the Property Development Division should participate in this team because the final use may impact the construction of the arena.

Write a description of the process for determining how Coastal Stampede will be used. Use plain paper rather than letterhead for this assignment. Save your work as *2D1si*. Remember to substitute your initials for *si* (student initials) and to save your file in the Shell Cove folder.

Job 2: Employee Communications

Sam has asked you to send a weekly group e-mail to Entertainment Division employees to keep them aware of current division activities and news. The e-mail should be upbeat and should include information that will interest and motivate the staff.

For your first e-mail, you have decided to draft two or three paragraphs on the entertainment venue analysis completed this week and on how plans for the Coastal Stampede arena are progressing. Since this is your first day in this division, you would like to show your draft to Sam and also ask if the Coastal Stampede information should be shared before you send it out as an e-mail. Save your work as *2D2si*. Use plain paper for this activity.

Team Activity

Internet Activity

Job 3: New Venue Team and Internet Project

The four entertainment venues at Coastal Stampede have excellent attendance and are already profitable. Therefore, the management team feels that it is time to add at least two more entertainment venues or attractions. Sam has asked you to lead a team that will begin developing ideas. You need at least three members of your class to work with you. Use the following process to complete this assignment:

a. Carefully review the venues that currently exist. Your proposed venues or attractions may be totally new, or they may be additions to existing venues. Try to have at least one totally new venue or attraction.

b. Use a brainstorming approach to come up with ideas for entertainment that would fit in with the Shell Cove development and that would appeal to the variety of customers that Shell Cove attracts. For example, some venues or added attractions might have broad appeal, while others might target specific groups like families or adults. Consider some activities that would appeal to specific groups, as well as others that would appeal to a broad range of ages and interests.

c. Use a brainstorming approach to determine the best way to obtain and evaluate all the information you need to make good recommendations to Sam.

d. Collect information about entertainment ideas and competitive upscale entertainment sites, including but not limited to beach sites. Use the Internet for this part of the project.

e. Choose three venues or attractions to recommend.

f. Write several paragraphs describing the three venues or added attractions that your team recommends. Give the advantages and disadvantages of developing each. Use plain paper for this activity, and save your work as *2D3tp-si* (remember, team projects are named with *tp* and one team member's initials).

3

GOOD-NEWS MESSAGES

OBJECTIVES

After you complete Chapter 3, you should be able to:

- Use a direct strategy for writing good-news messages.
- Adapt the strategy slightly for writing neutral messages.
- Edit messages more effectively.

OVERVIEW

Good writers know that both strategy and style determine the success of their writing. Chapter 3 teaches you to use a strategy that is based on the likely reaction the reader will have to your message. It also considers the situation that the message addresses. The key elements of this chapter include:

- Determining the reader's likely reaction.
- Planning good-news messages.
- Strategy for writing good-news messages.
- Planning neutral messages.
- Strategy for writing neutral messages.
- Using technology to share information.
- Using strategy wisely.

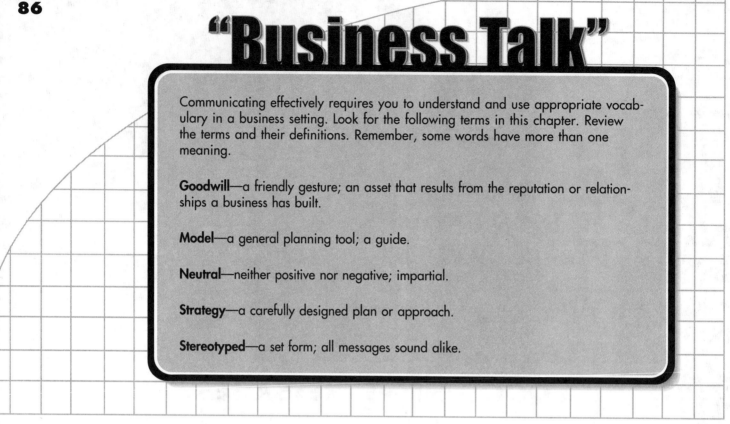

"Business Talk"

Communicating effectively requires you to understand and use appropriate vocabulary in a business setting. Look for the following terms in this chapter. Review the terms and their definitions. Remember, some words have more than one meaning.

Goodwill—a friendly gesture; an asset that results from the reputation or relationships a business has built.

Model—a general planning tool; a guide.

Neutral—neither positive nor negative; impartial.

Strategy—a carefully designed plan or approach.

Stereotyped—a set form; all messages sound alike.

STRATEGY AND READER REACTION

The writing **strategy** that you should use depends on the reaction that you expect from the reader and the situation. Style also impacts strategy. The purpose of any message is to convey information in such a way that the reader understands it as you intended. Always adapt your message to meet the needs of the reader rather than your own.

Determine the Reader's Likely Reaction

Readers react in different ways to messages they receive. Typically, they respond in one of four ways:

1. A reader may be pleased with the message. A reader who likes a message usually responds to it in a positive way. This type of message is known as a good-news or positive message.
2. A reader may react to a message with little or no emotion. The reader does not think of it as either good news or bad news. Most of the time such a message simply conveys information. This type of message is known as a **neutral** or routine message.
3. A reader may be displeased with the message. A reader who does not like a message typically responds to it in a negative way. This type of message is known as a bad-news or negative message.
4. A reader may question the content of the message and wonder what to do about it. This type of reaction differs from those in the first three situations. The reader may ask: Should I do this? Why? What is in it for me? Of what value is this? In such situations, you have to convince the reader to respond to your request. This type of message is known as a persuasive message.

Global Connections

Cultural Differences

Understanding cultural differences is important in building relationships, being able to communicate effectively, and being able to do business in other countries. The more you know about your international customers, the better you will be able to do business with them. The more you know about the international competition that you face, the better you will perform. The more you know about your fellow employees, the better you will work with them. Taking time to learn about other cultures shows your interest and helps you make a good impression.

How can you learn about different cultures? How about the Internet? Explore foreign Web sites. Read English versions of foreign magazines and newspapers that the Web makes available. Join a chat group in another country. Spend some time in an ethnic neighborhood in your area. Look around, sample foods, talk to people, or just sit and observe. Stop by a library and get some good books by writers from different cultures. Specific references such as books and Web sites can suggest things to do and not to do when conducting business in different parts of the world.

This chapter focuses on strategies for writing good-news and neutral messages. Chapter 4 teaches you strategies for writing bad-news messages. Chapter 5 covers strategies for writing persuasive messages.

Choose a Strategy

Remember, the strategy you should use depends on the situation and the reaction you expect from the reader. Each of the different types of messages calls for a different strategy. The reader's likely reaction gives you clues as to the best strategy to use. If you expect a negative reaction, the situation is likely to be a sensitive one that you must treat very carefully. If you expect a positive reaction, the situation is not likely to be a sensitive one.

PLANNING GOOD-NEWS MESSAGES

In Chapter 2, the first guide for effective writing, "Plan Messages Carefully," gave you general guidelines for planning messages. In this chapter, you must apply these guidelines specifically to good-news messages. You should plan messages carefully to ensure that you meet the specific needs of the reader and the situation. You need to think about the plan that will produce the best results before you start to write.

The planning stage gives you the opportunity to try to determine how the reader is likely to react and to understand the situation. Once you have clues about the reader's reaction and the situation, then you should compare your view of the situation to that of the reader. This will help you select the best strategy to use.

As you review the following steps in the planning process, which you learned in Chapter 2, think specifically about applying the steps to good-news messages.

Determine Objectives

What are you trying to accomplish when you write the message? What do you think the reader's objectives will be? Are your objectives and the reader's objectives the same? In a good-news message, your objectives and the reader's objectives tend to be very similar. Writing a message is much easier when both the reader and the writer want to accomplish the same thing.

Analyze the Reader

How do you visualize the reader? Keep in mind that the reader should be receptive to your message. Your challenge is to present the information in a way that makes it easy for the reader to understand and to use the information appropriately. Have you had any previous contact with the reader? Past contact—letters, personal visits, or telephone calls—gives the best clues about a reader's style and the style that might be best to use in the current situation.

Look for information on age, education, occupation, technical knowledge, and similar topics to help you visualize the reader. You would not use the same style to write to one of your peers that you would use to write to a much older person. The language you use for someone who has technical knowledge about a situation should be different than that used for someone who does not. Considering these factors helps you determine the vocabulary level, the amount of detail that should be provided, and ways to personalize the message.

Make Decisions

All decisions that are to be communicated to the reader should be made before writing begins. Once you decide that the message contains good news, then you need to follow the good-news strategy presented in the next section. This decision usually determines how long a message should be. When readers welcome your news, they typically do not want a long explanation. They simply want to understand the good news, and they are pleased with your message.

Success Tip

Be resourceful; locate information without having to ask for it.

Collect Information

You need two types of information to plan and write effective messages. When you analyzed the reader, you collected the first type of information—background information about the reader. The second type of information is that which you must supply to the reader. For example, a reader may ask about specific features of a product or service. You may need to get detailed information from files or from other employees. Having all the information you need before you begin writing enables you to organize your work effectively.

Develop a Writing Plan

A good plan ensures that all the information needed is available and organized effectively. The type of plan that works best usually depends on the experience of the writer. A written outline for each message helps an inexperienced writer prepare effective messages in an efficient manner. A more experienced writer may write effective messages using a few marginal notes or a mental outline.

Most writers enjoy writing good-news messages because they tend to be short and easy to write. The reader rarely questions good news when it is received. Therefore, you do not have to present detailed information.

STRATEGY FOR WRITING GOOD-NEWS MESSAGES

A direct, straightforward approach typically works best in writing good-news messages. Using a direct approach provides a distinct psychological advantage. The reader knows immediately that good news follows and looks forward to reading the remainder of the message. Use the following strategy:

1. State the good news very early in the message—preferably in the first sentence.
2. Provide supporting details and any needed explanation.
3. Use a positive, friendly closing paragraph designed to build **goodwill**.

People like to hear good news; therefore, telling them the good news immediately is logical. More important, presenting good news very early creates a good first impression and sets the tone for the entire message. First impressions tend to be lasting impressions. The reader—pleased with the good news—becomes comfortable with the message and is free to focus on the details.

A direct approach provides an additional benefit in that it applies techniques of emphasis effectively. In Guide 8 of Chapter 2, you learned that the beginning and end of paragraphs and messages are the key emphasis positions. The direct strategy uses emphasis techniques masterfully because it:

1. Provides the information the reader wants to hear at the very beginning of both the paragraph and the message.
2. Minimizes the detail and puts it in the middle, which is a less emphatic position.
3. Closes on a positive note.

The letter in Figure 3-1 on page 90 illustrates the use of the direct strategy for good-news messages. Analyze the letter carefully. Pay particular attention to the first paragraph. Note that presenting the good news in the opening paragraph sets the tone for the entire letter. The details are presented in the middle paragraphs—the ones that get the least emphasis. The final paragraph builds goodwill and leaves the reader with positive thoughts.

PLANNING NEUTRAL MESSAGES

Typically, neutral messages convey routine information that readers expect to receive. The message generally does not create any emotion. The reader simply receives the information and does not think of it as good or bad news. Inquiries, responses to inquiries, notices, and cover letters generally are considered neutral messages. For example, suppose you receive a message indicating that your car is due for its regular maintenance. Your reaction is likely to be, I need to schedule the maintenance. This type of message does not make you happy or unhappy.

You should use the same planning approach for neutral messages that you use for good-news messages. The planning process consists of the following steps:

1. Determine specifically what you want to accomplish and what the reader wants.
2. Try to visualize the reader so that you can present the information effectively.
3. Make all decisions before you begin to write.
4. Collect the information you need.
5. Develop a writing plan.

When planning a neutral message, you should analyze the information you must convey to determine what is most important. Since you are giving the reader routine information that is unlikely to arouse emotion, it is logical to begin with the important information and then move on to things that are not as important.

Figure 3-1: Example of a Good-News Letter

The **Hess** Center

www.hesscenter.com

October 15, 200_

Ms. Vanessa D. Penn
3927 Hutchins Avenue
Seattle, WA 98111-6475

Dear Ms. Penn

Congratulations! The Hess Scholars Foundation has selected you as one of eight full-scholarship participants in the Developing Creative Leaders program. More than 10,000 applicants competed for 100 seats in the program. The eight finalists will receive full scholarships valued at $20,000 each.

The nine-week program begins June 15 with a one-week session at the Hess Center in Dallas. Then you will return home for a three-week project in your local community. The second session is at the World Training Center in New York. After this weeklong session, you will spend the next three weeks at home completing your leadership project. The program ends with the final week at the Grand Resort on the Kona Coast of Hawaii.

The enclosed packet provides detailed information about preparing for and attending the Developing Creative Leaders program. One of our program coordinators will contact you to finalize all your plans.

With your outstanding leadership potential, we know that you will contribute as much to others in the program as you will gain from the program. Again, congratulations to you.

Sincerely yours

Jared C. Jordan
Program Director

pr

Enclosure

1493 Stemmons Avenue • Dallas, TX 75208-2301 • TEL: (214) 555-0187 • FAX: (214) 555-0129

Presents good news early and sets tone for entire letter.

Provides supporting information.

Closes on a friendly note that builds goodwill.

STRATEGY FOR WRITING NEUTRAL MESSAGES

Use the following strategy for writing neutral messages:

1. Present the most important information first, preferably in the first sentence or paragraph.
2. Present details and less important information next.
3. Close with a positive, friendly paragraph designed to build goodwill.

Using a direct approach for neutral messages has the same logical and psychological advantages as using it for good-news messages. When you tell the reader the most important news first, the reaction is likely to be favorable. Starting off with the most important news also sets the tone for the message.

A successful routine message presents the information in order of importance and in a concise, easy-to-read manner. You should try to build goodwill with every message you write. Therefore, use the closing paragraph to leave a good impression.

The direct strategy for good-news messages uses emphasis techniques effectively. The same is true when you use the direct strategy for neutral messages. The most important information is emphasized by putting it in the first sentence. Less important information is in the middle paragraphs, which receive less emphasis. The goodwill message is emphasized in the closing paragraph.

USING TECHNOLOGY TO SHARE INFORMATION

The information presented in Figure 3-2 could have been sent quickly and easily by e-mail. Two options could have been used. The first option is to substitute an e-mail for the memo. The second is to attach the memo to an e-mail for distribution. Because businesspeople get so many e-mails, a memo sometimes gets more attention.

Technology Connections

Instant Messaging

Instant messaging (IM) is a popular tool for determining if buddies are online and are willing to chat or play games. Now it is moving to the corporate setting. In a recent year the number of instant messages sent at work increased 110 percent.

With IM, messages fly back and forth, faster than e-mail. Workers use IM to get urgently needed information, send important news, signal that a client is waiting, and avoid telephone tag. Two problems with instant messaging have been lack of security and the inability to keep a record of correspondence. New business versions of IM software are addressing these issues.

Figure 3-2: Example of a Neutral Memo

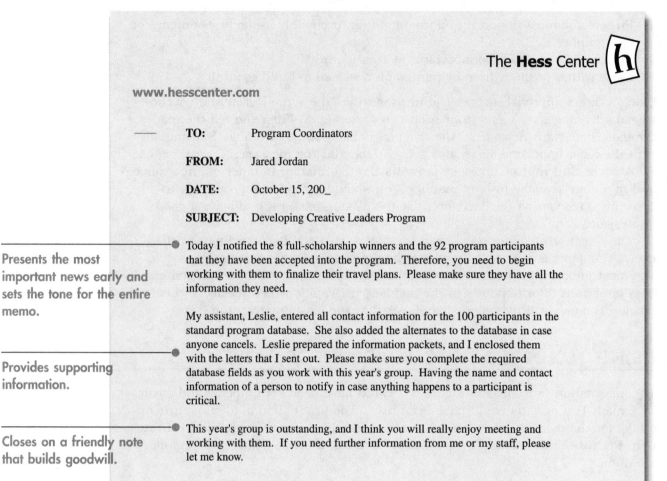

www.hesscenter.com

The **Hess** Center

TO: Program Coordinators

FROM: Jared Jordan

DATE: October 15, 200_

SUBJECT: Developing Creative Leaders Program

Presents the most important news early and sets the tone for the entire memo.

Today I notified the 8 full-scholarship winners and the 92 program participants that they have been accepted into the program. Therefore, you need to begin working with them to finalize their travel plans. Please make sure they have all the information they need.

Provides supporting information.

My assistant, Leslie, entered all contact information for the 100 participants in the standard program database. She also added the alternates to the database in case anyone cancels. Leslie prepared the information packets, and I enclosed them with the letters that I sent out. Please make sure you complete the required database fields as you work with this year's group. Having the name and contact information of a person to notify in case anything happens to a participant is critical.

Closes on a friendly note that builds goodwill.

This year's group is outstanding, and I think you will really enjoy meeting and working with them. If you need further information from me or my staff, please let me know.

pr

Companies expect their employees to be efficient. Having employees key the same information in different areas of the company wastes time and money. It also makes errors more likely. You learned in Chapter 1 that you can increase your productivity by using technology effectively to collect and share information. The memo you have just reviewed provides a good illustration of a situation in which many employees need access to the same information.

Two options are especially useful for sharing information. In this case, the information was placed in a database. Companies may also use a shared file location, so that all employees who work on a project have direct access to the information they need. With either option, the information is entered just once. Employees do not have to write memos and e-mail requesting or transmitting information. Updates can be made quickly and easily, with the assurance that everyone is working with the most current information.

Success Tip

You are often judged by the way you communicate with others. Keep this in mind when you send an e-mail. Ensuring the quality of an e-mail is just as important as ensuring the quality of a letter or memo.

USING STRATEGY WISELY

The strategy approach to writing helps you get started quickly and produce good results early on. Usually, the most difficult part of writing is getting started. Using a writing strategy makes it easy to determine what information should be presented in the first paragraph. Once you have written the first sentence or two, the rest of the message tends to flow smoothly. As you gain more experience writing, you will depend less on following specific strategies.

Some writers confuse strategies and **models**. A strategy differs from a model. The difference is subtle, but it is important. A model is a general planning tool that can be applied to all messages. A strategy may involve a model, but it does more. A strategy designed to meet the needs of a reader is more specific than a model.

A caution is in order, however, about using a particular strategy as a model or formula for writing. Using a strategy too often can lead to **stereotyped** messages. Stereotyped messages all sound alike. Good writers avoid stereotyped messages by planning carefully. The objective of each message is different, and each reader is different. A custom-designed message that is targeted to the needs of a specific reader and situation will be different from a message that is targeted to the needs of a different reader and situation.

Success Tip

Frequent communication enhances customer satisfaction.

! Points to Remember

About Good-News Messages

☑ The expected reader reaction and the situation should determine the best strategy for writing messages.

☑ Readers typically react to a message in one of four ways: they are pleased, are displeased, are neutral, or question the content of the message.

☑ You should plan messages carefully to ensure that you meet the specific needs of the reader and the situation.

☑ An effective strategy for writing good-news messages is to present the good news early, follow with the needed details, and close with a friendly paragraph that builds goodwill.

☑ An effective strategy for writing neutral messages is to present the most important information first, then provide the details, and close with a friendly paragraph that builds goodwill.

☑ Sharing a database or file location can make you more productive. It saves time and effort and reduces the chance of errors.

☑ Good writers avoid stereotyped messages by planning carefully and targeting messages to meet the objectives and specific needs of the reader and the situation.

Review Guide 1—Plan Messages Carefully

Review Guide 1 of Chapter 2 on pages 22–25, and then complete the following activities. You may need to create details for some answers.

1. Your company is scheduled to move to new offices over the weekend. Telephone and data lines will be disconnected at 6:00 on Thursday evening. The movers will begin packing at 10:00 on Friday morning. Employees who wish to pack some of their own belongings must do so before that time. All desks and furniture tops must be cleared before the movers begin packing. The movers plan to transport all furniture and boxes on Saturday.

The departmental moving committees reviewed and approved the layout for furniture placement last week. Employees should take appropriate measures to secure confidential documents. On Friday, employees may work from home or in the conference room in the new offices for their department. Plan a neutral memo that you will send to all employees conveying this information.

a. What objectives do you wish to accomplish?

b. What objectives do you think the employees want to accomplish?

c. What do you know about your employees that will help you write this memo?

d. What information should you present first?

e. What type of goodwill close would be appropriate?

2. Westfield University was one of 60 universities that placed a bid to host the USA Youth Soccer Tournament next year. You awarded Westfield the bid because its coaches have a great reputation for offering excellent soccer camps for youth and it has an outstanding soccer program, very good facilities, and terrific fan support.

The USA Youth Soccer Tournament Planning Team wishes to visit the
Westfield campus October 10–11 to finalize the contract and to begin
planning for the event. Plan the good-news letter you will write to Dr. Alex
Bryant, athletics director of Westfield University. In your letter, you will
note that you are enclosing a planning manual that explains the detailed
procedures the team uses in working with site coordinators. You will also
point out the checklist of tasks to be completed in Appendix A of the
manual.

a. What objectives do you wish to accomplish?

b. What objectives do you think Dr. Bryant wants to accomplish?

c. What do you know about Dr. Bryant that will help you write this letter?

d. What information should you present first?

e. What type of goodwill close would be appropriate?

3. Assume you are Dr. Bryant. You want to send an e-mail to all your soccer
coaches providing them with the information you just received about hosting the USA Youth Soccer Tournament. You also want them to attend a
reception at your home on the evening of October 10 to welcome the planning team. In addition, you need to tell your coaches that copies of the
planning manual with a checklist of the tasks you need to accomplish will
be sent to them this week.

Use the same five-step approach that you used for the first two activities to
plan the e-mail that you will send to all your soccer coaches. Then briefly
describe your writing strategy, following the three-step format for good-news
messages given in the chapter. Use the computer or a separate piece of
paper for this activity.

Editing and Language Arts Checkpoint

1. Carefully read the document that follows; it is packed with errors. Use proofreaders' marks to mark all errors in grammar, spelling, usage, word choice, capitalization, punctuation, and keying. If you need help with proofreaders' marks, refer to the table on page 53. Do not revise sentence or paragraph structure unless you find an error.

2. Access *File 3B* in the Chapter 3 folder on your student data disk and make the corrections. If you are not working with the data disk, key the document, making the corrections as you key. You may use online reference tools just as you would if you were editing this document as part of your job.

3. If you are not working with the data disk, format the document as a memo from you to Jan Marks. Date it June 8 of this year, and supply an appropriate subject line. Save as *3Bsi*.

Thank you for giving me a opportunity to review the Nova Web based training materials. I looked careful at the training package form the prospectives of both our mangers and our personal. I also tried to apprise the value relative to it's cost. In my opinion although this program is the more expensive of the 3 I have evaluated, it is is the better in terms of value.

The nova package does a real good job of meeting our employees needs. It includes interactive tutorials electronic quizzes, a trainee manual online video segments, links, and site specific graphics. The software is easy to use, concepts are presented in a clear concise way. From the prospective of managers, everyone completes teh training at their own pace.

One of the packages many features are tutorials for specific tasks,

that can be done on the job as needed An employee who I asked to

try a tutorial found it quiet helpful.

Curriculum development would cost $1,200.00. Training cost

4,500. For seventy-five employees, that comes too sixty dollars per

trainee. As you know these costs dont include our peoples' time.

I requested one more training proposal which should arrive on

June 14th. I plan to be at the training center in our Highway Ten

facility on the 15 of June and I will review the materials their. You

will recieve my final report on June 21st.

Writing Positive and Neutral Messages

In this application, you will write letters, memos, and e-mails. Letterhead for some activities is available in the Chapter 3 folder on the student data disk. Letterhead files are named with the letters *LH* followed by the activity number. For example, letterhead for Activity 3C1 is named *LH 3C1*. If you are not using the data disk or if letterhead is not provided, key the documents on plain paper.

Format your documents as shown on pages 47–49. Consult the database in Appendix A or on the student data disk (*Address Directory*) for addresses and contact information. Use the current date. For letters, supply an appropriate salutation and complimentary close. For memos and e-mail, add an appropriate heading. All documents are from you unless you are directed otherwise. You may need to create some details.

Your instructor may ask you to use the guide on page 102 for evaluating your documents. Your instructor may also use this form to evaluate your work.

1. Write the neutral memo that you planned in 3A1. Save the memo as *3C1si* (substitute your initials for *si*).

2. Write the good-news letter to Dr. Bryant that you planned in 3A2. Save the letter as *3C2si* (substitute your initials for *si*).

3. Write the good-news e-mail to all soccer coaches that you planned in 3A3. If you are using the data disk file *E-Mail Form*, use the group address Soccer.Coaches@Westfield.edu. Save the e-mail as *3C3si*.

4. Best Grills manufactures gas grills and ships them nationwide. Makalya Gortman, shipping manager, has asked you to find a new supplier for shipping containers for the grills. The shipping damage rate has risen to an unacceptable level. You have evaluated several containers and plan to recommend one made by Logan Containers, Inc. This container meets all specifications of the Shipping Department. It costs about the same as the container currently being used; however, it weighs 6 pounds more, which will have a slight impact on shipping costs. Savings from the lower damage rate will more than offset the additional shipping charges.

Plan and write a memo to Ms. Gortman recommending Logan Containers, Inc., as the new supplier. Suggest that, if she chooses Logan, the Shipping Team should meet with its representatives as soon as possible. Attach the cost analysis you have prepared and the technical specifications. Save as *3C4si*.

5. Ms. Gortman has chosen Logan Containers, Inc., as the new supplier. Plan and write a letter to Mr. Jonathan Logan giving him this news and telling him that Ms. Gortman has approved the specifications and price quotations that he supplied. Invite Mr. Logan or his representatives to meet with your Shipping Team next Tuesday at 2:30 p.m. to establish the procedures to be used for inventory management, quality control, and billing. Ask him to call and let you know if this date and time is acceptable. Save as *3C5si*.

6. Dr. Peter Chang has requested that Palm Atlantic Airlines sponsor the Kerry University MBA Case Competition team by providing its six members with round-trip airline tickets to the three cities hosting the competition. (*Note:* The Case Competition is an event at which students in MBA programs from various universities compete to see which team can analyze data and present the best solution to problems in a case about a specific company.)

Ryan Sparks, the marketing manager for Palm Atlantic Airlines, has asked you to prepare a letter to Dr. Chang. Indicate that the airline will be delighted to sponsor the team and to supply the tickets. Ask Dr. Chang to provide the names, addresses, and telephone numbers of the participants, as well as the preferred flight dates and schedules. Tell him that as soon as this information is received, a reservations agent will call him to finalize the arrangements. Prepare the letter for Mr. Sparks's signature. Save as *3C6si*.

7. Plan and write an e-mail from Dr. Chang to the six student members of the MBA Case Competition team informing them that Palm Atlantic Airlines is sponsoring their trips. Indicate that you are providing the airline with their names, addresses, and telephone numbers, as well as preferred flight dates and schedules. Tell students that they will receive additional information as soon as the travel plans have been finalized. Suggest that each student write to Mr. Sparks and thank him for sponsoring the team. If you are using the *E-Mail Form* file, use the group address <u>MBAteam@Kerry.edu</u>. Save as *3C7si*.

8. José Mendoza, M.D., has asked you to prepare a letter to Mr. J. T. Wang to give him the good news that the results of all the laboratory tests administered last week were negative. Dr. Mendoza wants you to remind Mr. Wang that it is important for him to follow the prescribed diet and exercise program carefully. He should schedule a follow-up appointment in six weeks and should contact Dr. Mendoza immediately if he experiences any problems before that time. Mr. Wang should call the office assistant at (208) 555-0164 to schedule his appointment or if he has any questions about the diet or exercise program. Prepare the letter for Dr. Mendoza's signature. Save as *3C8si*.

9. Team and Internet Project

Team Activity

Internet Activity

Form a trip research team consisting of yourself and two classmates to work on a group project. The Kerry University MBA Case Competition team is preparing for the first competition in Montreal in March. The team arrives on Tuesday, competes on Wednesday and Thursday, and returns home Sunday evening.

Your team has been asked to search the Internet for travel information about Montreal, a city in Quebec, Canada. The team already has hotel reservations near Olympic Park. Try to obtain information on attractions to visit, restaurants, weather, and other topics of interest. Your team will plan and write a memo to the MBA team sharing the information. As part of this process, your team should:

a. Determine what kinds of information would be of interest.
b. Assign specific topics to each person to research.
c. Collect the information.
d. Meet to analyze and organize the information.
e. Determine if further information is needed.
f. Develop a writing plan and implement it.

You may attach copies of material printed from the Internet to your memo. Save as *3C9tp-si* (team project and initials of one team member).

Application 3C: Guide for Evaluating Your Positive and Neutral Messages

Factors to Consider	Points	3C1		3C2		3C3		3C4		3C5		3C6		3C7		3C8		3C9	
Self-evaluation (SE), Instructor evaluation (IE)		SE	IE	SE	IE	SE	IE	SE	IE	SE	IE	SE	IE	SE	IE	SE	IE	SE	IE
Strategy—presents good or most important news very early	2																		
Strategy—presents supporting information needed	2																		
Strategy—ends with a friendly closing that builds goodwill	2																		
Writing Guide 1—evidence of good planning; organized	1																		
Writing Guide 2—meets the reader's needs; courteous	1																		
Writing Guide 3—uses positive language	1																		
Writing Guide 4—uses a clear, easy-to-read style	1																		
Writing Guide 5—complete; includes all needed information	1																		
Writing Guide 6—uses an efficient, action-oriented style	1																		
Writing Guide 7—uses specific, concrete language	1																		
Writing Guide 8—uses effective sentence and paragraph structure	1																		
Writing Guide 9—uses correct format and attractive placement	1																		
Writing Guide 10—has been edited and proofread; no errors	1																		
Overall assessment of document	4																		
Totals	**20**																		

Mastery Check for Chapter 3

1. How does the expected reaction of the reader to your message affect the strategy you use to write the message?

2. What can you do to avoid having stereotyped messages?

3. What is the best strategy to use for good-news messages?

4. How do neutral messages differ from good-news messages?

5. For each of the terms shown below, write a complete, correct sentence using the term.

Goodwill

Model

Stereotyped

Shell Cove—Property Development Division

Shell Cove delegates all property development to the Property Development Division, directed by Mr. Charles (Chuck) Austin. Once properties have been developed, they are managed by other divisions. Chuck has asked you to complete the following three projects.

Save all your work in your Shell Cove folder. Remember that the e-mail address for Shell Cove employees consists of the first name(period)last name@shellcove.com (example: Charles.Austin@shellcove.com). Use your title, assistant manager, for all communications you prepare with your name as the signature. Substitute your initials for *si* on the solution files.

Job 1: Tidewater Club Proposals

The evaluation team has selected the proposal submitted by Ms. Marissa Layden of Layden Properties to design and build the new clubhouse for the Tidewater Golf Course. The 30,000-square-foot Tidewater Club features a pro shop, a restaurant with a view of the cove and the 18th hole of the golf course, a very casual patio restaurant outdoors, upscale shower and dressing facilities, a state-of-the-art training room, offices, and a large conference room. The Layden Properties proposal was selected for the following reasons:

- The portfolio of previous projects Layden Properties has designed and built matches the level of quality expected at Shell Cove.

- The plans incorporate highly creative design concepts.

- The cost control and value engineering approach makes it likely that the final cost will remain in the $4.5 million range, which is important. (A cost control and value engineering approach involves finding a less costly way to build a facility of the same quality by using different techniques and materials.)

    a. Plan and write the good-news letter to Ms. Layden informing her that her proposal has been selected. Invite her and the Layden project team to a 9:30 a.m. meeting with the evaluation team one week from today to review all details and finalize the contract. Lunch will be provided. Save as *3E1asi*.

    b. Prepare an e-mail to Megan Garrett, director of the Golf/Tennis Division, telling her that Ms. Layden and her project team are scheduled to attend the meeting and inviting her and her senior staff to participate. Inform Ms. Garrett that the meeting will last through a working lunch brought in from Shell Cove's Blue Point Seafood House. Ask her to review the proposal before the meeting and to be prepared to talk about the design of each of the facilities in the club. Copy Chuck on the e-mail. Save as *3E1bsi*.

Job 2: Coastal Stampede Arena

Samantha (Sam) Howard, director of the Entertainment Division, has requested that the Property Development Division proceed with Phase 2 of the Coastal Stampede project, which you learned about in the last case study application. Sam has asked Chuck to send someone from Property Development to participate in the Arena Phase 2 team to determine the ultimate use of the arena, which may impact construction.

The evening functions at Coastal Stampede will include horse riding shows, drill troupes, and acrobatic and gymnastic riders. Sam wants to use the venue during the day up to 4:30 p.m. for additional rodeo events that would appeal to families and particularly to children. Rope tricks, clowns, trick riding, whip tricks, and pony rides are some possibilities. Sam does not want to include horseback riding, bucking horses, or anything dangerous.

Form a team with two classmates, who will represent the Entertainment Division. Use the Internet to research some of these activities and any similar kinds of entertainment you think would work well for Coastal Stampede. Try to locate similar venues on the Internet. If one is located nearby, you may want to call or visit it. Plan and write a neutral memo with your recommendations from the Arena Phase 2 team to both Sam and Chuck. Save as *3E2tp-si*. You may attach information from your research to support your ideas.

Job 3: Pat's at Shell Cove

Roger Brennan, manager of Pat's at Shell Cove, called Chuck Austin complimenting the Property Management Division for the quality of work done on the restaurant and on completing it three weeks ahead of schedule. He invited Chuck to select 12 employees to reward for this outstanding effort.

The employees and their guests are invited to a complimentary dinner next Friday evening at 7 p.m.—the night before the restaurant opens. You and Chuck have been asked to serve as hosts for the group. Chef Pat will prepare his six signature dishes for this fine dining restaurant as a tasting menu. This event will also give his staff an opportunity to ensure that everything works smoothly when the restaurant opens the next evening.

Chuck has asked you to write the good-news memo from him inviting the employees listed below to join him and you for the evening. Address each memo personally to each employee. For married employees, be sure to include their spouse's name (indicated in parentheses) somewhere in the memo. Provide enough detail to ensure that employees understand that this will be a very special evening for them. The restaurant requires gentlemen to wear coats and ties. Save all your memos in a single file as *3E3si*.

- Amy Tan (Lee)
- Dan Kane
- Josh Bailey (Susan)
- Lauren Woods
- Sarah Jones (Brad)
- Trinity Wharton
- Consuelo Miguez
- Jessica Cassidy (Jeff)
- Arturo Gonzales (Donna)
- Brian Johnson
- Ethan Matthews
- Carlos Rodriguez (Isabel)

BAD-NEWS MESSAGES

OBJECTIVES

After you complete Chapter 4, you should be able to:

- Use an indirect strategy for writing bad-news messages.
- Adapt the strategy for writing mixed-news messages.
- Determine when a direct strategy is appropriate for bad-news messages.
- Determine the appropriate media for bad-news messages.
- Edit messages more effectively.

OVERVIEW

Most people enjoy receiving good news. Virtually no one enjoys receiving bad news, yet bad news has to be delivered every day. When a payment is late, when an order will not arrive on time, when a request for a loan must be refused, or when an account must be canceled, someone has to communicate that information. Writing bad-news messages takes more planning and effort than writing good-news messages. Yet, being able to write an effective bad-news message is a valuable and important skill. The key elements of this chapter include:

- Planning bad-news messages.
- Strategy for writing bad-news messages.
- Strategy for writing mixed-news messages.
- An alternative strategy for bad-news messages.

"Business Talk"

Communicating effectively requires you to understand and use appropriate vocabulary in a business setting. Look for the following terms in this chapter. Review the terms and their definitions. Remember, some words have more than one meaning.

Buffer—something that softens or cushions the impact of a blow; a neutral statement that cushions bad news.

Claim—a demand for something that is due or that is one's right.

Legitimate—valid or acceptable; conforming to accepted standards.

Random—by chance; without a definite pattern or plan.

Tactful—diplomatic; saying and doing the right things.

WHY WRITE BAD-NEWS MESSAGES?

Bad-news messages must be delivered in some manner—written or otherwise. Organizations have limited resources and cannot agree to do everything that others ask of them. In some cases, a request may be **legitimate** and justified. In other cases, the request should never have been made; it is not legitimate or justified. Sometimes, the bad news is unexpected: a change in policy or the cancellation of a benefit. The following are examples of bad-news messages:

- Denying someone credit.
- Prompting a customer to make a tardy payment.
- Informing tenants about a rent increase.
- Complaining to a creditor about being billed for a service that was never received.
- Telling a customer that an order cannot be filled.
- Refusing a request from an employee to work flexible hours.

Writing is not always the best way to deliver a bad-news message. In some situations, it may be better to convey the information in person.

PLANNING BAD-NEWS MESSAGES

Planning a bad-news message differs significantly from planning a good-news message. People generally are eager to give and receive good news. Therefore, little time is spent trying to ensure that the message is justified and determining whether it should be put in writing. Rarely is anyone eager to give or receive bad news. Before bad news is communicated, efforts should be made to ensure that it is justified and to determine the best way to communicate the message.

Verify and Justify the Decision

Decisions should be made carefully, and the facts on which decisions are based should be verified for accuracy. Conveying bad news is difficult. Conveying bad news, only to find out later that an error was made and the bad news should not have been conveyed, can create a much worse situation.

Conveying erroneous bad news is not uncommon. Newspapers frequently print horror stories of bad news delivered in error. A recent article featured a picture of a woman who had returned to her home and was horrified to find that it had been bulldozed as part of an urban renewal project. The letter from the city notifying her of the pending action had been lost in the mail. Thus, she had no opportunity to notify the city that the letter was sent in error—the house slated to be destroyed was located in the next block. The bulldozer arrived and demolished the wrong house.

Once you have determined that bad news must be conveyed, make sure that all of the information that you are communicating is accurate. Any error in the message may cause the individual to question the decision.

> **Success Tip**
>
> Promptness is critical when writing bad-news messages. The recipient will be displeased with the bad news. Tardiness in responding just adds to the problem and gives the reader more reason to be unhappy.

Determine the Severity and Sensitivity of the Situation

The severity and sensitivity of bad-news situations vary widely. Some situations may be drastic, whereas others may result in only mild disappointment. The reaction to the house being bulldozed was not just one of being upset; it included major legal and financial consequences. The degree of sensitivity influences how a bad-news message should be written. Consider the following examples:

1. How do you think a reader who believes a **claim** was legitimate and expects to be paid will react upon receiving a letter indicating the claim was turned down because of a technicality?
2. How do you think a reader who ordered a product and receives a message that it is temporarily out of stock will react?
3. How do you think a reader who receives a very detailed complaint letter providing numerous examples of a problem in software purchased from the reader will react?

How would you react in each case? The range of reactions in these three situations would probably be from one extreme to another.

1. In the first situation, the reader is likely to be very angry. Expectations play a major role in reactions. Because the reader actually expected a positive response, the reaction to the negative response is likely to be more intense.
2. In the second situation, the reader might be disappointed but is not likely to be very angry unless the reader needed the product right away.
3. In the third situation, the reader might receive the bad news positively. Although no one is pleased to receive a complaint, the reader may believe that the information will help solve the problem.

Decide on the Best Media to Convey the Bad News

The degree of sensitivity influences the decision about the best way to convey bad news. In some cases, a written message may not be appropriate. Consider the best way to communicate information in the following examples:

1. A builder who placed a large order for one-way glass for observation windows in a research center has just learned that the window frames were positioned too high for observers to be seated while observing. Enlarging the glass is less expensive than reframing the windows. How should the builder notify the glass supplier to stop the order before the glass is cut?
2. A resort will close each of its buildings for one week at a time to change the HVAC systems. Hourly employees on both shifts will be without pay for the week that the building they work in is closed. How should the manager inform these hourly employees?
3. A company has decided to discontinue its Christmas party. The decision was made because some employees celebrate different holidays, attendance has dropped in recent years, and the company is trying to cut costs. How should the president notify employees?
4. A manager is going to fire an employee. How should the manager notify the employee?
5. A small business is two months late paying its printing bill. How should the printer notify this customer?

The best medium for these situations varies considerably. In some cases, the choice is clear-cut—one option is clearly better than all other options. In other cases, the choice is not clear-cut.

1. Two factors must be considered in canceling this large order. The first is that it is urgent to cancel before the glass is cut, and the second is making sure that the right order and the entire order are canceled. A fax, or a telephone call followed by a fax, offers obvious advantages. The message can be transmitted immediately, and a copy of the order to be canceled can be faxed with the message.
2. A fact that must be considered is that you have two work shifts. If one shift is informed, the grapevine will probably convey the news to workers on the other shift before you have an opportunity to inform them. To ensure that everybody receives the message at the same time, mail may be the preferred option. Employee expectations should also be considered. Employees may be aware that the HVAC systems will be replaced. The more knowledge you have of the circumstances and how employees are likely to react, the easier it is to decide how to convey the news.
3. The reasons for canceling the party are valid, and since the event is not well attended, this situation is not likely to be very sensitive. An e-mail message would be a very reasonable way to notify everyone of the change.

(continued on next page)

(continued)

4. Under most conditions, an employee who is being fired should be told in person rather than notified in writing. A brief written statement may be needed for documentation. The statement would be handed to the employee after the situation has been discussed.
5. A **tactful**, impersonal letter to remind the customer that the payment is late is preferable to other media at this stage. A fax would convey too urgent a message, and a phone call may embarrass a customer having temporary financial problems.

The use of e-mail for bad-news messages deserves special attention. Several factors need to be considered before deciding to use e-mail. Many people think of e-mail as a casual, informal way of communicating. Many also believe that e-mail is not a secure means of sending a message. People who are receiving bad news typically do not want the message to be casual, nor do they want it available to others.

On the other hand, when e-mail is frequently used to transmit information, the reader may not object to a bad-news e-mail. In most cases, you do not want bad news to be personalized. While you may have to say no in a particular situation, you do not want that situation to affect the professional relationship you have with a customer. E-mail is generally considered an impersonal way of communicating. The degree of sensitivity is also an issue. If a message contains bad news but is not likely to be very sensitive, then an e-mail may be acceptable.

An alternative that is sometimes used is to attach a message using a traditional format (letter or memo) and simply use e-mail as the delivery service. Knowing the reader and the reader's likely reaction to e-mail is usually the best guide in determining whether to use it.

Technology Connections

Digital Signatures

Many documents require signatures and dates. Traditionally, a fax has been used when it is urgent to transmit a copy of the signature and date. Then the original copy is sent by regular or overnight mail. Digital signatures provide an electronic alternative to this process. A digital signature is a series of **random**-looking letters and numbers generated with special software and a private electronic key. A certificate authorizes the signature, and a secure time stamp verifies when the signature was applied and sent. A document with a digital signature can be checked to determine if it has been altered.

Determine Who Should Convey the Bad News

Many employees have conveyed bad news to key customers, only to have those customers appeal successfully to someone with greater authority to overturn the decision. In situations that are extremely sensitive or that have a very negative impact on major customers, the best approach is to discuss the situations with managers in positions of higher authority before making final decisions. You may even be asked to prepare a letter for the signature of someone in a position of higher authority.

Prepare the Reader

Most people can accept bad news more easily when they have been prepared appropriately for it. Surprises, particularly negative ones, generally are not received very well. Usually, when bad news is presented, obstacles must be overcome before the negative news can be communicated effectively.

Use Empathy

Perhaps the best way to think about the difference between writing a positive message and writing a negative one is to place yourself in the position of the reader. Try to visualize what your reactions would be if you were in each of the following situations:

- Suppose you had just been told by your employer that you would receive a 15 percent increase in salary. What would your reaction be? Most people would be very pleased. Would you ask why you got such a generous raise? Would you question the judgment of the person making the decision? Most people would express pleasure in the result and would not question the process at all.
- Suppose the situation were reversed—you had just been told by your employer that you would receive no raise or, even worse, your salary would be cut by 15 percent. What would your reaction be? Most people would be very displeased and maybe even angry. What would your first question be? Most people would want to know why. Because most people immediately react to bad news by wanting to know the reasons why, a good strategy usually is to explain the reasons before you present the bad news.

Readers of good-news messages rarely question the logic of the situation. Therefore, lengthy explanations serve no useful purpose. Because readers of bad-news messages usually do question the logic of the situation, adequate explanations are necessary. Thus, bad-news messages tend to be longer than good-news messages.

Choose a Strategy

If the situation is sensitive and the reader is likely to react negatively, an indirect style usually works best. If the situation is routine or if the reader is likely to receive the information without being upset, a more direct style would be appropriate. If the reader is likely to accept the news positively even though it is bad news, use a direct style.

A few readers prefer a direct style because of their personality type. They tend to be open, frank, and even blunt in their communication to others, and they expect the same type of communication in return. Providing information in a roundabout way to such people may upset them more than providing negative information without preparing them adequately for it. They want the information immediately, regardless of whether it is good or bad. A caution is in order, however. Just because you may prefer a direct approach does not mean that it is the best approach to use with others.

Develop a Plan

Remember, good strategy depends on both the situation and the anticipated reaction of the reader. The situation may be bad, but the reader may like the way it is being handled. Also remember the key questions to ask during the planning process:

- Is the bad news justified?
- Is a written message the best way to convey the bad news?
- Who should convey it?
- What strategy is likely to be most effective?

Clients, customers, and even friends may make requests that are not in your best interests or the best interests of your company. Although you cannot do what they ask, you value the patronage and friendship of these individuals. Therefore, when you disagree with them, you do not want to be perceived as being disagreeable. Good writers master the art of disagreeing without being disagreeable.

STRATEGY FOR WRITING BAD-NEWS MESSAGES

No one likes to receive bad news. Therefore, the writer should make a special effort to present the bad news as tactfully and sincerely as possible. The way something is said may be more important than what is said. Tone is especially important. A strong or undesirable tone often produces a strong emotional reaction on the part of the reader. Bad news presented in a milder manner is less likely to create a strong emotional reaction on the part of the reader.

Global Connections

Language Usage

Although English is the international language of business, remember that your reader may have limited English skills. Use words that are very familiar and that can be translated easily. Avoid nonstandard English, slang, and idioms such as *get cold feet* or *see eye to eye*. These expressions often have no equivalent in foreign languages and are likely to be misinterpreted. Provide more detail and clarifying information than you might if the reader's first language were English.

Success Tip

Honesty and sincerity are always important, but never more so than when you have to convey bad news.

Success Tip

How you say something may be more important than what you say.

Honesty and integrity are critical. Getting bad news from an honest and sincere writer is difficult; getting it from a dishonest or insincere writer is intolerable.

The most appropriate strategy for writing negative messages usually is an indirect approach. Here are the steps to using an indirect approach for negative messages:

1. Begin with a buffer to soften the bad news.
2. Explain the reasons for your decisions in a logical manner, using a positive tone.
3. Present your refusal clearly as an outgrowth of a logical, fair decision-making process, and communicate it in a positive, tactful manner.
4. Offer helpful suggestions or alternatives when they are appropriate.
5. Close on a positive—or, at least, a neutral—note.

A **buffer** is a neutral statement that enables you to explain the situation logically before you present the negative news. An effective buffer is a reasonably short statement that enables you to begin on an agreeable note but does not mislead the reader into thinking that the message contains good news.

The best use of a buffer is to establish that you have been logical, fair, and reasonable in making the decisions you are conveying. Consider this example:

You are a logical, fair person who receives a request to replace merchandise that the customer states is defective.

1. What would you do first to begin resolving the problem?

   Most logical people would begin by examining the merchandise to determine the actual problem. The reported problem may be the same as the actual problem, or the actual problem may be something different than was reported.

2. What would you do next?

   You would try to determine the best course of action to solve the problem. If the merchandise was defective, you would have it repaired or replaced. If the merchandise was damaged by the customer, you would probably decline to repair or replace it without charge. You might offer other alternatives if they are available.

Assume in this scenario that you sent the merchandise to quality control, and the inspector found that it had been damaged by the customer. Therefore, company policy will not allow you to replace the merchandise without charge. Remember, however, that just because you have to follow company policy does not mean that the reader cares about your company's policy. Most readers want a logical explanation.

What type of buffer could you use in this situation that would enable you to explain the logical process you used to make a decision and that would also prepare the reader for a negative decision? An appropriate buffer might be as follows: *Our quality control inspector carefully checked the merchandise you returned to us.*

This opening statement establishes that you used a reasonable approach to determine the problem. At this point, however, the customer does not know what decision the quality control inspector has made. Note that the buffer relates to the situation—the problem with the merchandise. It does not mislead the reader into thinking that a positive response will follow.

The next logical step would be to present the inspector's findings. Review the facts and give the reasons for the decision before actually disclosing the decision. If you present good, logical reasons, the reader is likely to have an open mind and view the facts objectively. A fine line exists between presenting negative information too quickly and delaying it too long.

Reasons differ from policy statements. Giving reasons is very different from stating that your company's policy does not permit you to do what was asked. Customers are not interested in a policy as such. They want to know why you made the unfavorable decision. Therefore, present the reason you have the policy rather than just stating the policy.

Carefully stated reasons should lead logically to a gentle statement of refusal. It should be clear that the request cannot be granted, but rarely is it necessary to refuse in a negative or high-impact tone. A good technique is to focus on what you can do rather than on what you cannot do. An example of this might be as follows: *The features you need are part of the professional version, not the standard version, of our software that you purchased. We can offer you the opportunity to upgrade to the professional version at a discount.*

On some occasions, you will have no reasonable alternative to offer the reader. In those situations, try to close the letter on a positive—or, at least, a neutral—note. On other occasions, you may have an alternative to suggest or a way to assist the reader. Provide alternatives only if they are reasonable and helpful. Providing a workable alternative enables you to close the letter on a positive note.

An example of a reasonable alternative in this scenario would be to offer to repair the merchandise and charge only for the parts or to offer a replacement at a substantial discount. Although you were not responsible for the problem, you would probably build goodwill by trying to accommodate the customer. Most companies value the goodwill of customers and will try to accommodate them when it is possible to do so.

De-emphasize Bad News

Most often, the best approach in dealing with bad news is to use a low-impact style that will minimize the attention placed on the negative aspects of the situation. In Chapter 2, you learned about techniques that you can use to emphasize ideas. When you present negative information, you should strive to give it as little emphasis as possible. In effect, you reverse those six techniques to de-emphasize ideas.

- **Mechanical techniques.** Use a regular font. Avoid attributes such as bold, all capitals, and underline.

- **Space.** Limit the amount of space devoted to the negative information, and avoid repeating it.

- **Isolation.** Bury negative statements in paragraphs consisting of several sentences. Do not draw attention to them by setting them as separate paragraphs.

- **Sentence structure.** Use compound and complex sentences to present negative information. These types of sentences provide less emphasis than simple, direct sentences. In complex sentences, placing negative information in the dependent clause gives it less emphasis than placing it in the independent clause.

- **Language.** Use general language and the passive voice to de-emphasize negative information.

- **Position.** Put negative information in the middle paragraphs of a message because they receive less emphasis than the first and last paragraphs. Likewise, put negative information in the middle sentences of a paragraph because they receive less emphasis than the first and last sentences.

Handle Mistakes Effectively

Bad-news messages often deal with mistakes that were made by the writer or the writer's company, the reader or the reader's company, or both. Depending on who is responsible, these mistakes can be handled effectively in different ways:

1. The writer or the writer's company made the mistake.

   The most effective way to handle a mistake made by the writer or the writer's company is to admit the mistake, apologize for it, and emphasize what is going to be done to correct the mistake. The apology should be simple and straightforward. It should be given quickly and only once. The apology should not be repeated or positioned in the closing paragraph. The reader should remember the corrective action that has been taken, not the mistake that was made.

2. The reader or the reader's company made the mistake, but the reader is unwilling to accept responsibility for it. The reader expects the writer's company to correct the mistake, even though the writer's company was not responsible for it.

   The most effective way to handle a mistake made by the reader or the reader's company is to use the indirect strategy for writing bad-news messages.

3. Both the reader and the writer contributed to the mistake.

   The writer should accept responsibility for the writer's role (or the company's) and use the indirect approach for handling the areas that are the responsibility of the reader.

The following scenarios illustrate the situations just discussed:

Scenario	Analysis
Our order for a specially beveled mirror specified that it was to be 36 inches high and 32 inches wide. The mirror you sent was 39 inches high and 32 inches wide. Please provide the correct size that we ordered.	You made a mistake. Admit it, apologize for it, and correct it.
The 30– × 48-inch specially cut one-way glass we ordered is not large enough. Please exchange it for 39– × 48-inch glass. Although your order form states that special orders may not be exchanged, we know you want satisfied customers and will make an exception in this case.	The customer admits the mistake but still expects your company to correct it. Use the indirect strategy for bad-news messages.

(continued on next page)

(continued)

Scenario	Analysis
Our order specified #39 light yellow carpet, but the carpet you shipped us was #39 ivory. We wanted and specified light yellow. Therefore, please exchange the ivory for the light yellow carpet.	You ship carpet by color number—39. The customer used the wrong number for the color specified. Your company, however, should have noted that the number and color did not match and then questioned the customer. Both of you contributed to the problem. A workable solution should be negotiated.

The writer gains no advantage by accusing or lecturing the reader, regardless of the situation. For example, the following sentence would not be appropriate:

> If you had verified the number in the color brochure we sent you last week, you would have ordered the correct color. Light yellow is clearly listed as Color 37.

Use an Effective Closing

Close a negative message with care. The closing provides the last impression—use it to build goodwill. Stereotyped closings that writers use in most of their letters often end a message on the wrong note. Make sure that the closing does not include statements that imply the problem will happen again, ironic statements (statements that say one thing but mean the opposite), or statements that invite prolonged correspondence. Review the following examples:

Closing statement	Analysis
Please let me know if you have problems with our service in the future, and I will deal with them personally.	Implies that you expect to have problems and your staff may not handle them effectively.
We are sorry we were unable to grant your request this time, but please let us know if we can help you again in the future.	The statement is ironic. It implies you helped the reader when you did not do so. You turned down the request.
If you have further questions about our decision not to replace your carpet, please let us know.	Encouraging the reader to try again means that you will have to say no again.

Now compare them with the following examples of effective closing statements:

Scenario	Closing statement
You had a service problem and corrected it.	Our employees work very hard to ensure that service problems do not recur. They are always happy to assist you.

(continued on next page)

(continued)

Scenario

A customer brought in a worn briefcase that had been out of stock for six months and wanted you to replace it with a larger one. You declined to do so.

Closing statement

We are sure you will receive many years of excellent service from this top-quality briefcase. A catalog featuring our entire line is enclosed should you wish to order an additional, larger briefcase.

Figure 4-1 on page 120 illustrates the use of an indirect style to give negative information—the rejection of a proposal. Review it and the margin comments.

STRATEGY FOR WRITING MIXED-NEWS MESSAGES

A mixed-news message contains both good and bad news. The reader is likely to be pleased with part of the information and displeased with the rest. The best approach is to use a direct writing style for the good news and modify it slightly to accommodate the bad news.

1. Present the good news first.
2. Explain the reasons for the negative portion of your message.
3. Let the reasons lead logically to the negative information.
4. Present the negative information in as positive a tone as possible.
5. Close with a statement that builds goodwill.

This strategy follows the same principles that you learned in Chapter 3 and in this chapter. The opening and closing paragraphs are reserved for positive information. The reasons are presented before the negative news, and the negative news is buried in the middle.

Figure 4-2 on page 121 illustrates the strategy that is generally most appropriate for a mixed-news message. Pay particular attention to the way that the bad news is introduced after the good news has been presented. When you present good news in a mixed-news message, keep in mind that bad news follows; therefore, use a conservative approach.

AN ALTERNATIVE STRATEGY FOR NEGATIVE MESSAGES

Some negative situations can be handled very effectively using a direct strategy. The emphasis in this chapter on using an indirect style for writing most bad-news messages does not imply that all situations require an indirect style. In certain situations, a direct style may, in fact, be the most effective style to use. Letters that report problems with products or services to the supplier or manufacturer present bad news, but the response to this bad news is usually very positive. These letters are generally called claims letters. Most organizations are very eager to correct problems for several reasons:

- Their reputations depend on good products and services.
- Customer feedback helps to improve products and services.
- They want to maintain good relationships or even partnerships with their customers.
- They want to keep their customers.

Therefore, a high-impact style is not needed to get action. If a claim is justified, presenting the information factually is all that is necessary. A good tone is important in maintaining good relations with suppliers and manufacturers.

The following strategy is generally used for reporting problems with products and services:

1. Present the problem factually, giving enough information to allow the reader to identify the situation.
2. Provide additional details that are necessary to explain the situation and justify your request for action.
3. Request the action that you desire.
4. Close on a friendly note.

Figure 4-3 on page 122 illustrates the effective use of a direct strategy for presenting negative information. Review the letter carefully. Pay particular attention to the tone.

! Points to Remember

About Bad-News Messages

☑ Bad-news messages require a different planning approach than other types of messages. Decisions should be made with great care and verified for accuracy. Often, others in your organization should be consulted, and the message may be sent out over the signature of someone with a position of higher authority than your position.

☑ Tone is extremely important in writing bad-news messages. Use techniques to de-emphasize negative ideas.

☑ The best way to handle a mistake you made is to admit it, apologize for it, and focus on correcting it.

☑ An indirect strategy usually works best for bad-news messages.

☑ Give special attention to the closing paragraph of a bad-news message to ensure that it does not imply the problem will happen again, is not ironic, and does not invite future discussion about it.

☑ Mixed-news messages include both good and bad news. A good strategy for mixed-news messages is to present the good news before you explain the reasons for the bad news.

☑ A direct strategy is appropriate for claims letters even though they contain bad news. Most businesses want the opportunity to correct legitimate problems with their products or services.

Figure 4-1: Indirect Approach for Bad-News Messages

METRO MANUFACTURING, INC.

WWW.METROMANUFACTURING.COM

November 6, 200_

Mr. Miguel C. Devarez
Cadillac Lake Security Fencing
2583 Sunnyside Drive
Cadillac, MI 49601-9383

Dear Mr. Devarez

Opens with a buffer to set the tone of logical decision making.

Your proposal is unique, and we have compared your security provisions and costs with the security measures we currently use at our other sites. We appreciate the comprehensiveness of your proposal. What makes your proposal unique is that it combines security fencing with random monitoring by security rangers.

Presents the basis for making the decision.

For many years, our company used only security fencing at our plant sites. Last year, we experimented with random monitoring on several large projects. The reduction in loss on the plant sites, however, was less than the cost of monitoring. Therefore, we now limit the use of monitoring to those days on which we have specially designed products or extremely expensive materials on site. Typically, monitoring is used about 10 percent of the time.

Presents the facts that justify the decision.

Although the costs you proposed for the combined system are less than what we incurred in our test projects, they are still higher than the loss reduction we experienced. Therefore, we plan to continue using just our current fencing system and add random monitoring only in carefully selected situations.

Closes on a friendly note that builds goodwill.

We plan to review our costs and our need for random monitoring periodically. Should our situation change, we will contact you for an updated proposal.

Sincerely

Daniel Wexford
General Manager

xx

2653 WEST 13TH STREET • CADILLAC, MI 49601-8487 • TEL: (231) 555-0070 • FAX: (231) 555-0008

Figure 4-2: Modified Direct Approach for Mixed-News Messages

METRO MANUFACTURING, INC.

TO:	Jeremiah Howell
FROM:	Vanessa Bailey
DATE:	March 12, 200_
SUBJECT:	Facilities Request

Presents the positive information first.

The four offices and the conference room that the marketing group vacated have been reassigned to your department as you requested. This added space should accommodate the additional staff you plan to hire. The offices and conference room are being painted now and will be ready for occupancy next week.

Explains the reason for the negative information.

We have also reviewed your request for new furniture for these facilities. Our facilities staff has checked the furniture carefully. The furniture can be restored by cleaning and touching up scratched areas. Facilities has elected this option as it is much more cost-effective in our limited budget situation. You may, of course, use your own departmental funds to replace the furniture.

Presents a realistic alternative.

The facilities staff plans to complete the work on the furniture next week, before your employees move into the offices. If you elect to replace the furniture, please notify Facilities this week.

Closes on a friendly, optimistic note.

We hope that the additional space will improve the working conditions in your department.

xx

Figure 4-3: Direct Strategy for Claims Messages

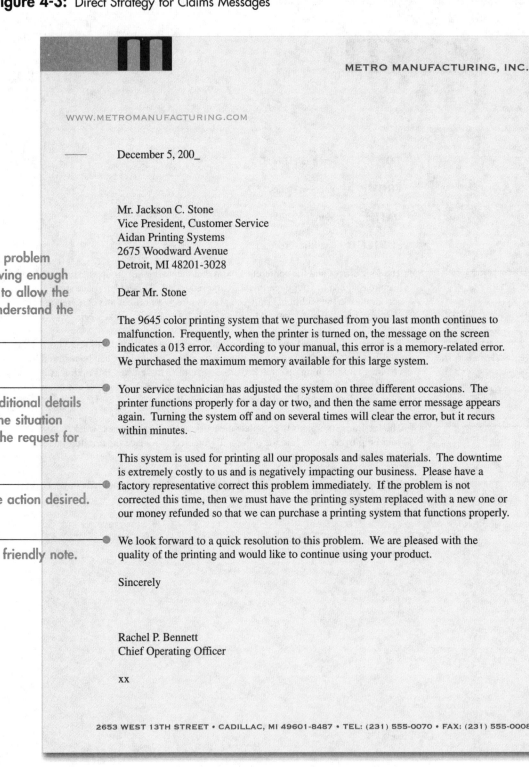

METRO MANUFACTURING, INC.

WWW.METROMANUFACTURING.COM

December 5, 200_

Mr. Jackson C. Stone
Vice President, Customer Service
Aidan Printing Systems
2675 Woodward Avenue
Detroit, MI 48201-3028

Dear Mr. Stone

Presents the problem factually, giving enough information to allow the reader to understand the problem.

The 9645 color printing system that we purchased from you last month continues to malfunction. Frequently, when the printer is turned on, the message on the screen indicates a 013 error. According to your manual, this error is a memory-related error. We purchased the maximum memory available for this large system.

Provides additional details to explain the situation and justify the request for action.

Your service technician has adjusted the system on three different occasions. The printer functions properly for a day or two, and then the same error message appears again. Turning the system off and on several times will clear the error, but it recurs within minutes.

This system is used for printing all our proposals and sales materials. The downtime is extremely costly to us and is negatively impacting our business. Please have a factory representative correct this problem immediately. If the problem is not corrected this time, then we must have the printing system replaced with a new one or our money refunded so that we can purchase a printing system that functions properly.

Requests the action desired.

Closes on a friendly note.

We look forward to a quick resolution to this problem. We are pleased with the quality of the printing and would like to continue using your product.

Sincerely

Rachel P. Bennett
Chief Operating Officer

xx

2653 WEST 13TH STREET • CADILLAC, MI 49601-8487 • TEL: (231) 555-0070 • FAX: (231) 555-0008

Review Guide 2—Write for the Reader

Review Guide 2 of Chapter 2 on pages 25–27. Then revise each of the following sentences or paragraphs so that it will be written from the perspective of the reader—which includes being courteous, fair, and unbiased.

1. I like the way you rearranged your office, and I want you to do the departmental office in a similar manner.

2. That black, female attorney always insists on making the presentation.

3. If you had started early and finished your project on time, you would not have to be worried about how you can get it to me at the convention site. You can get the contact information from the girl at the reception desk.

4. Call Jed and tell him to give you a copy of the audit. Tell him I said to do it if he questions you.

5. I want each department head to ensure that his expenditures are within his budget.

6. If you had read the instructions carefully, you would not have messed this project up. Correct it immediately.

Editing and Language Arts Checkpoint

1. Carefully read the document that follows; it is packed with errors. Use proofreaders' marks to mark all errors in grammar, spelling, usage, word choice, capitalization, punctuation, and keying. If you need help with proofreaders' marks, refer to the table on page 53. Do not revise sentence or paragraph structure unless you find an error.

2. Access *File 4B* in the Chapter 4 folder on your student data disk and make the corrections. If you are not working with the data disk, key the document, making the corrections as you key. You may use online reference tools just as you would on the job.

3. If you are not working with the data disk, format the document as a memo from you to Members, Board of Directors. Use the current date, and supply an appropriate subject line. Save as *4Bsi.*

---

the Board of Directors of the Economic Alliance have

scheduled a meeting on [insert date two weeks from today] at one

p.m. with Robert West, Mayor of Horrell Hill Judy Ledbetter,

President of County Council and Wayne Roxbury Director of the

state Film Office. The primary purpose of the meeting is to discuss

the exciting agreement among the city and roselawn studios to film

the movie "North Star Nights" here.

Mr Roxbury said recently that the film, 'Will give a boost to

the cities diverse economy. The production will spend money on

food housing, offices, utilities, furniture, equipment, personnel,

security, rentals transportation, and many other goods and

services.' He estimated that "North Star Nights" will bring $50,000 in revenues to the area. Incidently, the producer plans to hire seventy-five local people mostly high school and college students as extras.

The alliance will also review Bob Smith's and Tom Graham's proposal to upgrade the conference room and shift form portable projection equiptment to a stationery multimedia platform for presentations to visiting prospects. The funds are available for the project permission is needed to build a base platform which is twelve feet long, six feet deep, and ten inches high. The multimedia podium will be mounted on this base platform.

The last item proposed is a plan to beautify rosewood boulevard between 1st Street and 9th Street. This area is the gateway too our city and needs to be enhanced with landscaping, benches,and appropriate lighting to create a postive first impression for visitors. The landscape architect who we have consulted has provided a cost estimate for the project. We have 2/3 of the amount on hand. a architectural drawing of the area will be on display at the meeting.

The Board welcome your comments or suggestions on these topics before the meeting. Please send them to Anita or I as early as possible.

Application 4C

Writing Bad-News and Mixed-News Messages

In this application, you will write letters, memos, and e-mails. Letterhead for some activities is available in the chapter folder on the student data disk. If you are not using the data disk or if letterhead is not provided, key the documents on plain paper.

Format your documents as shown on pages 47–50. Consult the database in Appendix A or on the student data disk (*Address Directory*) for addresses and contact information. Use the current date. For letters, supply an appropriate salutation and complimentary close. For memos and e-mail, add an appropriate heading. All documents are from you unless you are directed otherwise.

Your instructor may ask you to use the guide on page 130 for evaluating your documents. Your instructor may also use this form to evaluate your work.

1. Dr. Peter Chang has asked Palm Atlantic Airlines to sponsor the Kerry University MBA Case Competition team by providing six round-trip airline tickets to Montreal, leaving on December 27 and returning on January 3. You would like to do so, but the holiday time period is your peak season, and demand is so high that you even have to block out tickets for your frequent fliers during this time. Therefore, you are unable to provide the tickets during the holiday period. You would be happy to provide six tickets to any destination you fly to if the team has a competition scheduled at another time. Plan a letter to Dr. Chang by answering these questions:

   a. How is the reader likely to feel about your decision?

   b. What objectives would you like to accomplish?

   c. What buffer would be appropriate to open the letter?

   d. What reasons support your decision?

   e. What alternatives, if any, can you offer?

   f. What would be an appropriate closing to build goodwill?

2. Write the mixed-news letter to Dr. Chang using an indirect approach. Prepare the letter for the signature of Ryan Sparks, the marketing manager. Save as *4C2si*.

3. A number of employees have sent you e-mails requesting that Pathmark Construction provide an employee cafeteria to serve breakfast and lunch at its Lake Charles facility. You do have cafeterias at some of the large industrial facilities, but providing a cafeteria to serve breakfast and lunch at a small facility with fewer than thirty employees would not be cost-effective. You will, however, expand the employee lounge, providing a microwave oven and adding several vending machines with a variety of sandwiches, cereals, snacks, and beverages appropriate for breakfast and lunch. The expansion work will begin immediately.

Plan and write the memo that you will send as an e-mail attachment to all employees at the Lake Charles facility. Save as *4C3si*. Prepare the cover e-mail that will be used to transmit the memo. Tell employees that the attached memo addresses the issue of an employee cafeteria, which many of them have requested. If you are using the data disk file *E-Mail Form*, address the e-mail to lcemployees@pathmarkcon.com and save as *4C3asi*.

4. Today you received an application from Roger Johns, with a $10,000 check for tuition, for the Developing Creative Leaders Program at the Hess Center. Although Mr. Johns's profile meets the admission criteria for the program, all the available seats have already been taken, and the applicants have been notified. Enrollment was closed several weeks ago, and you will have to return his check. Plan and write a bad-news letter telling Mr. Johns that the program has been filled. Invite him to apply for the same program next year, but do not guarantee his admission because the profile of the group that applies next year may be different. Indicate that he should submit an application by September 15 of next year. Save as *4C4si*.

Team Activity

Internet Activity

5. Several months ago, Pathmark Construction purchased Construction-CostEstimator, a software package designed to estimate the amount of supplies needed for construction jobs. Pathmark has used the software for six different projects. On the three large projects, the quantity of supplies was grossly underestimated. On the three small projects, the quantity of supplies was grossly overestimated. Ms. Kathryn James has asked you to evaluate the software and determine what to do to solve the problem.

At your request, a technician from Custom Construction Software reviewed the procedures you used and verified that you were using the software properly. You had to pay restocking fees when you returned the excess supplies that were ordered on the small projects. On the large projects, the underestimates caused you to lose time by having to order additional supplies and then wait for them to be delivered. You have purchased several other software packages from Custom Construction Software and have been very pleased with them; but these errors are extremely costly to your construction business, and you are dissatisfied with the software.

You would like to return ConstructionCostEstimator for a full refund of the $995 you paid for it. However, before you ask for a refund, you want to make sure that a similar product that you can use instead of ConstructionCostEstimator is available. Form a team with two or three classmates. Search the Internet, using keywords such as *construction estimation software* and *building costs software*. If you conclude that other appropriate products are available, plan and write the letter to Mr. Taku Patel at Custom Construction Software. If you conclude that no similar products are available, plan and write a memo to Ms. James telling her that you cannot find an appropriate replacement for the software. Save as *4C5tp-si*.

6. Ms. Emma Garrison, an owner of several small apartment complexes, has requested that Midlands Appliance increase her current $5,000 line of credit to $15,000 so that she can purchase appliances as needed for apartment units. Ms. Garrison was granted the $5,000 line of credit nine months ago. You base credit decisions on income and credit record. Ms. Garrison's income justified only $5,000 when you extended the credit, and her payment record has not been satisfactory. During the past nine months, she has been late with her payments three times and did not pay the minimum required on two occasions. You would reconsider her request after she has maintained her account properly for one year. Plan and write a letter declining Ms. Garrison's request to extend her credit limit. Sign your name and use the title *credit manager*. Save as *4C6si*.

7. When your employer, Mr. Bradley E. Jones, returned from a business trip on Palm Atlantic Airlines Flight 485 from Miami to Baltimore last week, his luggage was not on the flight. A delivery service dropped off his suitcase later that day at the main desk of your company. When Mr. Jones picked up the suitcase, he found that it had been badly damaged. The baggage had tire marks and appeared to have been run over by a baggage trailer.

Mr. Jones called the airline. A customer service representative instructed him to take his suitcase to Joey's Repair Shop for repairs and have the shop bill Palm Atlantic Airlines. The repair job left deep scars on the bag and was not acceptable to Mr. Jones. Joey's Repair Shop indicated that Mr. Jones should contact Ms. Amanda A. Burke, manager of customer service at Palm Atlantic Airlines. Mr. Jones paid $275 for the luggage less than six months ago. He wants the airline to send him a check for $275 by the 15th of next month so that he can replace the suitcase before his next business trip. Plan and write a claims letter to Ms. Burke for Mr. Bradley's signature. Save as *4C7si*.

8. Shaun Jackson, an employee of Grand Vista Professional Services, requested and was granted permission to attend a two-day telecommunications training seminar offered by Leeway Community College. The $350 fee was paid by the Training Department, of which you are the manager. A week after the seminar was held, Leeway refunded $250 to the Training Department because the employee did not attend the seminar. A nonrefundable $100 fee was retained for failure to cancel his registration. You had no notification from the employee. Therefore, you called the college and verified that Shaun Jackson did not attend the seminar either day or call to cancel his registration. You have also determined that he did not come to work on those two days.

Company policy requires that an employee who does not attend a scheduled training program notify the Training Department and reimburse the company for any fees incurred. Exceptions are made only in circumstances beyond the control of the employee. As training manager, you must notify the employee of the amount that must be refunded (in the form of a check sent to you and payable to the Training Department) and the reasons why. A copy of the memo is sent to the employee's supervisor (Demetrius Jervey). Any disciplinary action will be taken by the supervisor. Plan and write a bad-news memo to Shaun Jackson. Save as *4C8si*.

Application 4C: Guide for Evaluating Your Bad-News Messages

Factors to Consider	Points	4C2		4C3		4C4		4C5		4C6		4C7		4C8	
		SE	IE	SE	IE	SE	IE	SE	IE	SE	IE	SE	IE	SE	IE
Self-evaluation (SE), Instructor evaluation (IE)															
Strategy—uses appropriate indirect or direct strategy	2														
Strategy—presents supporting information needed	2														
Strategy—closes on a positive—or, at least, a neutral—note	2														
Writing Guide 1—evidence of good planning; organized	1														
Writing Guide 2—meets the reader's needs; courteous	1														
Writing Guide 3—uses positive language	1														
Writing Guide 4—uses a clear, easy-to-read style	1														
Writing Guide 5—complete; includes all needed information	1														
Writing Guide 6—uses the passive style when appropriate	1														
Writing Guide 7—uses general language when appropriate	1														
Writing Guide 8—uses effective sentence and paragraph structure; uses techniques to de-emphasize ideas	1														
Writing Guide 9—uses correct format and attractive placement	1														
Writing Guide 10—has been edited and proofread; no errors	1														
Overall assessment of document	4														
Totals	**20**														

Mastery Check for Chapter 4

1. Why is it important to verify a bad-news decision before you write a bad-news message?

2. How do you determine the best medium to use in writing bad-news messages?

3. Describe the strategy that is generally most appropriate to use for bad-news messages.

4. Describe three techniques that you can use to de-emphasize bad news.

5. A direct strategy may be most effective for what type of bad-news message? Why?

6. For each of the terms shown below, write a complete, correct sentence using the term.

Buffer

Claim

Random

Shell Cove—Rental/Condominium Division

Shell Cove delegates all responsibilities for rental and condominium units to the Rental/Condominium Division, directed by Ms. Trinity McBride. For this rotation of your training program, you are assistant manager to Trinity. Crescent at Shell Cove is a rental complex, and Captain's Watch is a condominium complex. All of the condominium units in the Captain's Watch have been sold. The occupancy rates for the Crescent and the Captain's Watch for the past year are as follows:

	Season	**Off-Season**
Crescent at Shell Cove	85%–90%	60% or higher
Captain's Watch	95%–100%	75% or higher

Trinity has asked you to complete the following three projects this week:

Job 1: Increase in Captain's Watch Regime Fees

Regime fees are fees paid by condo owners for the maintenance and upkeep of the exterior of all units and the shared and common areas (halls, pool, clubhouse, patios, boardwalk, lawn, etc.). The regime fees have never been raised since the Captain's Watch was developed. A combination of property tax increases, labor cost increases, and damage from several storms makes it necessary to increase fees 10 percent effective the first of next month. This increase is consistent with the provisions of Shell Cove's legal agreement with owners. Current monthly fees are as follows:

2-bedroom units	. . . .	$180
3-bedroom units	. . . .	$225
4-bedroom units	. . . .	$250

Plan and write a memo to all Captain's Watch owners telling them about this increase. Use a table to show the current fees and the new fees for each type of unit. Fees are always assessed in increments of $5. Therefore, when you list new fees, calculate them at 10 percent rounded to the next $5 amount (example: $180 × .10 = $18; rounded to $20; $180 + $20 = $200).

You may use either an indirect or a direct approach for this memo. The owners are aware of increasing costs and know that a well-maintained unit enhances the rental opportunities for investors. Save as *4E1si*. Attach a copy of your memo to an e-mail and send it to Trinity for her comments before mailing it to the Captain's Watch owners. Save the e-mail as *4E1asi*.

Job 2: Request for Reservations

The Wilsons are among your best customers. The family has rented a four-bedroom unit at the Crescent at Shell Cove for at least one week each quarter since it was built. Usually the Wilsons make reservations early. Today your reservation associates received a request from them for a four-bedroom unit for a week starting two weeks from Saturday, and you do not have one available. You have two 2-bedroom units on the same floor, which would cost them a total of $3,500 ($1,000 more for the week than a four-bedroom rental unit). You also have a four-bedroom condo in the Captain's Watch that would rent for $3,500. The condominium units are larger and more luxurious than the Crescent at Shell Cove units.

Because the Wilsons are such good customers, you are willing to reduce the rental cost of the two units at the Crescent to $3,000 so that the difference would be only $500. You cannot reduce the cost of the condo because the rental price is specified in the owner's agreement. Plan and write a letter to Mr. and Mrs. James S. Wilson telling them you do not have the accommodations they requested, and offer them alternatives. Save as *4E2si*.

Team Activity

Internet Activity

Job 3: Proposal From Investors to Convert Crescent at Shell Cove to Condos

Trinity has asked you to form a team with three classmates to study whether it would be better to build a new rental complex or a new condominium complex. She has also asked you to propose several possible names for the new complex.

Your team has analyzed the current situation with the rental and condominium units. Here are the results you have obtained thus far:

- For the past six quarters, Shell Cove's rental units have been at least 20 percent more profitable than its condo units. The difference is that rent is shared with the condo owners.

- The occupancy rate is lower at the Crescent than at the Captain's Watch. You could rent more luxury units like those in the Captain's Watch if you had them available.

- Demand for new luxury condos is very high, from both investors who rent their units and owners who do not rent their units.

- Condos require a smaller Shell Cove investment than new rental units do.

Your team has concluded that it would be better to build new condos and work to increase occupancy on the lower-priced Crescent rental units.

In the meantime, Trinity sent you a proposal from Ocean City Resort Investors, Inc., with an offer to convert Crescent at Shell Cove to condos for you. Your team analyzed the proposal and, based on your previous results, decided that it did not meet Shell Cove's needs. The most important consideration was that you need additional high-end luxury condos. Crescent was designed to appeal to a market seeking more affordable rates in an upscale development. It is also more profitable than the Captain's Watch condo units are. Therefore, the team agreed that you will recommend to Trinity that she turn this proposal down.

Your team has decided to send Trinity an e-mail explaining the team's results and recommending that she develop a new condo project rather than accept the offer to convert Crescent to condos. Your team will brainstorm and include in the e-mail three alternative names for the proposed complex. One requirement of a name is that it is not already in use by a similar business. Search the Internet to ensure that the names you propose are not already taken.

Draft a bad-news letter from Trinity to Mr. Robert L. Cash of Ocean City Resort Investors, Inc., to tell him that the project does not meet Shell Cove's needs. However, invite his group of investors to a meeting one week from today at 9:30 to discuss the possibility of purchasing condos in the new development being planned. Note that investors who have purchased units in the Captain's Watch are very pleased with the occupancy rate and the returns on their investment. Attach the draft letter for Trinity's review to the e-mail you send her. Save the e-mail as *4E3tp-si*. Save the draft letter as *4E3asi*.

PERSUASIVE MESSAGES

OBJECTIVES

After you complete Chapter 5, you should be able to:

- Use logical appeals for writing persuasive messages.
- Use psychological appeals for writing persuasive messages.
- Determine when to use each type of appeal.
- Edit messages more effectively.

OVERVIEW

To *persuade* means to induce or convince someone to do something. Writers use persuasion for many different types of messages. Persuasion is involved if you are trying to convince a person to buy a product or service, donate to a charitable cause, do a favor for you, pay a bill, or hire you. These situations vary significantly, but they all require elements of persuasion.

The type of situation determines the most appropriate appeal to use in a persuasive message. The degree of persuasion can vary from a minor element of persuasion to a very persuasive message. The key elements of this chapter include:

- Goal of persuasive messages.
- Ethical implications of persuasion.
- Planning persuasive messages.
- Factors that influence persuasion.
- Strategies for writing persuasive messages.

"Business Talk"

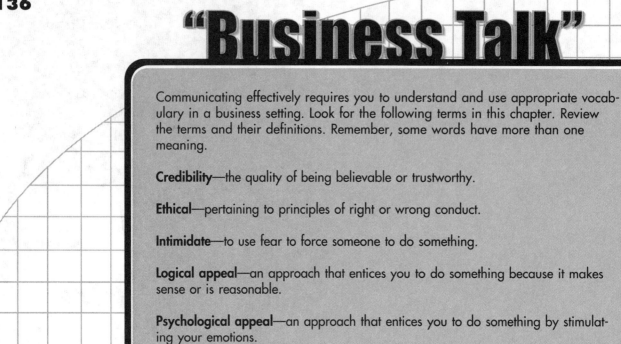

Communicating effectively requires you to understand and use appropriate vocabulary in a business setting. Look for the following terms in this chapter. Review the terms and their definitions. Remember, some words have more than one meaning.

Credibility—the quality of being believable or trustworthy.

Ethical—pertaining to principles of right or wrong conduct.

Intimidate—to use fear to force someone to do something.

Logical appeal—an approach that entices you to do something because it makes sense or is reasonable.

Psychological appeal—an approach that entices you to do something by stimulating your emotions.

GOAL OF PERSUASIVE MESSAGES

The goal of persuasive messages is to get readers to do something—to buy insurance, upgrade Internet service, support diabetes research, or grant a job interview—that they might not otherwise do. The need for persuasion implies that the reader may not do what you ask unless convinced to do so. Very little, if any, persuasion is needed if the reader is already likely to do something. A routine request is all that is necessary. In other cases, however, a persuasive strategy is required.

Individuals and organizations often make requests of other individuals or organizations. Many requests involve the commitment of resources, such as money, time, or effort. Most individuals and organizations rightfully tend to guard their limited resources very carefully.

When you write persuasive messages, you ask readers to do things they might not be likely to do. Therefore, you should expect and prepare for some resistance. In some cases, a reader may like your request or think it is reasonable but may be concerned about committing the time or resources involved. In other cases, the reader may not like your request but could be convinced that it is in his or her best interest—or the best interest of the organization—to grant it.

In many organizations, writing specialized messages, such as sales and collection letters, is handled by specialists within the organization or by external consultants who write only those types of messages. This chapter focuses on general persuasive messages.

ETHICAL IMPLICATIONS OF PERSUASION

Persuasion often involves **ethical** issues. Techniques used to persuade people to do things may be ethical or unethical. Think about the following question:

Is it ethical to persuade or convince someone to do something that you know is not in that person's best interest?

You might respond by asking yourself, "Why would I do something that is not in my best interest?" Many answers exist. You may not have enough information to determine that the action is not in your best interest. The information you have may not be accurate. You may feel that you have no choice but to do what was asked.

Persuasion does not involve force. A person in a position of power (such as a supervisor) who uses force to cause another person to take a certain action is trying to **intimidate** rather than persuade that person. Intimidation is different from persuasion and is never ethical.

Persuasive techniques that manipulate, misrepresent, mislead, or take advantage of the reader are not appropriate. Messages must be honest. Deliberately withholding information may be just as deceitful as presenting incorrect information. The following are some examples of unethical persuasive tactics:

- Creating a debt collection letter that looks and reads like a legal document, to scare the recipient into paying.
- Claiming your product "works faster" or "lasts longer," when you have no proof that it does.
- Offering a sale on an item you know you will run out of (or don't have at all), with the intent of getting customers to purchase a similar higher-priced product.

Intent or motive is a key issue in ethical situations. The intent to deceive a reader by providing incorrect information or by withholding needed information obviously represents an unethical situation. At the same time, as a writer, you should take care that your persuasive messages do not unintentionally mislead the reader.

PLANNING PERSUASIVE MESSAGES

Many different types of messages fit into the broad category of persuasive messages. The approach that works best for one type of persuasive message may differ from the approach that works best for another type. For example, the approach used to persuade someone to buy a product differs from the approach used to persuade someone to pay a delinquent bill or devote time to work on a community service or charitable project.

These situations all have similarities and differences. They are similar in that you have to get the reader's attention before you can present the request. They are also similar in that in each case the main objective is to convince the reader to take action. They are different in terms of the knowledge needed to be effective in each situation.

- In the sales situation, planning requires you to analyze the customer's needs, determine how your product fits those needs, analyze competitive products, and understand the market. Convincing the customer of the need for the product may even be required.
- The collection letter may require that you understand the reasons why the person did not pay the bill. Often a series of letters is required to get that information. Once you know the cause of the problem, you can focus on potential ways to solve it. Then you can provide options that might persuade the individual to take the necessary steps to pay the delinquent bill.
- In the last situation in which you want to convince the reader to devote time to a community service or charitable project, you may have to appeal to the reader's emotions. Most people who contribute to charitable causes do so because they feel good about helping others or giving back to their community.

The planning process for a persuasive message differs slightly from the process you used in previous chapters. With persuasive messages, you are focusing on trying to get the reader to do what you are asking rather than trying to understand and meet the needs of the reader. Use the following steps to plan persuasive messages:

1. Focus on options that might be used to get the reader's attention.
2. Think of ways to develop interest in the request and create the desire to do what is asked.
3. Think about ways to make it easy for the reader to do what is requested.

In Chapter 2, you learned that both individuals and groups can brainstorm to generate ideas. Brainstorming is especially effective in stimulating the type of creative thinking that is needed to be persuasive. A freewheeling, questioning tactic is helpful. Ask yourself (or your group) questions such as these:

- What benefit, if any, does this request have for the reader?
- How important is the benefit? Is it a direct benefit or an indirect benefit?
- If I were the reader, would I be likely to do what is being asked?
- Why would anyone who does not have to do what I am asking be willing to do it?
- Would the reader grant the request because it makes good business sense to do so or because it is a good thing to do?
- What reasons would convince me to do what is being asked of the reader?
- What would motivate me to take action on the request?
- What would convince the reader of my **credibility**?
- What would be the most effective way to appeal to the reader?

Remember that the purpose of brainstorming is to generate as many ideas as possible. During the brainstorming process, accept all ideas without being judgmental about them. Resist the temptation to criticize; rather, try to build on the ideas that you generate. An idea may have no value on its own, but it may lead you to think of other ideas that could prove to be valuable.

Once you have generated as many ideas as possible, evaluate them to determine their strengths and weaknesses. As you evaluate the ideas, do a quick credibility check. Ask questions such as these:

- Would I believe this idea? If not, why not?
- Would I think this is a good reason to do what I am asking?
- How could I change this idea so that it would be believable?

The ideas that you select as the basis for your appeal should be given a final check for credibility. Some writers try to use a gimmick to open a message and get the reader's attention. An idea may be clever or cute, but if the reader does not believe it, the opening will not be effective. Here are some examples of gimmicks:

Success Tip

Building effective relationships is an important part of doing business in any culture.

- Are you ready to make the deal of a lifetime? If so, call within 24 hours.
- The dollar that is enclosed may not mean much to you as an executive, but give it to the first child you see and watch the reaction you get.
- Would you like an opportunity to win $10,000? By subscribing to our magazine, you could be the lucky winner.

Technology Connections

Technology Bridges Geography and Time

When you do business with individuals who live in different locations around the world, time zones, holidays, and distance can create major barriers to communications. Electronic communications become more important. Voice mail, fax, videoconferencing, computers with high-speed modems, e-mail, and the Internet make it possible to communicate frequently and in a relatively inexpensive manner. However, technology does not replace face-to-face communications.

FACTORS THAT INFLUENCE PERSUASION

Earlier in this chapter, persuasive messages were defined as messages that ask readers to do something that they might not be likely to do. When you write a persuasive message, you are trying to influence or change the behavior of the reader. Two key factors that determine your effectiveness in persuading the reader to do what you ask are:

- Your credibility as the writer.
- The appeal you use in the message.

Credibility

Both you and your message must have credibility. For you to have credibility, the reader must perceive you as:

- Knowledgeable or having expertise on the topic.
- Sincere, honest, and forthright.
- In control of the situation.

If any of those elements is missing, the reader is not likely to believe you. If you are not credible, the reader is not likely to believe your message. Even if you are credible, your message may not be credible unless the reader judges it to be:

- Accurate.
- Clear and easy to understand.
- Supported with adequate information to make a decision.

Note that the reader is the one who judges your credibility and that of your message. You may think that you are credible and that your message is very credible, but unless the reader agrees with that belief, you are not likely to persuade the reader to take action.

Appeal

A message can have a **logical** or a **psychological appeal**. In some cases, the logical and psychological appeals can be combined. A message has a logical appeal when the reader believes good reasons exist for taking the action requested. To be logical, the message must make sense; the request must seem reasonable to the reader.

To develop a message with a logical appeal, you must:

1. Present facts and supporting evidence.
2. Analyze the evidence.
3. Draw logical conclusions based on the evidence.

You will be believed if your reader perceives the facts to be accurate, the analysis to be proper, and the conclusions to be justified by appropriate analysis of the facts.

A message has a psychological appeal when it stimulates the reader's emotions or satisfies the reader's goals, values, or perceived needs. A psychological appeal makes the reader feel good or righteous about taking the action that was requested. Psychological appeals often focus on fair play, appreciating one's good fortune, helping the less fortunate, and doing things just because they are good things to do. Figures 5-1 and 5-2 illustrate the use of logical and psychological appeals.

Global Connections

Credibility

Building credibility in a different culture is far more challenging than in your own. Factors such as age, rank, social status, and gender make a difference in credibility in many cultures. In some Asian and African countries, young people have a difficult time establishing credibility. Knowledge and wisdom are attributed to older people. In India, Great Britain, and some Eastern cultures, high professional rank and social status enhance credibility. For a business deal to be closed, someone in a high-ranking position may have to be involved. In many Middle Eastern countries, women have a far more difficult time establishing credibility than men.

Usually it is easier to overcome such barriers in written messages than in face-to-face communications. You can use techniques such as the following to minimize these factors:

- President John Smith and I are pleased to present this proposal for your consideration. (Adds rank and male influence.)
- My company's position on establishing local offices is . . . (Uses the power of the company rather than the individual.)
- Mr. Jones, the senior member of our team, recommended that we test the product in the local area for two weeks. (Adds age and rank.)

STRATEGIES FOR WRITING PERSUASIVE MESSAGES

In Chapters 3 and 4, you focused on writing positive and negative messages. The primary emphasis was on conveying information. The strategy you used was determined by the reaction you expected from the reader and the situation. In this chapter, the strategies are different, because the goal of a persuasive message is to get the reader to do something. However, you can build on what you learned in Chapters 3 and 4 because persuasive messages can have either positive or negative overtones.

The best strategy for writing a persuasive message depends on what you are trying to accomplish and how difficult the task is. Many different types of messages require an element of persuasion. However, some messages require more persuasion than others do. No one best approach exists for all situations. The degree of persuasion needed is the key element to use in determining the strategy that is likely to produce the best results.

Direct Strategy

The best strategy for a simple request that requires very little persuasion is the direct strategy that you learned in Chapter 3 for positive and routine messages:

1. State the request early in the message—preferably in the first sentence.
2. Provide supporting details and any needed explanation.
3. Use a positive, friendly closing paragraph designed to build goodwill.

The key is to present the reasons for the request effectively so that the reader will believe that the reasons are good and that the request is justified.

Indirect Strategy

The best strategy for messages that require more persuasion is an indirect strategy similar to the strategy you used in writing negative messages. This type of strategy is used most frequently in persuasive messages. An indirect strategy works better in persuasive situations because the reasons or justification is presented before the request is made. Use the following strategy for messages requiring more persuasion:

1. Attract the reader's attention and interest.
2. Explain the request carefully, and make sure that it is fully justified.
3. Minimize the obstacles, and make it as easy as possible for the reader to act.
4. Request the desired action confidently.

Attracting the reader's attention is not always easy. In some cases, the reader may have an interest in your message, and attracting attention is relatively simple. In other cases, creativity and imagination are crucial in gaining the reader's attention.

Getting attention is only the first step. The opening paragraph must also prepare the reader for the justification that follows. Using the right appeal for the situation is important. Most people respond to requests that appeal to either their emotions or their reasoning power.

As a rule of thumb, use a logical appeal when the situation has some direct benefit to the reader. Use a psychological appeal when the benefit is indirect or when the request does not benefit the reader. Analyze the situation carefully before deciding which type of appeal to use. Be creative in developing appeals.

Busy people often can accept only a few of the many requests they receive. Creativity and persuasiveness often determine which requests they accept.

© JOSE LUIS PELAEZ, INC./CORBIS

Sincerity and Empathy

Sincerity is especially important in persuasive messages. Warm and friendly messages that contain factual information tend to build trust. Some writers exaggerate to make a point in persuasive messages. Effective writers avoid this temptation because they do not want to risk jeopardizing their credibility with the reader.

Empathy is a great technique for evaluating sincerity. Read the message carefully. If you received the message, would you believe it? If it does not seem sincere to you, it probably will not seem sincere to the reader.

Review Figure 5-1 on page 144. Note the following points as you examine this letter:

- The letter contains a reasonable request that could benefit the reader. However, granting the request would cost him money and time. Therefore, combining a psychological and a logical appeal is appropriate.

- The first paragraph is designed to get attention and stimulate interest. The information in this paragraph is likely to please the reader.

- The first paragraph also prepares the reader for the justification of the request.

- The second paragraph makes the request, using an approach designed to appeal to the reader's emotions.

- The third paragraph uses a logical, commonsense approach to explain how granting the request could benefit the reader.

- The last paragraph shows that you are confident the reader will grant the request, but it also provides a reasonable way for him to decline.

- The last paragraph makes it easy for the reader to grant the request. Calling also makes it more difficult for him to refuse.

- Note that an indirect strategy was used to make the letter more persuasive.

Review Figure 5-2 on page 145. Note the following points as you examine the letter:

- This letter offers no direct benefit to the reader. A significant amount of persuasion will be required to convince the reader to take the action requested. Therefore, an indirect style with a psychological appeal is appropriate.

- The first paragraph uses a psychological appeal to get attention and lay the groundwork to make the request.

- The second paragraph also uses psychological appeals. It implies that successful business leaders are participating in the program; therefore, if the reader thinks of herself as successful, she should, too. This paragraph notes that mentoring can be personally satisfying. In addition, it focuses on the limited amount of time involved to make it easier for the reader to take action.

- The third paragraph presents the request in a low-key way and makes it easy to accept.

- The last paragraph builds goodwill and reinforces a positive decision.

Success Tip

The only good substitute for hard work is working both smart and hard.

Figure 5-1: Persuasive Letter With Combined Psychological and Logical Appeals

GRAND VISTA PROFESSIONAL SERVICES

October 14, 200_

Mr. Sam J. Phelan
Phelan and Associates, Inc.
867 Highland Avenue
Butte, MT 59701-2958

Dear Mr. Phelan:

Your staff has conducted a number of excellent training programs for Grand Vista Professional Services over the last few years. Our employees have reacted very favorably to the training, and our company has benefited immensely from the investment in these training sessions. Today, when the Board of Directors of Butte Community Services agreed that training our volunteers must be our first priority, I immediately thought of Phelan and Associates and the outstanding training programs you offer.

Would you please consider contributing one day of training in early November for all volunteers working with Butte Community Services? As you know, Butte Community Services and its volunteers have improved the quality of life for many of the less fortunate members of our community.

In addition to knowing that you have made a major contribution to our community by helping our volunteers do an even better job, you will have an opportunity to showcase your training to leading companies in the Butte area. Many of these leading companies provide the volunteers who work with Butte Community Services.

Please check your calendar, and I will call you next week to see if we can work out an appropriate time for you to conduct the training session.

Sincerely yours,

Student's Name
Chair, Board of Directors

xx

4286 Western Boulevard
Butte, MT 59701-6705
Tel: (406) 555-0156
Fax: (406) 555-0182
www.grandvistaprofessional.com

Attracts the reader's attention and stimulates interest.

Explains the request and begins with a psychological appeal.

Adds a logical appeal to help persuade the reader to act.

Requests action confidently; makes it easy for the reader to act.

Figure 5-2: Persuasive Letter With a Psychological Appeal

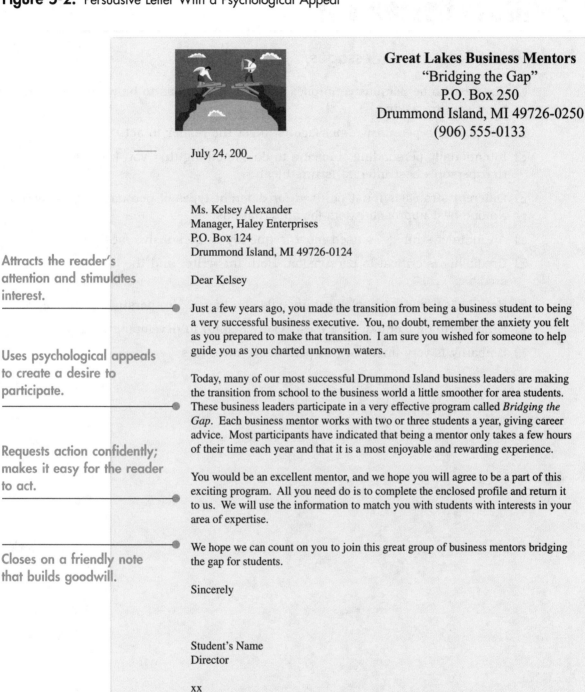

Attracts the reader's attention and stimulates interest.

Uses psychological appeals to create a desire to participate.

Requests action confidently; makes it easy for the reader to act.

Closes on a friendly note that builds goodwill.

Great Lakes Business Mentors
"Bridging the Gap"
P.O. Box 250
Drummond Island, MI 49726-0250
(906) 555-0133

July 24, 200_

Ms. Kelsey Alexander
Manager, Haley Enterprises
P.O. Box 124
Drummond Island, MI 49726-0124

Dear Kelsey

Just a few years ago, you made the transition from being a business student to being a very successful business executive. You, no doubt, remember the anxiety you felt as you prepared to make that transition. I am sure you wished for someone to help guide you as you charted unknown waters.

Today, many of our most successful Drummond Island business leaders are making the transition from school to the business world a little smoother for area students. These business leaders participate in a very effective program called *Bridging the Gap*. Each business mentor works with two or three students a year, giving career advice. Most participants have indicated that being a mentor only takes a few hours of their time each year and that it is a most enjoyable and rewarding experience.

You would be an excellent mentor, and we hope you will agree to be a part of this exciting program. All you need do is to complete the enclosed profile and return it to us. We will use the information to match you with students with interests in your area of expertise.

We hope we can count on you to join this great group of business mentors bridging the gap for students.

Sincerely

Student's Name
Director

xx

Enclosure

! Points to Remember

About Persuasive Messages

☑ The need to be persuasive implies that the reader has to be convinced to do what you are asking.

☑ The goal of a persuasive message is to get the reader to act.

☑ Intentionally persuading someone to do something that you know is not in that person's best interest is unethical.

☑ Different strategies must be used for different types of persuasive messages. No one best approach exists for all situations.

☑ An indirect strategy is used most frequently in persuasive messages.

☑ Credibility is critical to persuasion. Both the writer and the message must be credible.

☑ Both logical and psychological appeals can be used in persuasive messages.

☑ Brainstorming techniques are especially helpful in developing creative ideas.

☑ Empathy is very important in persuasive messages.

Review Guide 3—Present Ideas Positively

Review Guide 3 of Chapter 2 on pages 28–29, and then complete the following activities. Revise each sentence or paragraph to make it positive or at least to minimize the use of negative words. Disagree when it is necessary to do so, but do not disagree in a disagreeable manner.

1. We regret that we did not send you adequate information to determine whether or not you could support the Community Nurturing Center.

2. Do not complete these forms if you have not read the instructions carefully.

3. We do not use post office box numbers on mailing labels because delivery services do not deliver to postal boxes; they do not accept anything without a full street address.

4. Why don't you call Bill and see if he doesn't have a day open in the next week or two when he can spare time to have lunch with us?

5. Leslie did much worse on the English section of the examination than on the math section. Her math scores were not so bad; in fact, they were quite good.

6. Jack is never in the office on Friday, but he is here the other days if he does not have to go out of town on business.

Editing and Language Arts Checkpoint

1. Carefully read the document that follows; it is packed with errors. Use proofreaders' marks to mark all errors in grammar, spelling, usage, word choice, capitalization, punctuation, and keying. If you need help with proofreaders' marks, refer to the table on page 53. Do not revise sentence or paragraph structure unless you find an error.

2. Access *File 5B* in the Chapter 5 folder on your student data disk and make the corrections. If you are not working with the data disk, key the document, making the corrections as you key. You may use online reference tools just as you would on the job.

3. Format the document as a letter, which will be sent to Ms. Teresa Ramos from you, as an employee of Rosselot Fitness Solutions. You can get both addresses from the address directory on the student data disk or in Appendix A. Use the current date. Save as *5Bsi*.

---

aAs a Benefits Manger, rising health-care costs are impacting

your companys bottom line and you ability to provide effective

medical coverage for your employees. 1 of the most cost effective

methods of improving your employee's health is at your finger

tips—a in-house fitness program.

Corporate fitness programs decrease health-care costs, studies

show they have other positive affects as well. As employees loose

weight and become more physically fit there health improves. They

are better at managing stress. And preforming physical tasks.

These workers have increased morale, are absent less, and are

more productive.

Rosselot Fitness Solutions provides on sight fitness programs for many of Baltimores' finest companies. Our system consists of these 5 steps, private employee consultations and advise, fitness evaluations custom designed exercise programs, fully supervised training, and periodic follow-up visits. The enclosed brochure describes the services we provide, and include testimonials from several leading Baltimore firms.

You're employees are your most importent asset. Shouldnt you and them enjoy the many benefits Rosselot Fintess Solutions has to offer. I will call next friday to explain the features of our proven popular programs and discuss how they can meet your needs.

Writing Persuasive Messages

In this application, you will write persuasive letters, memos, and e-mails. Use the appeal that would be most effective. Letterhead for some activities is available in the chapter folder on the student data disk. If you are not using the data disk or if letterhead is not provided, key the documents on plain paper.

Format your documents as shown on pages 47–50. Consult the database in Appendix A or on the student data disk (*Address Directory*) for addresses and contact information. Use the current date. For letters, supply an appropriate salutation and complimentary close. For memos and e-mail, add an appropriate heading. All documents are from you unless you are directed otherwise.

Your instructor may ask you to use the guide that appears on page 156 for evaluating your documents. Your instructor may also use this form to evaluate your work.

1. Mr. Mark C. Moore, vice president of human resources at Palmetto State University, was recently made aware of the need for a high-level professional development program for the executive assistants in the administrative offices. This program will be part of a larger branding effort being made across campus.

   The goal is to develop a consistent professional image and to use a consistent document style in every office on campus. A major outcome of the program will be the development of an office manual that can be used as a reference for temporary employees when regular employees are out of the office and as a training guide for new employees. Once the program has been developed and tested, the training department will offer it to other administrative employees.

   A former faculty member, Dr. Joyce S. Glenn, who has expertise and a lot of experience in this area, is a senior administrator now. Plan a memo from Mark to Joyce that will persuade her to take a leadership role in designing and pilot-testing this professional development program. Mark would assemble a team to work with her. Joyce would not expect extra pay, but she has a very busy job and this project would take a lot of time.

   a. What direct and/or indirect benefits would Dr. Glenn gain from agreeing to this request?

b. What factors might cause Dr. Glenn to turn down the request?

c. How could you overcome these factors?

d. What type of appeal do you think will work best?

2. Draft the persuasive memo to Dr. Glenn for Mr. Moore. Save as *5C2si.*

3. Mr. Moore wants his assistant, Ann Major, to review the memo before he sends it to Dr. Glenn. He has asked you to send Ann an e-mail requesting that she review the memo and make suggestions to you for improving it. Indicate to Ann that Mr. Moore would like her to work very closely with Dr. Glenn on this project and handle most of the administrative work. You do not need to explain the project to Ann, as she already knows about it. Attach the memo you drafted in the previous activity to your e-mail. Although Ann will feel that she must do what Mr. Moore asks, be persuasive in convincing her that this is a very important project so she will give it extra effort and attention.

E-mail addresses at Palmetto State University consist of the first name(period)last name@PSU.sc.edu (example: Ann.Major@PSU.sc.edu). Copy Mark on the e-mail. Save as *5C3si.*

Team Activity

Internet Activity

4. Dr. Glenn has accepted Mr. Moore's request to take a leadership role in developing and pilot-testing the program. She has asked you to form a team with two classmates to research topics for the Professional Development Program for Executive Assistants for her review.

Dr. Glenn has suggested that the team use the Internet to find training programs for executive and administrative assistants and review the topics being covered. She has indicated that individuals, consulting teams, and professional organizations offer these types of programs. The team should make a list of the topics that are addressed most frequently in training programs. You have also decided to talk with some of the executive assistants at PSU and get their opinions on the most important topics. Then you will analyze your data and choose the four or five topics that you feel are most important to include.

Write a memo to Dr. Glenn persuading her to accept your topics. List the topics in the memo. Use a logical appeal because Dr. Glenn is very knowledgeable in this area. Save as *5C4tp-si.*

5. You are manager of community relations for VanHuss Associates, Inc. You want to encourage all employees to contribute to the Community Chest Fund. The Community Chest supports more than fifty local charitable agencies. The bulk of all funds are collected through the workplace. Employees can donate through payroll deductions, check, or credit card.

VanHuss Associates wants to be viewed as a good corporate citizen and matches each gift an employee makes. At the same time, the company does not want to pressure employees to donate. VanHuss Associates prefers to appeal to people's sense that they should help take care of the homeless, the hungry, the abused, the neglected, and many other groups needing community support.

Plan and write a letter that will be sent to each employee encouraging him or her to contribute generously to the Community Chest Fund. Refer employees to an enclosed brochure that describes the various agencies that receive support from the fund and to a form, also enclosed, that they can fill out to make their contribution. Prepare the first letter for Ms. Elizabeth Hudson, chief financial officer of VanHuss Associates, Inc. Use her first name in the salutation. Save as *5C5si.*

6. You are a professor of human resources management at Southwestern State University writing a textbook on principles of human resources management. You also work as a consultant. Recently, one of your clients showed you a compensation survey sent to him and other human resources directors of large companies within the state. The survey instrument included short job descriptions for benchmark jobs. You feel the survey is constructed very effectively, and the job descriptions are concise and clear. In fact, this is one of the best examples of a compensation survey that you have ever seen.

You would like to include the survey and job descriptions as examples in your textbook. You will give full credit to Ms. Brenda Crum, human resources director of The Hess Center, who designed the survey instrument. Write Ms. Crum asking if you may use the survey instrument with the job descriptions. Enclose a permission release form and a stamped, self-addressed envelope. Save as *5C6si.*

7. For some years Metro Manufacturing, Inc., has had a compensation plan for sales representatives in their first three years that consists of 25 percent salary and 75 percent commission. After three years, the compensation changes to 50 percent salary and 50 percent commission. Your sales managers have reported to you, as marketing manager, that they have lost several candidates for sales positions to competitors who offered more salary but less commission than you offer. You have also noted that turnover in the sales force is much greater in the first few years of employment, with employees leaving for the same reason.

The company has always felt that commissions provided a greater incentive than salary for new hires. You have given a lot of thought to the issue and believe that concern about economic security is now a factor that is offsetting the commission incentive.

You propose changing the ratio of salary and commission for new hires to 50 percent salary and 50 percent commission. The total dollar amount paid to new sales representatives is not expected to change significantly. Plan the persuasive memo to the Compensation Committee.

a. What benefits, if any, would Metro Manufacturing gain from changing the compensation plan?

b. What obstacles would you anticipate in trying to persuade the Compensation Committee to change the compensation to 50 percent salary and 50 percent commission for all sales representatives?

c. How can you overcome these obstacles?

d. What appeal do you think will produce the best results?

8. Write the memo to the Compensation Committee. Save as *5C8si.*

9. As a business communications instructor at Central Technical College, you would like to secure examples of the types of letters, memos, and reports that are written in local businesses. You plan to use these documents as illustrations in your classes. You would protect the confidentiality of the company by changing the company name and any other identifying information.

To determine the type of response you might get, you have selected Meekins and Meekins, an advertising, public relations, and marketing consulting firm. This firm has a great image and an excellent reputation for being a good corporate citizen. Write a persuasive letter to Mr. Roger Meekins asking for examples of letters, memos, and reports used in his company. You need the materials within two weeks. Enclose an envelope, but also offer to pick up the materials at Mr. Meekins's convenience. Save as *5C9si.*

10. Think of a situation in which you would have to persuade someone to do something. Write a brief paragraph describing the situation. Then prepare the persuasive letter that you would send persuading the person to do what you ask. Design and use your own personal letterhead for this job. Save as *5C10si.* Save your letterhead for use in Chapter 9.

Application 5C: Guide for Evaluating Your Persuasive Messages

Factors to Consider	Points	5C2 SE	5C2 IE	5C3 SE	5C3 IE	5C4 SE	5C4 IE	5C5 SE	5C5 IE	5C6 SE	5C6 IE	5C8 SE	5C8 IE	5C9 SE	5C9 IE	5C10 SE	5C10 IE
Self-evaluation (SE), Instructor evaluation (IE)																	
Strategy—uses appropriate logical or psychological appeal and is credible	2																
Strategy—attracts attention and interest and justifies the request	2																
Strategy—requests action confidently and makes it easy for reader to act	2																
Writing Guide 1—evidence of good planning; organized	1																
Writing Guide 2—meets the reader's needs; courteous	1																
Writing Guide 3—uses positive language	1																
Writing Guide 4—uses a clear, easy-to-read style	1																
Writing Guide 5—complete; includes all needed information	1																
Writing Guide 6—uses an efficient, action-oriented style	1																
Writing Guide 7—uses specific, concrete language	1																
Writing Guide 8—uses effective sentence and paragraph structure	1																
Writing Guide 9—uses correct format and attractive placement	1																
Writing Guide 10—has been edited and proofread; no errors	1																
Overall assessment of document	4																
Totals	20																

Mastery Check for Chapter 5

1. Describe the most appropriate strategy for a persuasive message. Justify your choice.

2. Describe two types of appeals normally used in persuasive messages.

3. Describe the situation in which each type of appeal is most effective.

4. Why is credibility of major importance in persuasive messages?

5. Describe both ethical persuasion and unethical persuasion.

6. For each of the three terms shown below, write a complete, correct sentence using the term.

Credibility

Ethical

Intimidate

Shell Cove—Conference Center Division

The Conference Center Division, directed by Mr. Henry Tassin, handles all conference and meeting marketing and management. For this rotation of your training program, you are assistant manager to Henry. The Conference Center focuses on three goals:

- Ensure meetings are totally hassle-free for the corporate executives who bring their employees and clients to Shell Cove.

- Provide a setting that helps make meetings productive.

- Make the free time participants have so memorable that they will want to come back for vacations or to buy condos.

Shell Cove facilities are very flexible and make it possible to:

- Handle groups ranging from 10 to 600 participants—meetings for groups of more than 100 are held in the hotel and of fewer than 100 people in the Conference Center.

- Host 20 different groups at the same time depending on group size.

- Give participants the option of staying in the hotel or in rental units and condos.

The Conference Center Division markets conference facilities to corporate groups, negotiates facilities and services, and coordinates all activities with other Shell Cove divisions for participants. Henry has asked you to complete the following three projects.

Job 1: The Marbex Corporation

Ms. Isabella Cabrera, president of Marbex Corporation, is considering Shell Cove and three other sites to host the Marbex Corporation President's Club award trip this year. Each year the President's Club awards the 50 top sales representatives and their spouses or guests an all-expense-paid, one-week trip to an outstanding resort. The event provides an opportunity for senior executives to spend time with the most productive salespeople in a relaxed, casual setting.

Typically, the event includes:

- Two or three short meetings (required to make the trip tax-deductible for the company).

- A formal awards dinner/dance on the final night.

- One afternoon/evening special event that features fun games and ends with a very casual outdoor dinner.

- Unlimited access to golf, tennis, spas, fishing expeditions, and any other amenities offered by the resort selected (Shell Cove offers all these features).

- Rental cars for participants who want to explore the surrounding area.

- A hospitality room available from 8 a.m. to midnight for breakfast, snacks, and beverages.

- A $300 allowance for participants to have meals on their own.

Write a letter to Ms. Cabrera persuading her to select Shell Cove as the site. You will enclose a package of materials from the marketing department that includes beautiful color brochures of Shell Cove describing the many features it offers her group. The package also includes a special group pricing plan based on her needs. Although the group rates are good, for this type of event, focus on the quality of the experience you can offer at Shell Cove. Invite Ms. Cabrera and three guests to spend two days as your guests to preview the facilities and services you offer. Tell her that you will call to schedule her visit after she has had an opportunity to review the materials. Save as *5E1si*.

Job 2: Camp Kemo at Shell Cove

Shell Cove President Michael Brewer has agreed to partner with Cove Medical Center in sponsoring and hosting Camp Kemo. Children who have cancer and are taking chemotherapy and one guest (often a brother or sister) spend a week at the camp at no charge. The Conference Center provides all facilities for the use of campers and volunteers. Cove Medical Center provides medical care and some volunteers. The community raises money to help defray the costs of this fun experience for children who are very sick.

Write an e-mail to all Shell Cove employees asking them to consider volunteering five hours of their time during the week of the camp at Shell Cove. Use a psychological appeal. Employees would supervise activities, serve as mentors, and take the children to various sites. Employees were sent an e-mail telling them about the camp, the dates, and the activities, so you do not have to include that type of information. Tell employees that they can sign up this week at the Conference Center office or by sending you an e-mail. Use the group address employees@ shellcove.com. Save as *5E2si*.

Job 3: Special Events Project

Team Activity

Internet Activity

Shell Cove often gets requests for special events for large corporate groups, such as the afternoon/evening event for Marbex Corporation, and family groups and special occasions, such as bar/bat mitzvahs, weddings, birthdays, and reunions. In the past, Shell Cove hired outside party and event planners to stage these events. They were well done, but they cost a lot and produced little or nothing in terms of profits for Shell Cove. Clients have requested food events such as Hawaiian luaus, pig pickings, clambakes, lobster boils, barbecues, and picnics of various sorts. They have requested events and activities such as beach and carnival games, theme parties, Olympic-style sports events, and volleyball.

Henry has asked you to work with a team of three classmates to research some popular events and activities that are appropriate for these events. Use the Internet and keywords such as *party planners* or *event planners* for your search. Also try to find information that would help you decide whether Shell Cove should hire outside event planners or establish a Shell Cove special events team. Make a team decision and use a logical appeal to write a memo to Henry trying to convince him to accept your recommendation. Attach a list and, if needed, a brief description of the events and activities that Shell Cove could offer clients. Save as *5E3tp-si*.

TEAM WRITING

OBJECTIVES

After you complete Chapter 6, you should be able to:

- Work with team members to reach a consensus on issues.
- Use technology for collaboration.
- Write effective messages documenting teamwork.
- Edit messages more effectively.

OVERVIEW

A key trend in organizations is to use teams extensively. Companies assign projects to teams because they tend to produce better results than individuals do. The types of teams used vary widely. Writing as a team presents challenges that are different from just working together on a project. Major advances in technology make team writing much easier. The ultimate goal of team writing is to produce high-quality documents that achieve the team's objectives and read as if they have been written by one person. The key elements of this chapter include:

- Working as a team.
- Strategies for team writing.
- Message consistency.
- Technology for team writing.

"Business Talk"

Communicating effectively requires you to understand and use appropriate vocabulary in a business setting. Look for the following terms in this chapter. Review the terms and their definitions. Remember, some words have more than one meaning.

Collaborative writing—writing accomplished by two or more persons cooperating on the document.

Consensus—general agreement.

Cross-functional teams—teams from different departments or specialties, such as marketing, finance, or legal areas.

Leaderless teams—teams that do not have assigned leaders; a member of the group usually emerges to lead the team.

Synergy—the whole being greater than the sum of the parts; combined or cooperative action that produces better results than individuals could produce working separately.

WORKING AS A TEAM

Working in groups or teams is the norm in organizations today. The team concept emerged because many projects are complex and require more and different kinds of expertise than one person is likely to have. The main benefit from teamwork is the **synergy** that results. People who work together on a project can produce better results than they could if they worked on it separately.

Teams differ from groups. Being on a team implies working cooperatively as a unit. A group can work on a project by dividing the project into parts, with individuals doing a portion of the project and not ever working together.

Creating Teams

Organizations create different types of teams. Some teams consist of members of the same department or work unit, and they work together on all projects. Other teams, called **cross-functional teams**, are from different work groups or areas of the company. This type of team is typically formed to work on one specific project. Everyone benefits by having input on a project from many different areas, such as production, marketing, finance, legal, and technical areas.

Teams formed from one department or work unit usually have an assigned leader. That person performs the typical role of a manager. In some cases, a team is formed without a leader being named. This type of team is often called a **leaderless team** or a self-directed team. A manager might ask a group of employees to get together and come up with a solution to a particular problem. Usually, someone in the group will emerge as the leader even though that person may never have the title of team leader.

Characteristics of a Good Team Member

Most people give a lot of attention to the role of team leader, and leadership is important. However, a team is only as strong as its weakest member. The way to build successful teams is to focus on making every team member a strong contributor to the team effort. Here are some steps that you can take to be a good team member:

- Understand the goals the team is trying to accomplish.
- Put the goals of the team above your personal goals.
- Help to determine ways in which team goals can best be met.
- Recognize the role that you must play if the team is to accomplish its goals.
- Meet commitments; do your share of the work or even a little more.
- Participate actively in making decisions.
- Support team decisions once they have been made.
- Be results-oriented; focus on solutions, not problems.
- Respect every member of the team.
- Share in both the successes and the failures of the team.
- Feel comfortable as a member of the team and have "team spirit."

> **Success Tip**
>
> Learning to work effectively with team members is a critical career skill.

Characteristics of a Good Team Leader

Before you can be a good team leader, you must be a good team member. The job of a good team leader is to coordinate the work of the team and to be a facilitator. A facilitator is simply a helper. Here are some steps that you can take to be a good team leader:

- Understand the team's goals.
- Guide the team in determining how goals can be met.
- Encourage every team member to play an effective role.
- Do not permit any member, including yourself, to dominate the team.
- Share credit with your teammates.
- Accept responsibility for your mistakes.
- Work to gain the respect of others, and show your respect for them.
- Help every member feel comfortable on the team.

Structure for Teamwork

The guides for effective planning and writing that you studied in Chapter 2 apply to team writing as well. However, the writing process is likely to be different. A structure for working as a team must be created before the team can begin to think about writing the message.

A team leader (appointed or one who emerges from the group) usually assumes responsibility for coordinating the entire project. One of the first things that must be accomplished is to get organized and determine how the team will function. Use these steps to structure the process:

1. Solve the problem that has been assigned to you, or at least agree on what information is needed to solve it. Usually, the problem has to be solved and all decisions must be made before the document can be written.
2. Divide the project into tasks that need to be done. The leader usually helps with this step.
3. Agree on what needs to be done and on how to accomplish the tasks. The leader usually helps the team make these decisions.
4. Determine who will do each task.
5. Agree on the information to be included.
6. Decide on the best way to present that information.
7. Determine how the final product will be reviewed and approved.

Managing Differences

Working as a team member is very different from working as an individual. Members of a team bring different points of view to a situation and may think that it should be handled in different ways. A real benefit that organizations reap from teamwork is the different views that are brought to bear on a situation. Teams make better decisions than individuals do because they are more likely to consider a wider range of factors than any one person would consider.

Since team members view situations from different perspectives, some disagreements about issues are very likely to happen. Disagreement on issues is not bad; in fact, it can be very healthy. As you learned in Chapter 2, however, the way that you disagree does matter. Learn to disagree without being disagreeable. When team members respect the opinions of each other, they can approach a project with an open mind and work to reach the best possible solution.

Making Decisions

Teams have to work together to solve problems and make decisions. The following steps will help you to be a good problem solver:

1. Gain a clear understanding of a problem and all its parts.
2. Collect as much information as possible.
3. Evaluate the information to make sure it is accurate and complete.
4. Use the information objectively to make decisions.
5. Explore as many good alternatives as you can.
6. Look at the pros and cons of each option to determine the best course of action for all.

Being able to communicate ideas effectively is important. Some team members are able to present their ideas more persuasively than others are. A caution to all team members is to make sure that the option selected is truly the best one—not one that was not as good but was sold more effectively by the team member proposing it. Good teams do not make decisions by voting on issues or options. They work together until they reach a **consensus** about the best solution.

Global Connections

Collaborating With People of Different Cultures

Collaborative writing is challenging within a culture and even more challenging across cultures, but the results can be very rewarding. The keys to successful team writing across cultures are good listening skills, good interpersonal skills, respect for the ideas of others, patience in trying to understand differences, a willingness to help others understand differences, and courtesy. Most people respond positively to those who show that they are interested in the ideas of others. Working with people from other cultures provides a great learning opportunity to those who will take advantage of it.

STRATEGIES FOR TEAM WRITING

Teams usually have to document their work in some way. The writing stage comes after the problem has been solved. The documents that teams write include letters and internal company documents, such as memos, short and long reports, policies, procedures, proposals, and specialized documents of various types. Often the work done by the team must be submitted to a superior in the organization to be approved before it can be implemented.

Steps for Team Writing

The following is an effective set of steps that a team can use for writing long documents:

1. Prepare a detailed outline, specifying the content to be included.
2. Prepare a style sheet for everyone to follow in drafting the document. The section on message consistency provides details on what to include in the style sheet.
3. Make writing assignments for each section of the outline; specify writing deadlines.
4. Produce a draft of the document.
5. Review the document as a team to evaluate content and stylistic elements.
6. Refine the document based on the team's review.
7. Edit and finalize the document.

Team members must assume responsibility for the entire document. Some team members tend to pay attention only to the sections for which they are responsible. Every section of the final product represents the entire team, not just the person who wrote it.

Document Type Often Determines Strategy

Strategies for writing must be adapted to the type of document. Strategies that work well for letters and memos may not be effective for reports or procedures manuals.

Often the length of a document determines the best strategy to use for writing the document. Short reports are often formatted as letters or memos. Once the team agrees on a solution to a problem that can be documented in a short letter or memo, a very brief outline can be used to ensure that the appropriate content is included. Long reports are normally prepared in standard report format or in a standardized style for certain types of documents such as policy or procedures manuals. In Chapter 7, you will learn effective strategies for writing different types of reports.

Writing Plan

On very short documents, a good strategy is to have one person write the document and then have other team members review and edit it to ensure that it represents the team's view. If the team produces documents regularly, team members should rotate the writing assignment. However, if one team member has superior writing skills, that person may be selected to write the document, while other team members assume more of the other responsibilities to balance the workload.

On long documents, the writing responsibility is usually shared. Many decisions have to be made before a team can write a long document. In addition to the decisions made to solve the problem, decisions must be made about how much detail to include in the report and how you will ensure that the content and the format are consistent. A detailed outline of the entire document must be prepared.

MESSAGE CONSISTENCY

Team writing presents a special challenge because the document should not read as if it were written by different people. The style should be consistent throughout the document. A reader should not be able to tell where one person stopped writing and another started.

For example, if throughout the document one writer uses the percent sign and another writes the word *percent*, it will be obvious that two people worked on the document. Or if one writer uses an acronym to refer to the company and another uses the full company name, it will be obvious that two different people wrote the document. Documents must be consistent in the use of tense, headings, writing style, and other attributes to avoid the appearance of being written by more than one person.

Team writing should be consistent in both content and appearance. Consistency is easier to achieve by planning ahead for it than by trying to edit an inconsistent document to make it consistent.

Content Consistency

Many issues relating to the content of the message must be discussed before a team writes a document:

- The most important issue relates to information that must be included and information that is specifically excluded. For example, if your team was asked to design a seminar to teach employees how to make effective presentations, you would have to determine whether you would simply provide the content that needs to be included in the seminar or whether you would develop the training material to be used in the seminar.

- The level of detail is also important. If several sections of a document are equivalent in importance, the amount of copy devoted to each should be similar.

- The best way to ensure that everything that should be included is included in the document and that content is not duplicated is to prepare a detailed outline. Once the outline has been developed, the writing project can be divided into segments that can be handled by different team members.

- The style of writing should be similar throughout. An action-oriented writing style usually works best unless the report is negative or controversial. Team members also have to decide if the writing style is going to be objective or personal. You will learn more about this topic in Chapter 7.

- Team members should ensure that sections fit together and flow smoothly. An effective way to ensure coherence is to open each section with a brief overview statement indicating what is covered in the section and to close each section with a very brief summary statement.

- Team members should use a consistent pattern to present charts, graphs, tables, and other visuals. A good way to accomplish this is to have each team member introduce a visual by its name or number before presenting it and follow up a visual with a statement about its content after it has been presented. Terms used to refer to visuals should be the same. Teams should discuss options and make style decisions such as "Use *figure* for graphs, charts, and other illustrations and use *table* for information in tabular form."

Technology Connections

Wikis

A *wiki* is a collaborative writing Web site. The term is also applied to the software used to create the site. Some people refer to wikis as social software. The software allows any visitor to the Web site to create or edit the content using any browser. Anyone can edit anything on the Web site regardless of who wrote it.

Wiki comes from the Hawaiian word for *quick*. The largest wiki currently on the Web is *Wikipedia*, a free encyclopedia. You can create a new article to add to the hundreds of thousands already on the site, or you can edit any of the articles that exist. Wikipedia visitors both write and edit articles. If you do not think an article is accurate, you can change it. Users have developed policies and style guides for using the site by consensus.

Format Consistency

All parts of a document should have a consistent appearance. To ensure a consistent appearance, the team should decide on stylistic elements before writing, and all team members should follow the styles selected. One person should be asked to list all decisions the team makes about style in a style sheet and to provide copies of it to all team members to use as a reference in preparing drafts of the document. Error-free documents are more likely to be produced when the entire team pays attention to style issues during the writing phase rather than waiting for editing to correct style differences. The following are examples of stylistic elements that must be considered:

- Font, font size, margins, and general layout.
- Format for numbering pages.
- Type of headings and the style in which they are formatted.
- Use of italics or underlining for titles.
- Use of headers or footers.

TECHNOLOGY FOR TEAM WRITING

Effective teamwork depends heavily on the ability to share information easily. When people work together on a project, it is essential that they be able to brainstorm to generate ideas and to review and critique each other's work. In some cases, team members meet in face-to-face situations to work on a project. In others, they work in different geographic areas and must communicate electronically. Today's technology makes sharing information much easier than in the past.

Two types of technology are especially useful for producing documents jointly. The first is word processing software features that facilitate the writing, review, and revision of documents. The second is technology such as e-mail and FTP sites

(FTP, or **f**ile **t**ransfer **p**rotocol, provides a simple way to transfer documents to and from a site where they can be stored for shared access on a network). This technology makes it easy to send documents to team members, store them, and give members access to both the documents and the comments made on them.

Word Processing Software

Features called track changes, annotations, comments, redlining, and revisions are designed for documents that will be reviewed or edited by different people. These features allow you to mark through the original text and suggest changes. Each person editing or commenting on the document can use a different color or his or her initials to indicate who suggested the changes. The writer can accept or reject suggested changes. Figure 6-1 shows a document that has been edited using these features.

A special merge feature allows a writer to pool two versions of the same document—for example, the writer's original draft and a copy that has been edited by a reviewer—and see at a glance where they differ.

Document Distribution, Storage, and Access

Documents can be distributed to team members or stored where members can access the documents whenever they are needed. Drafts for review can be distributed by e-mail, instant messaging, computer fax, and posting in an accessible location such as a shared network or an FTP site. Company intranets, special servers, subscription-based services, and the Web can be used to store information for easy access.

A type of software called groupware offers many features useful for team writing, including scheduling, workflow automation, and document management. Document management enables the team to have access to documents and to send comments about them to a central point. The entire team can review all comments from every member and can respond to them. A key advantage of groupware is that team members can be in remote locations.

Success Tip

Good problem-solving skills and good interpersonal skills are required to be an effective team member.

Technology Connections

Blogs

Blogs are Web logs (personal journals) that are owned and maintained by one person. A blog gives its owner a place to write about any topic of interest. It is typically updated frequently, much as a travelog or diary would be. Only the owner can edit, delete, or add to the content of a blog. Visitors can comment about the content, but they cannot change it. Wikis differ from blogs in this respect, since anybody can change anything in a wiki.

Figure 6-1: Using Collaborative Writing Features

Word Processing Features for Team Writing

This document illustrates the use of collaborative writing features in word processing software. The comments and changes made in this document are added by those who have reviewed the document. Different reviewers can use their initials or different colors to distinguish their comments and changes from those made by others.

This document is stored on your student data disk as *Figure 6-1*. If you are using the data disk, open the document and view it on screen.

Note that the original document has not changed. The suggested revisions are shown, but the person who created the document has the option of accepting or rejecting each change suggested.

Team members typically propose content changes and mark corrections in grammar, style, usage, and format. Content changes usually appear in comments, whereas editorial corrections are made directly on the copy. Often comments contain specific text for inclusion.

Teams can save time and effort by transmitting documents electronically rather than by distributing printed versions. When a document is routed from one member of the team to the next, all comments and corrections appear on the same document. Sometimes each team member edits an individual copy of the document. The writer can use the compare and merge documents feature to pool two versions of a document, with the differences between them automatically marked for easy review.

Comment: Should this apply to groupware as well?

Comment: **I agree with Karen.**

Deleted: Collaborative

Comment: I think this only applies to word processing; groupware should be handled separately.

Deleted: **state-of-the-art**

Comment: **Some software versions show initials; some versions use color only.**

Deleted: **authors**

Deleted: is

Deleted: **changes in**

Deleted: **mechanical**

Deleted: s

Deleted: **are**

Deleted: **to all**

Deleted: s

❗ Points to Remember

About Team Writing

- ☑ The main benefit from teamwork is the synergy that results. People who work together on a project can produce better results than they could if they worked on it separately.

- ☑ Teams make better decisions than individuals because they are more likely to consider a wider range of factors than any one person would consider.

- ☑ Learn to disagree without being disagreeable. When team members respect the opinions of each other, they can approach a project with an open mind and work to reach the best possible solution.

- ☑ Good teams do not make decisions by voting on issues or options. They work together until they reach a consensus about the best solution.

- ☑ Team members must assume responsibility for the entire document. Every section of the final product represents the entire team, not just the person who wrote it.

- ☑ On very short documents, a good strategy is to have one person write the document and then have other team members review and edit it to ensure that it represents the team's view. On long documents, the writing responsibility is usually shared.

- ☑ Team writing presents a special challenge because the document should not read as if it were written by different people. The style should be consistent throughout the document. A reader should not be able to tell where one person stopped writing and another started.

- ☑ Effective teamwork depends heavily on the ability to share information easily. Today's technology makes sharing information much easier than in the past.

Review Guide 4—Write in a Clear, Readable Style

Review Guide 4 of Chapter 2 on pages 29–33, and then complete the following activities. Revise the sentences and paragraphs by using a conversational tone, simplifying words and sentence structure, and using lists, charts, or tables.

1. The manager gave notification to employees that compliance with the provisions of the policy of adhering to smoking exclusively in designated areas was now mandatory rather than voluntary.

2. Pursuant to our discussion this morning, I herewith enclose a copy of the proposal you requested; and I trust that you will kindly advise me when you are ready to discuss it.

3. The Executive Committee will meet in the morning in the Vista Conference Room to discuss the location of the new facilities. Then we will have lunch in the Vista Dining Room and then we will return to the Vista Conference Room to finalize our decision on the location of the new facilities.

4. Please send us your complete name, including middle initial; your complete address, including street address, city, state, and postal code; the name of the county in which you reside; your Social Security number; your telephone number, including the area code; and two credit card references.

5. An investigation of the circumstances precipitating the incident revealed no apparent way to anticipate or prevent the occurrence of the assault.

Editing and Language Arts Checkpoint

1. Carefully read the document that follows; it is packed with errors. Use proofreaders' marks to mark all errors in grammar, spelling, usage, word choice, capitalization, punctuation, and keying. If you need help with proofreaders' marks, refer to the table on page 53. Do not revise sentence or paragraph structure unless you find an error.

2. Access *File 6B* in the Chapter 6 folder on your student data disk and make the corrections. If you are not working with the data disk, key the document, making the corrections as you key. You may use online reference tools just as you would on the job.

3. Save as *6Bsi*.

Presentation To Selected Staff—november 15 200_

Would you like to have twelve extra hours a week to devote to the reponsibilities you think are the more important of every thing you do in your job. Dr. Ashu Sopios an imminent expert did a communications audit for our company. His conclusion was that staff members in the business services department and the Claims Department could save an average of 12 hours per week. If the company developed an extensive file of form documents for situations that lend themselves too form applications.

As a way of preceding with this task, dr. Sopios suggested that we first identify situations in which from letters could be used affectively. The second step is to determine the type of form that wouldbe best for each situation. Then form letters can be drafted by a team of employees whom are knowledgeable in the area. A cross functional team will review the letters before approving them.

10 supervisors identified about 50 situations in which form letters would save a significant amount of time. For a situation to qualify as requiring a form letter an average of 5 letters a week must be written to customers refering to that situation. Variable forms—letters with minor variations in information—could be used affectively in many of the situations. Another good option is form paragraphs. To create a letter, a series of stored form paragraphs are combined by an employee with teh appropriate opening and closing. Teams can choose among these two types of forms.

Dr Sopios described some other types of form letters. He said, "complete forms are identical letters sent to different readers. Guide forms are model documents the company provides for various situations.' An employee apprises a situation, selects the appropriate guide form, and writes a letter patterned after them. Complete forms are impersonal an guide forms are inefficient, therefore the supervisors recomended that neither complete forms or guide forms be used.

Supervisors plan to name five four-member teams this week to develop the first draft of the form letters. Each team will be asked to prepare 10 form letters. Than the cross functional team will review the letters and either approve them or or suggest revisions. Employees who's jobs require them to draft such letters will recieve copies by E-Mail with an explanation of how to use them.

Team Writing

In all jobs in this application, you will be a member of the HRM Team (human resource management) at VanHuss Associates, Inc., writing memos to the Staff Development Committee. Letterhead for these activities is available in the chapter folder on the student data disk. If you are not using the data disk, key the documents on plain paper.

For each of the following scenarios, work with a team of three or four people. Use brainstorming techniques to get started. Then use the library, the Internet, and other sources that may be available to search for information. After your team has reached a consensus on the topic, write a memo summarizing your results. Determine the strategy you will use for the team-writing portion of your work. Involve as many team members as possible in the writing process. Everyone should read and edit the memos.

Format your memos as shown on page 49. Use the current date. Add an appropriate subject line for each memo.

Your instructor may ask you to use the guide that appears on page 176 for evaluating your documents. Your instructor may also use this form to evaluate your work.

Team Activity

Internet Activity

1. The Staff Development Committee has asked your team to work on a project designed to improve meetings throughout the company. Collect information on how to make meetings at VanHuss Associates, Inc., more effective. Use the keywords *effective meetings* to begin your Internet search. Save as *6C1tp-si.*

2. VanHuss Associates is working with several clients to help them build better relationships with their customers. Clients have indicated that they would like to increase their use of voice mail because it is cost-effective. However, some of their customers have complained about the way voice mail is used. The Staff Development Committee has asked your team to research the topic "Use and Abuse of Voice Mail." Save as *6C2tp-si.*

3. While you were discussing voice mail, members of your team brought up the idea of looking at ways to improve employees' telephone skills. The team decided to examine the topic "Keys to Effective Telephone Calls." Save as *6C3tp-si.*

4. Your team will be involved in presenting short employee development segments in an orientation and training program. Training programs at VanHuss Associates typically use slides created in the Microsoft® PowerPoint® presentation graphics program. They occasionally use overhead transparencies. The team has decided to compile a set of guides for preparing effective visuals. Save as *6C4tp-si.*

5. Your team has been asked to provide guides for managing time effectively. Save as *6C5tp-si.*

Application 6C: Guide for Evaluating Your Team-Written Messages

Factors to Consider	Points	6C1		6C2		6C3		6C4		6C5	
		SE	IE	SE	IE	SE	IE	SE	IE	SE	IE
Self-evaluation (SE), Instructor evaluation (IE)											
Strategy—uses appropriate strategy for message	2										
Strategy—has developed good ideas to solve the problem	2										
Strategy—uses consistent style and content	2										
Writing Guide 1—evidence of good planning; organized	1										
Writing Guide 2—meets the reader's needs; courteous	1										
Writing Guide 3—uses positive language	1										
Writing Guide 4—uses a clear, easy-to-read style	1										
Writing Guide 5—complete; includes all needed information	1										
Writing Guide 6—uses an action-oriented or a neutral style as appropriate	1										
Writing Guide 7—uses specific or general language as appropriate	1										
Writing Guide 8—uses effective sentence and paragraph structure	1										
Writing Guide 9—uses correct format and attractive placement	1										
Writing Guide 10—has been edited and proofread; no errors	1										
Overall assessment of document	4										
Totals	20										

Mastery Check for Chapter 6

1. What are the main benefits a company gains by having employees work as a team?

2. Diverse teams tend to have more conflict than teams from the same work unit. Knowing this, why do companies use cross-functional teams on projects?

3. How does the length of a document affect the strategy a team uses to write that document?

4. Describe several issues that relate to making the content of a document written by a team consistent.

5. Describe how technology can be used to facilitate team writing.

6. For each of the three terms shown below, write a complete, correct sentence using the term.

Collaborative writing

Consensus

Synergy

Shell Cove—Hotel Management Division

The Hotel Management Division, directed by Ms. Emily Ellison, is responsible for marketing and managing the Inn at Shell Cove. The Inn at Shell Cove has two target markets: (1) groups of 100 or larger and (2) business and leisure travelers who prefer hotels to condos and beach rental units. For this rotation of your training program, you are assistant manager to Emily.

The Hotel Management Division interacts extensively with the other divisions of Shell Cove. Inn and Conference Center staff work together to meet the needs of the various groups that visit. Some Inn guests take advantage of the amenities offered, such as the golf and tennis facilities, restaurants, and entertainment options. If rooms are not available in the Inn, prospective guests are offered accommodations in condos and rental units. Emily is a strong believer in using cross-functional teams, and your work in this division will be team projects.

The Inn has the following amenities:

- 300 guest rooms and 25 suites.

- 1 large ballroom that seats 600 for a meal and 850 for a reception.

- 1 smaller ballroom that seats 450 for a meal and 650 for a reception.

- 10 meeting rooms that accommodate 50 to 125 depending on the layout.

- A dining room and a casual restaurant near the pool.

- 2 lounges, retail outlets, and rentals (sailboats, bicycles, beach umbrellas, and surfboards).

Job 1: Cross-Selling Other Venues
Shell Cove wants to encourage Inn guests to patronize both Inn facilities and other Shell Cove venues. Most Inn guests have one or more meals in the Inn. Data collected over the past six months indicate the following usage rates for guests who spend three or more nights at the Inn:

Team Activity

- 40 percent eat at Shell Cove restaurants other than Inn restaurants.
- 28 percent use the tennis courts.
- 22 percent use the golf course.
- 52 percent visit one or more of the entertainment venues.

Shell Cove has set a goal of increasing each of these categories by 15 percent. Emily has asked you to work with team members representing the Restaurant Division, the Golf/Tennis Division, and the Entertainment Division to develop plans to cross-sell these venues. Your task is to make recommendations on how to reach the 15 percent goal. Use brainstorming techniques to get started. Collect data, make decisions on recommendations, and prepare a memo from the Sales Team to Emily summarizing them. Save as *6E1tp-si.*

Team Activity

Internet Activity

Job 2: Hotel Security

The Inn at Shell Cove takes guest security very seriously and has invested in the latest security equipment and training. Shell Cove has not had any security problems. However, Emily works diligently to maintain this excellent security record. Every three months, she reviews information on security at other hotels across the country and compares it to what is being done at the Inn at Shell Cove.

Emily has asked your team to do some research on the Internet to find out what hotel security experts are recommending and what steps are being taken in other hotels to ensure the security of guests. Your research can include interviewing a hotel security manager (in person if a local hotel has a security manager, or by e-mail or telephone if no one is available locally). You may also use security information from hotels in which you have been a guest. Limit your search to suggestions for hotels in the United States, as security varies by country. Emily has asked you to focus on these two questions:

a. What are other hotels telling their guests to do to be safe?

b. What security measures and equipment should hotels have to ensure guests' security?

Use the keywords *hotel security* to begin your search. Your team should compile two lists to attach to a memo to Emily. The first list should be called "Advice to Enhance Your Safety in a Hotel." This list should have recommendations from security experts and advice that other hotels are giving their guests on how to be safe. The second list should be named "Security Features Provided by Hotels." This list should contain steps that hotels should take to ensure the safety of their guests. Write an e-mail to Emily explaining what your team did, how you did it, and the results of your research. Most of your results will be contained in the two lists that you will attach. Save the e-mail as *6E2atp-si*. Save the lists as *6E2btp-si*.

Team Activity

Internet Activity

Job 3: Pets and Hotel Accommodations

Shell Cove has had numerous inquiries about allowing guests to bring pets (limited to cats and dogs) with them to the Inn at Shell Cove. Currently the Inn at Shell Cove does not allow pets. Emily has read in industry publications that more and more upscale hotels are becoming "pet-friendly." She has asked the Sales Team to use the Internet to see what other hotels are doing and to recommend whether or not the Inn at Shell Cove should accept pets. She wants you to include topics such as the following:

- What special accommodations are needed for pets?
- Should size and weight limitations be placed on pets?
- Should you require deposits or charge extra for pets?
- Are pet owners willing to pay for special services for their pets?
- Should specific rooms be designated as rooms that accommodate pets?
- What health and cleaning requirements must be considered?

After your team has completed its research, write a memo summarizing the information you found on the topics listed above and other issues that you discussed. Make a recommendation on whether or not the Inn at Shell Cove should become a pet-friendly hotel. Save as *6E3tp-si*.

LETTER AND MEMO REPORTS

OBJECTIVES

After you complete Chapter 7, you should be able to:

- Write effective messages that can be used to make decisions.
- Use both personal and objective styles for writing reports.
- Choose appropriate organizational styles for reports.
- Edit messages more effectively.

OVERVIEW

Most companies consider reports to be key documents for conducting business. Reports usually are used for decision making or to document activities, events, or transactions. Because reports are used for decision making and documentation, they must be accurate and objective. Good decisions result from careful analysis of accurate information.

The key elements of this chapter include:

- Types of reports.
- Formality and writing style.
- Report content and format.
- Technology for presenting data.
- Report organization.

"Business Talk"

Communicating effectively requires you to understand and use appropriate vocabulary in a business setting. Look for the following terms in this chapter. Review the terms and their definitions. Remember, some words have more than one meaning.

Analytical—examining data to draw conclusions and make recommendations.

Benchmark—a point of comparison; a standard or reference point.

Functional—related to an operation or function.

Qualitative—based on judgment or quality analysis.

Quantitative—based on numerical or statistical analysis.

TYPES OF REPORTS

Reports are used to provide a record of activities, events, or actions or to transmit information for decision making within or outside an organization. An external report may be a letter informing a customer that a project is about two weeks behind schedule because the shipment of materials needed has been delayed.

The customer may then use the information to decide what other action must be taken, such as rescheduling other phases of the project, to accommodate this two-week delay.

An internal report may be a memo to the crew leader working on the project reporting that a delayed shipment of materials has put the project about two weeks behind schedule and stating that the project schedule must be adjusted. This type of report is often called a progress or status report.

Usually reports move up the chain of command. A superior requests that a subordinate collect and analyze data about a particular problem and report back with recommendations for solving that problem.

Success Tip

Internal reports move up the chain of command; therefore, they give you a chance to showcase the quality of your work to managers.

FORMALITY AND WRITING STYLE

The degree of formality of a report often determines the best writing style—objective or personal—for that report. Formal reports tend to be written in objective style, and informal reports tend to be written in personal style.

A report written in objective style uses third-person pronouns (such as *they, he, she, them,* and *it*) and formal language. A report written in personal style uses first- and second-person pronouns (such as *I, we, our, us,* and *you*) and informal language. Formal language is more precise and professional than informal language. Contractions, as well as colorful and conversational language, are part of informal style and would not be acceptable in a formal report.

Reports written in objective style **appear** to be more objective than those written in personal style. However, just because a report is written in objective style does not mean that the report is actually objective or unbiased. On the other hand, just because a report is written in personal style does not mean that the report is biased. Regardless of style, care must be taken to ensure that all information is accurate and is presented in an objective manner.

As you learned in Chapter 1, style is a matter of choice. Some companies tend to be more formal than others are. An important fact to consider in selecting a writing style is that objective style is more persuasive than personal style. Using only third-person pronouns makes a report appear to be objective, whereas using first-person pronouns makes it appear to be the writer's opinion. Information presented with words such as *I believe*, *I think*, or *I feel* is often interpreted by readers as being the writer's opinions rather than conclusions drawn from an objective analysis of facts.

Compare the following pairs of sentences. The sentences on the left are written in personal style, and the sentences on the right are written in objective style.

Personal Style

I evaluated the three alternatives, and I believe that the first one is the one we should use. It generates more revenue for us over a three-year period than the other two alternatives do.

I studied the data carefully, and I strongly believe that the training program improved productivity.

I feel that it is time for us to change the name of the organization so that we can broaden our appeal to a wider group.

Objective Style

A careful evaluation of the three alternatives shows that the first one produces greater revenue over a three-year period. Therefore, the first alternative is recommended.

The data clearly show that the training program improved productivity.

The timing is ideal to change the name of the organization so that it will appeal to a wider group.

In the first example, a reader who does not agree with the first alternative may respond by saying, "I believe the second alternative is better because . . ." The issue then becomes personalized. Objective style places the emphasis on the issue studied rather than on the person who studied the issue. Some writers trying to use objective style substitute terms such as *the writer* or *the researcher* in place of first-person pronouns. Good writers avoid this practice. Writing in objective style is a little more difficult than writing in personal style, but the results make the extra effort worthwhile.

REPORT CONTENT AND FORMAT

Reports may be formatted as letters, as memos, or in standard report format. Typically a cover letter, memo, or e-mail is included with reports prepared in report format. These formats are illustrated in Figures 7-1, 7-2, and 7-3 on pages 189–192. The best format for a report varies depending on the length of the report, the difficulty of the data, the level of formality, and the report's destination. Consider the following examples:

- A report with several charts, tables, and graphs or a report that is three or more pages long would usually be prepared using standard report format.

- External reports tend to be more formal than internal reports and are usually prepared in standard format with a cover letter.

- Internal reports tend to be more informal and may be prepared in memo or standard format and attached to an e-mail for distribution.

- Reports that consist of text with no graphics are more likely to be formatted as a letter or memo report.

Most reports contain headings, visuals (charts, tables, graphs, pictures, or diagrams), and summaries. If the report is short or simple, these elements may be omitted. Headings may be **functional** or may relate to the content of the report. The following examples illustrate both types of headings that could be used for the report in Figure 7-2:

Functional Headings	Content Headings
Purpose	Status of Nature Trails Project
Methods	Project Oversight
Data Analysis	Comparison of Budget and Actual Expenditures
Conclusions	Costs Exceeded Budget
Recommendations	Funding Options

Report content varies depending on the length, complexity, and type of report. The following categories of information are frequently included. These categories are often combined depending on the information that must be presented.

Identifying Information

Most readers want to know who prepared a report, the title of the report, the date it was prepared and, in some cases, who authorized or requested the report. For long reports in standard report format, a title page is prepared that contains this information. For shorter reports, the cover letter, memo, or e-mail supplies it. When memo format is used, the memo heading contains the identifying information.

A letter report may or may not provide all the identifying information. Standard letter format requires the date and signature of the person who prepared the report. The person who requested or authorized the information is generally the person to whom the letter is addressed. The title of the report may be included in a subject line. The subject line is formatted in the same way as it is in a memo, except that the word *Subject* is not included and capital letters are used. The subject line appears between the salutation and the first body text paragraph, separated by two line returns from each. In some cases, the first paragraph of the letter presents the identifying information.

Purpose

The purpose, or problem, statement should clearly present what you are trying to accomplish in the report. Often, a brief summary of the background information

Global Connections

Ethics

Do ethics differ from culture to culture? That is a very difficult question to answer. Rules for conducting business vary from one culture to another. What is legal in one country may not be legal in another country. Child labor laws and human rights issues are two examples. While companies and their employees have to be flexible and sensitive to cultural differences, employees should not have to compromise their integrity or morals. Sincerity and honesty are important regardless of cultural differences. If a severe ethical conflict exists, then the whole issue of doing business in that particular culture needs to be examined.

that led to the problem is provided. Background information is particularly useful when the reader is not familiar with the reasons for studying the problem. Care must be taken not to repeat information the reader already knows.

Methods

Methods consist of a brief statement indicating where and how you obtained the information used to solve the problem.

Data Analysis

The data analysis consists of the information collected and used to solve the problem. This section includes a discussion of the facts and an interpretation of how those facts can be applied in solving the problem. Both **qualitative** (judgment) techniques and **quantitative** (statistical) techniques may be used to analyze data. The following example shows how both qualitative and quantitative data might be collected:

Qualitative Analysis
Please evaluate the meeting and provide specific information about its effectiveness.

First response: The meeting was excellent. It was well organized, the topics were relevant, and the information presented was useful. The handouts supplemented the information presented and will be especially helpful in our companies. The facilities were perfect for the type of meeting.

Quantitative Analysis
Please evaluate the meeting using the following criteria. Use a scale from 1 to 5, with 5 as the highest and 1 as the lowest.

1. Was the meeting well organized? ____
2. Were the topics relevant? ____
3. Was the information presented useful? ____
4. Were the facilities effective? ____

To analyze the qualitative data, you would have to read all responses, put them in categories, and then summarize them. To analyze the quantitative data, you would have to total the number of respondents who gave the same rating for each item and compute percentages. Qualitative data are more difficult to summarize, but respondents may provide information on topics you did not think to ask about when you prepared the questions. In this example, questions were not asked about the handouts.

Conclusions

Conclusions are the results obtained by analyzing and interpreting the facts. Each conclusion presented should be supported by data included in the data analysis section. Some reports, such as progress or status reports, may not contain conclusions. These reports simply convey information to the reader.

Recommendations

Suggested actions based on conclusions are called recommendations. Generally the writer of a report is in the best position to recommend specific action to take. However, not all reports contain recommendations. Reports that contain conclusions and recommendations are called **analytical** reports.

Conclusions and recommendations are often confused. The following examples show the differences between them:

> ### Success Tip
>
> Remember, your organization will use your reports to make decisions. If your information is not accurate, you may be held accountable for any bad decisions that are made.

Conclusions	**Recommendations**
The cost of having the annual report prepared by McVie Communications is 50 percent higher than the cost of preparing it internally. The quality, however, is significantly better.	McVie Communications should be contracted to prepare the annual report because the quality justifies the cost.
The *Using Technology to Improve Office Productivity* training program is highly effective. Supervisors have documented productivity increases for employees who participated in the program.	The *Using Technology to Improve Office Productivity* training program should be offered to all support staff.

Summary

The summary consists of the highlights of the report. It should contain a brief statement of what you studied, how you studied it, and your results. In short or simple reports, if a summary is included, it is often part of a conclusions and recommendations section. In long reports, it is usually a separate section.

An executive summary is frequently included with long reports (ten or more pages). An executive summary presents a brief statement of the problem studied, a statement of how it was studied, and a summary of the results, conclusions, and recommendations. Executive summaries are prepared as stand-alone documents; that is, they do not relate to specific pages of the report. The summary can be read and understood as a separate document by people who do not have access to the complete report.

TECHNOLOGY FOR PRESENTING DATA

Visuals help to simplify complex data and help the reader understand the concepts being presented. Word processing and spreadsheet software provide easy-to-use features for presenting statistical information in tables, charts, and graphs. The adage "A picture is worth a thousand words" applies to reports. When it is appropriate to do so, you should include visuals in the data analysis section of your reports and in other sections as needed.

Many organizations prefer to have written reports accompanied by oral presentations. Presentation software, such as the Microsoft® PowerPoint® presentation graphics program, makes it easy to present data using graphs, charts, tables, sound, video, and animations.

Technology Connections

Information Overload

Both e-mail and the Internet provide quick access to information. In fact, many companies say the problem is too much information. With e-mail, often the information is neither needed nor requested. Internet searches produce volumes of information, and verifying its accuracy can be a major task. Often information is disguised to look official, but it is produced from a biased source with less than honorable intentions. Sorting through information and compiling it in a useful format are also major tasks.

REPORT ORGANIZATION

Information contained in a report can be organized in different ways, and the way that it is organized may influence the results obtained. Any organizational style can be applied to any type of report. Each style has both pros and cons. Four frequently used organizational styles are described and compared in the following paragraphs. The best style to use depends on the content and complexity of the report. The four styles are illustrated in Figures 7-1, 7-2, 7-3, and 7-4 on pages 189–193.

Narrative Style

A narrative report simply gives an account of events in the sequence they occurred. The advantages of a narrative style are that this type of report is easy to write and it provides a record of events that took place. The disadvantages are that it does not facilitate comparing information and does not emphasize ideas effectively. The first and last paragraphs of a document should be used to emphasize key ideas. The activities that occur first and last in a narrative may not be the ones that deserve emphasis. This approach is most effective when the order in which events occurred makes a difference.

Indirect, or Inductive, Style

A report written using an indirect approach presents the facts and supporting information first; then it lets those facts lead to logical conclusions. The primary advantage of the indirect style is that it is a persuasive style—it presents facts in an objective manner before telling the reader the conclusion. This approach is most effective when the reader is likely to disagree with the conclusions and recommendations presented. The reader is more likely to consider facts objectively and less likely to raise objections if the conclusion is not known. The primary disadvantage of the indirect style is that it is a roundabout, slow-moving style.

Direct, or Deductive, Style

A report that uses the direct approach presents the key information, conclusions, or recommendations first and then presents the data that support them. Many people in industry like this approach and often refer to it as the bottom-line approach because you get to the heart of the matter immediately.

The advantages of the direct style are that it is straightforward and it places emphasis on the most important information. The primary disadvantage is that the style is not persuasive. The direct style is best used when the reader is likely to agree with the conclusions of the report. If the reader disagrees with the conclusions presented at the beginning of the report, the reader is likely to question the facts as they are presented rather than read them with an open mind.

Weighted Style

A report that uses the weighted approach presents the information in order of importance. The most important information is presented first; then the second most important information is presented. This procedure continues until all information has been presented. A closing statement summarizing the two or three most important points is essential to avoid ending the report with the least important information. The primary advantages of the weighted style are that it effectively uses position as an emphasis technique and that it makes comparing data easy. The primary disadvantage is that it is not a very persuasive style.

Figure 7-1: Narrative Report, Personal Writing Style, Letter Format, No Headings

▲ **VanHuss Associates, Inc.**

6974 Garners Ferry Road
Columbia, SC 29209-2101
Tel: (803) 555-0164
Fax: (803) 555-0138
www.vanhussassociates.com

November 16, 200_

Mr. Zachary Taylor, President
Vista Technology Training, Inc.
2584 Piedmont Road, NE
Atlanta, GA 30324-3007

Dear Mr. Taylor

This report summarizes my October 26 visit to Houston to evaluate the Burge
Computer Center as a potential site for a Vista Authorized Training Center (VATC).
Mr. Lee Burge met with me first, and then I met with three staff members. I
reviewed the Vista philosophy, needs, and approach for establishing a VATC with
Mr. Burge and his staff.

My next meeting was with Julie Cox, the technical manager. She has a staff of 12
and manages all computer facilities in six centers in Houston. The Burge Computer
Center has state-of-the-art technology that exceeds your requirements for a VATC.

My third meeting was with Debbie Jensen, who manages the main Burge Computer
Center. Debbie had studied our materials and had developed an excellent plan for
integrating the VATC into their current operations.

My final meeting was with Cyndi White, the training manager. She invited me to
observe the impressive training programs that were being conducted. The trainers
have the technical expertise needed; they would only need to learn our systems and
materials.

Mr. Burge has a superior staff and operation. I recommend that you contract with
his organization for a VATC. The enclosed site evaluation form shows that the
Burge Center is comparable to the best VATC of the 24 that I have helped you
establish.

Sincerely yours

Michael B. Hess

prv

Enclosure

Figure 7-2: Indirect Report, Objective Writing Style, Two-Page Memo Format

▲ VanHuss Associates, Ínc.

TO: Executive Committee

FROM: Megan M. Davis

DATE: November 17, 200_

SUBJECT: Nature Trails Project

The Executive Committee authorized a study of the Nature Trails project that was approved in March 2002. The study has been completed, and the results are summarized in this report.

Purpose

The purpose of this report was to determine the status of the Nature Trails project and the total cost of the project. The project was initiated by training managers who requested that nature trails be developed on the 125-acre campus of VanHuss Associates. The Nature Trails project was designed to enhance the conference center facilities and to provide employees with a family-friendly environment for evenings and weekends. Employees and training managers have requested that a swimming pool be added to the project.

Methods

Company records were obtained to determine the status of the project. The former training manager was responsible for overseeing the project budget and coordinating the development of the project. Records documenting expenditures were available, but sources of funds to cover the excess expenditures were not identified in the records.

Data Analysis

The initial budget for the project was $650,000. The expected completion time was March 2003. The table and chart on page 2 show a comparison of budgeted and actual costs. The project was completed in October 2003.

Figure 7-2 *(continued)*

Executive Committee
Page 2
November 17, 200_

Nature Trails Budget		
Component	**Budget**	**Actual**
Trail design	$ 35,500	$ 38,700
Entrance	45,200	56,450
Parking lot	28,350	27,964
Pavilion	100,000	135,860
Walking trails	90,050	105,200
Bike trail	350,900	441,875
Total Project	$650,000	$806,049

The project was over budget by $156,049. The excess costs were distributed across all components except the parking lot, which was completed within budget. Currently, the account shows a deficit, and sources of additional funding have not yet been identified.

The project took approximately seven months longer than estimated to complete. During that time, costs rose significantly. Change orders on the length of the bike trail accounted for much of the increased cost on that item. Cost estimates have not been provided for the swimming pool that employees and training managers have requested.

Conclusions

The Nature Trails project has been completed, and the quality of the project meets all expectations. The main issue that must be resolved is finding a source of funds to cover the deficit. Adding a swimming pool at this time would compound the funding problem.

Recommendations

Two options are recommended to solve the funding problem. The first option is to assess a one-time usage fee to each department to cover the costs, since all employees have access to the nature trails. The second option is to charge the excess to next year's Training Department budget. The swimming pool should be deferred until funds to cover costs have been identified.

Figure 7-3: Direct Report, Objective Writing Style, Standard Report Format

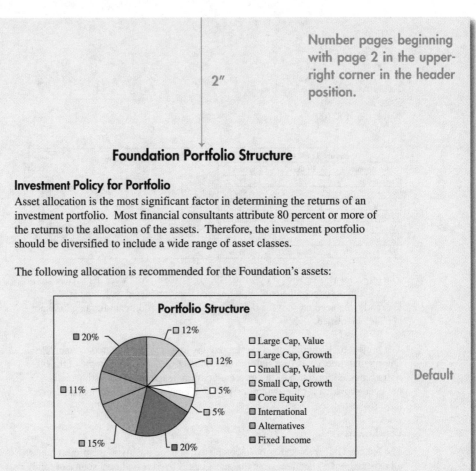

Number pages beginning with page 2 in the upper-right corner in the header position.

2"

Foundation Portfolio Structure

Investment Policy for Portfolio

Asset allocation is the most significant factor in determining the returns of an investment portfolio. Most financial consultants attribute 80 percent or more of the returns to the allocation of the assets. Therefore, the investment portfolio should be diversified to include a wide range of asset classes.

The following allocation is recommended for the Foundation's assets:

Default

Portfolio Structure

- 20%
- 12%
- 12%
- 11%
- 5%
- 5%
- 15%
- 20%

- ☐ Large Cap, Value
- ☐ Large Cap, Growth
- ☐ Small Cap, Value
- ☐ Small Cap, Growth
- ☐ Core Equity
- ☐ International
- ☐ Alternatives
- ☐ Fixed Income

Default

Asset Allocation Studied

The purpose of this study was to determine the asset allocation that would provide the highest returns with an appropriate level of risk for the Foundation portfolio. The investment policy must establish both the asset classes and the percentage of the portfolio invested in each class.

Returns and Risk Analyzed

The Investment Committee analyzed data showing returns based on asset class for the past 20 years. The risk associated with each class was also evaluated. Benchmark data from comparable foundations were examined. All of the data analysis charts are available for review in the Foundation's Office.

About 1"

Figure 7-4: Weighted Report, Personal Writing Style, Memo Format

▲ VanHuss Associates, Inc.

TO: Julie Jameson, Director of Human Resources

FROM: Miguel Rodriguez

DATE: November 17, 200_

SUBJECT: Professional Development for Executive Assistants

The findings of my study on the training needs of executive assistants support my recommendation that we offer a full-scale professional development program immediately. A program modeled after our Management Development Program for Technical Employees should be used for our executive assistants.

The recommended program meets the perceived needs of both the executive assistants and the executives they support. High-priority needs are highlighted in yellow on the attached outline of the program contents.

A small group of executive assistants participated in the program to test it. Results were excellent. Executives were pleased with the human relations skills, the productivity skills, and the conceptual skills their assistants developed.

A secondary requirement of all professional development programs is to give participants an opportunity to improve their communication skills. The proposed program includes both written and oral communication components.

The program was compared to other high-quality programs. Many of the benchmark programs had similar program components. We believe the program we outlined and modeled after the Management Development Program for Technical Employees meets our needs better than any of the benchmark programs we reviewed.

Attachment

! Points to Remember

About Reports

- ☑ Reports are used to make decisions or to document activities, events, or transactions.

- ☑ Organizations use both internal and external reports for problem solving.

- ☑ Typically a subordinate prepares a report at the request of a superior who wants recommendations for solving a particular problem.

- ☑ Reports may be written in objective or personal style. Objective style should be used for situations that require persuasion.

- ☑ Reports typically contain the following components: identifying information, purpose, methods, data analysis, conclusions, recommendations, and a summary.

- ☑ Headings may be functional or may relate to the report content.

- ☑ The graphics and table features of word processing, spreadsheet, and presentation software should be used to simplify complex data.

- ☑ Reports may be organized using four styles: narrative, direct, indirect, or weighted. Each style has pros and cons. The best style to use depends on the content and complexity of the report.

Review Guide 5—Check for Completeness

Review Guide 5 of Chapter 2 on pages 34–35. Then read the following sentences and paragraphs and provide the information requested.

1. You currently use word processing, graphics, and presentation software from the Office Pro suite and spreadsheet software from the Office Master suite. You want to change to Office Pro spreadsheet software. You already have the software, but you need permission to convert all the departmental documents that are in Office Master to Office Pro.

   Information you must provide:

   Questions you should anticipate:

2. You are planning a memo inviting the members of your department to attend a football game and a tailgate celebration before the game. You will provide tickets to the game.

   Information you must provide:

   Questions you should anticipate:

3. You are planning a memo to inform three managers that you have made all travel and hotel reservations for their three-day trip to the corporate office across the country next month.

Information you must provide:

Assumptions you could logically make:

Questions you should anticipate:

Editing and Language Arts Checkpoint

1. Carefully read the document that follows; it is packed with errors. Use proofreaders' marks to mark all errors in grammar, spelling, usage, word choice, capitalization, punctuation, and keying. If you need help with proofreaders' marks, refer to the table on page 53. Do not revise sentence or paragraph structure unless you find an error.

2. Access *File 7B* in the Chapter 7 folder on your student data disk and make the corrections. If you are not working with the data disk, key the document, making the corrections as you key. You may use online reference tools just as you would on the job.

3. Format the document as a report with a memo heading. The report will be sent to the Executive Committee from you. Use the current date. The subject line should be Addendum to Outsourcing Printing Report. Save as *7Bsi.*

Data from section 2 of the Outsourcing Printing Report clearly showed that the cost of printing could be reduced substantially by manageing many of VanHuss Associates printing jobs in-house. Therefore, a second phase of the report was authorized to determine the feasability of setting up a in-house electronic publishing system.

Problem

The primary purpose of this phase of the project was to determine the percentage and type of work, which could be handled internally. This information can then be used to determine the better and most cost-affective system too meet the needs of

VanHuss Associates.

Methods

All the request forms for outside printing for the passed year was

collected and analyzed to determine the typeand volume of printing.

In many cases, job samples had to be obtained and analyzed by

the printing production team who determined whether or not the

job could be handled internally. Like the report directed four

electronic printing system proposals from local vendors were

obtained and examined to determine capabilities and prices.

Data Analysis

The analysis of the request forms for outside printing showed that

during the the past year ninety percent of the black and white

printing and forty percent of the color printing could have been

done internally on an electronic publishing system. Each of the

systems that was demonstrated to the evaluation team could have

handled the internal jobs.

All four systems include high resolution laser printers with the capability of handling color as well as black and white copy. The proposals form all four vendors include software scanners, and 2 workstations with 2-page display monitors. The Hess system use two seperate printers—one for color printing but the other for black and white printing. The Hess system costs $41,750.00. This is two thousand dollars more then the other systems however the Hess system has advanced features and equiptment that make it feasible to do additional jobs internally. Specifications for the four systems and a complete cost analysis is attached.

Conclusion

The conclusion of the Outsourcing Printing Report indicated that a in-house system could be justified at a cost of eighty thousand dollars if at least forty percent of the printing volume could be shifted internally. The volume of printing that could be shifted internally for excedes the minimum requirements and all systems evaluated meet the cost restrictions. The Hess electronic publishing system meets the needs of VanHuss Associates more better than the other 3 systems.

Recommendation

The Hess system should be purchased and installed within the next 6 weeks. This time frame allows time far personal in the Printing Center to be adequately trained before the outsourcing contract non-renewal notice must be given.

Writing Letter and Memo Reports

You will write various types of reports. Letterhead for some activities is available in the chapter folder on the student data disk. If you are not using the data disk or if letterhead is not provided, key the documents on plain paper.

Format your documents as shown on pages 47–50 and 192. Consult the database in Appendix A or on the student data disk (*Address Directory*) for addresses and contact information. Use the current date. For letter reports, supply an appropriate salutation and complimentary close. For memo reports, add an appropriate heading. All documents are from you unless you are directed otherwise.

Your instructor may ask you to use the guide on page 204 for evaluating your documents. Your instructor may also use this form to evaluate your work.

1. You manage Wayne's Fitness Center. Each week, you prepare a report summarizing the activities of the previous week and send it to Anne McKay, the operations manager at the parent company, Markland Fitness Centers. Use the sketchy notes below to write a weighted memo report for last week using personal writing style and no headings.

   - This past week was the best you have had in the two years you have managed the center. Memberships sold: 4 lifetime, 10 one-year, and 6 three-year.
   - Participation rate: high also. Weight room used by 300 members; handball and racquetball courts used an average of 9 hours per day; 3 aerobics classes each day with average attendance of 22 per class; 6 special fitness programs with average of 18 per program.
   - Problem: inadequate number of handball and racquetball courts to meet demand, especially from 4 to 10 p.m.
   - Expansion plans have been taken to 3 contractors for price estimates for building 2 more handball and 2 more racquetball courts. Expect bids within 10 days. Other services: babysitting services and vending operations continue to be profitable.

   Attach the standard financial report for the week and save as *7C1si*.

2. Revise the report you just completed in the previous activity. Use standard report format, direct organization, objective writing style, and content headings. Prepare an e-mail to Ms. McKay telling her that you are sending the weekly report to her and that you believe she will be very pleased with the results achieved this past week. Use the e-mail address A.McKay@MarklandFitness.com. Attach the report to your e-mail. Save the report as *7C2si* and the e-mail as *7C2asi*.

3. Local companies work with Sterling Technical College in a program called Business Mentors. This program is designed to help students with the transition to the workplace. Executives from four businesses have been working with a team of eight students (you and seven classmates) for the past year. At their last meeting, the executives talked about doing business with clients over lunch or dinner. They mentioned that they often take job candidates to lunch or dinner to evaluate the candidates' social skills and the way they would fit in and interact with clients.

Instead of the regular meeting, the companies have offered to take the team to a business dinner at 7:30 p.m. a week from today. You have been asked to evaluate restaurants that you think would be appropriate for a business meal with a client and to make a recommendation justifying your selection to Ms. Mary Turnquist, leader of the Business Mentors team, for approval. You plan to use this opportunity to showcase your report-writing skills and good judgment because you would like to be considered for a position at one of the four companies when you graduate in June.

You researched restaurants using the telephone directory, local advertisements, and the Internet, as well as ratings from diners who had eaten there recently. You have narrowed the options to three restaurants that are taking reservations on the date needed. Each restaurant can accommodate a group of 12 at one table in a private room (or one table of 12 or two tables of 6 in the main dining room), and each is suitable based on the broad general guides discussed at the last meeting. Your rough notes follow:

- *Chez Csiszar.* Very formal, small French restaurant with fancy, hard-to-pronounce names for all menu items. Great food and atmosphere. Ad indicated coat and tie required. Prices for entrées at the very top of the acceptable price range. All items are à la carte (priced separately).
- *Chateau Alyssa.* Very popular; ribs and a wide variety of pastas are the primary items (but not the only items) featured on the menu. Nice atmosphere. Most people dress casually (not jeans) because ribs can be messy. Prices in the middle to upper middle of the acceptable price range. Food is very good. Trip to salad bar and garlic bread are provided with all entrées. Known for large servings.
- *The Frozen Bay.* Reasonably formal, very nice restaurant with a pleasant atmosphere. Menu is varied, with a broad range of seafood, chicken, beef, and vegetarian items. Great food. One or two side dishes and a salad are served with each entrée. Diners generally dress nicely. Entrée prices in the middle to upper middle of the range.

Decide which restaurant you will recommend, justify your choice, and write a letter report using the style you believe would be best. Copy the Business Mentors. Save as *7C3si.*

Team Activity 4. Work with two classmates to select and modify one of the reports the three of you completed for the business mentors. Use actual restaurants in your town or a nearby city. The team should determine the best style to use for this report. Save as *7C4tp-si.*

5. As an employee in the human resources department of Linder Advertising Agency, you have been asked by Mr. Richard Meekins, vice president of human resources, to take on a sensitive assignment. He is concerned that clients may view the attire worn by many employees as unprofessional. He wants you to recommend an appropriate dress code.

Mr. Meekins has identified 12 **benchmark** companies that he would like you to visit to inquire about specific services they offer. While you are at the companies, your plan is to observe the attire worn by various types of employees. You were also asked to talk with clients you know well and with employees at Linder Advertising Agency to get their reactions on appropriate attire for employees.

You visited the 12 companies and found that in 9 companies, the managers and sales staff dressed very professionally. Men wore coats and ties, and women wore business suits or tailored dresses. Attire worn by office staff also was professional but a little less formal. The attire of technical people tended to be more casual than that of other employees. In most cases, men wore slacks with shirts that had collars, and women wore slacks or skirts and blouses. In 3 of the companies, employees did not dress as professionally. A few employees wore jeans or jogging outfits. You also learned that 6 of the companies you visited had casual days on Fridays only but that 3 of them were planning to eliminate casual Fridays.

Most of the clients (75 percent) whom you talked with indicated that they preferred to deal with companies whose employees had a professional appearance, 15 percent preferred casual attire, and 10 percent did not have a preference.

Employee reaction at Linder was varied: 55 percent said employees dressed too casually; 35 percent liked the comfortable, if somewhat sloppy, attire worn at Linder; and 10 percent did not think attire mattered.

Your initial reaction is to propose a very general dress code for Linder Advertising Agency. Employees who have contact with clients should wear professional attire—coats and ties for men and suits or tailored dresses for women. Employees who do not have contact with clients may dress more casually; slacks and shirts with collars for men and slacks or skirts and blouses for women would be appropriate. You have not yet decided what to do about casual Fridays. You will either recommend that employees have the option of dressing more casually on Fridays, but that T-shirts, shorts, jeans, or jogging outfits should not be worn to the office, or you will propose that casual Fridays not be an option in the dress code.

Your assignment is to decide what you will do about casual Fridays and write the report proposing a dress code. Use an indirect organizational approach, memo format, functional headings, and objective style. Include charts or tables in your report. Save as *7C5si*.

6. Your company, Carolina Promotions, provides Centex University with a $10,000 fellowship to be awarded to an incoming MBA student. Mr. Nicholas Csiszar, vice president of community relations, asked you to represent the company and participate as a judge in the final selection of the recipient.

    You were provided with copies of the applications of the ten finalists a week before the event. Last Thursday evening, you attended a get-acquainted dinner for finalists, judges, and administrators of the School of Business. On Friday, you and the other judges, who were administrators and faculty of the MBA program, conducted 30-minute interviews of the finalists. The judges ranked candidates on a point system based on the criteria for the fellowship. Then the judges met and agreed on the recipient.

    The recipient was announced at a large reception at the Faculty House Friday evening. Susan J. Walker was selected as the Carolina Promotions MBA Fellowship recipient. Twenty fellowships sponsored by various companies were awarded at the reception.

    Write a narrative report to Mr. Csiszar using memo format, personal style, and no headings. Be sure to convey to him that all ten finalists were highly qualified and that Centex University handled the entire event in an extremely professional manner. Your overall assessment was that Carolina Promotions gained excellent public relations benefits from this activity. Attach a copy of Susan's biographical sketch. Save as *7C6si*.

Application 7C: Guide for Evaluating Your Reports

Factors to Consider	Points	7C1		7C2		7C3		7C4		7C5		7C6	
Self-evaluation (SE), Instructor evaluation (IE)		SE	IE	SE	IE	SE	IE	SE	IE	SE	IE	SE	IE
Strategy—uses appropriate writing and organizational style for report	2												
Strategy—develops good ideas to solve the problem	2												
Data—analyzes and presents data effectively	2												
Writing Guide 1—evidence of good planning; organized	1												
Writing Guide 2—meets the reader's needs; courteous	1												
Writing Guide 3—uses positive language	1												
Writing Guide 4—uses a clear, easy-to-read style	1												
Writing Guide 5—complete; includes all needed information	1												
Writing Guide 6—uses an action-oriented or a neutral style as appropriate	1												
Writing Guide 7—uses specific language when appropriate	1												
Writing Guide 8—uses effective sentence and paragraph structure	1												
Writing Guide 9—uses correct format and attractive placement	1												
Writing Guide 10—has been edited and proofread; no errors	1												
Overall assessment of document	4												
Totals	20												

Mastery Check for Chapter 7

1. Explain the differences between the personal and objective styles of writing for reports.

2. Describe the differences between a direct (deductive) and an indirect (inductive) organizational approach for writing reports. Indicate the type of situation in which each is most effective.

3. Explain the differences between functional and content headings.

4. Describe a narrative organizational approach and indicate the type of situation in which it is most effective.

5. Explain the difference between conclusions and recommendations in a report.

6. For each of the terms shown below, write a complete, correct sentence using the term.

Analytical

Benchmark

Qualitative

Shell Cove—Restaurant Division

Shell Cove delegates all responsibilities for restaurants to the Restaurant Division, directed by Mr. Kenneth Opsahl. For this rotation of your training program, you are assistant manager to Ken. Shell Cove has two stand-alone restaurants: Pat's at Shell Cove (fine dining—lunch and dinner) and the Blue Point Seafood House (casual, buffet—dinner only).

The average occupancy for each restaurant is listed below. "Early bird" consists of one seating from 5:30 to 6:30 p.m. at a reduced price. It typically appeals to older guests or families with young children. Regular seating is from 7 to 10:30 p.m. Typically tables turn over at least once during regular seating, enabling the restaurants to accommodate more than double the seating capacity.

Restaurant	Capacity	Lunch	Early Bird	Regular Seating
Pat's at Shell Cove	75	70	35	140
Blue Point Seafood House	60	0	40	95

During the busy season (normally about eight months of the year), Pat's at Shell Cove operates at full capacity at least five days a week and usually turns reservations down at least two days a week at both lunch and regular seating times. Blue Point is closed at lunch and does not require reservations in the evening. During the busy season, guests rarely have to wait more than 20 minutes for a table.

The Inn at Shell Cove has two restaurants: an excellent dining room and a very casual sandwich and salad restaurant at the pool. Inn guests provide 90 percent of the business for these two restaurants.

Ken has asked you to complete the following two projects this week:

Job 1: Pat's at Shell Cove

Ken has been asked to determine whether it is better to expand Pat's at Shell Cove or to build another restaurant to accommodate guests that Pat's at Shell Cove turns away. He wants you to do research and prepare a report making a recommendation. You have interviewed the manager at Pat's, Chef Pat, and the director of the Property Development Division. You have also talked with a number of customers. You have made the following notes based on these interviews.

Facts supporting expansion:

- The restaurant could be expanded to accommodate 25 more customers.
- Business at Pat's would be expected to increase 15 percent in the slow season and 25 percent in the busy season.
- Customers would not have to be turned away.

Facts against expansion:

- Chef Pat believes it would be difficult if not impossible to maintain the high quality of food and service at Pat's with a larger capacity. The manager agrees.

- Customers have expressed concern that enlarging Pat's may destroy the quality and the atmosphere that make it so popular.

- Pat's would be closed for six months during the expansion.

- Adjacent parking would not accommodate the additional guests; valet service would have to be used.

- Three years would be required to recover the costs of the expansion.

- Additional staffing would be required, with added costs and training demands.

Use standard report format and appropriate organizational and writing styles. Save as *7E1si*. Attach the report to an e-mail to Ken. Save as *7E1asi*.

Team Activity

Internet Activity

Job 2: New Restaurants

Ken has decided not to expand Pat's at Shell Cove. He has asked you to work with employees of the Property Development and Rental/Condominium Divisions to research the need for new restaurants. You will search the Internet to determine the most popular types of restaurants in the Ocean City, Maryland, area. You will also use the results of a survey of 300 guests who stayed at least one week in a rental or condo unit last month. The survey results are summarized below. The numbered columns refer to number of times per week. In a previous survey, condo owners requested an Italian restaurant, so this type was included in the survey questions.

Question	0	1–2	3–5	6–7	Total*
How often did you eat breakfast out?	90	68	83	57	298
How often would you eat breakfast at a new restaurant at Shell Cove?	41	90	107	62	300
How often did you eat lunch out?	30	102	118	50	300
How often would you eat lunch at the new restaurant if it offered brunch items, salads, and deli sandwiches?	28	101	114	56	299
How often would you eat lunch at the Blue Point Seafood House if it opened for lunch?	104	126	56	12	298
How many nights did you try unsuccessfully for reservations at Pat's?	109	105	75	8	297
How often would you eat at a new Italian restaurant in Shell Cove?	20	172	85	20	297

*Some respondents did not answer all questions.

Analyze the survey and Internet data. Remember that local residents and visitors who stay in accommodations other than Shell Cove also eat at Shell Cove restaurants. Draw conclusions and make recommendations on the following topics:

a. Should Shell Cove open a new restaurant that would serve breakfast and lunch?

b. Should the Blue Point Seafood House open for lunch?

c. Should a new Italian restaurant be built if the cost can be justified?

Prepare the report in the style of your team's choice. Save as *7E2tp-si*.

GOODWILL MESSAGES

OBJECTIVES

After you complete Chapter 8, you should be able to:

* Plan goodwill messages.
* Write effective goodwill messages.
* Edit messages more effectively.

OVERVIEW

All business correspondence should be designed to build goodwill, as well as to accomplish the specific purpose of the message. In addition, some messages are intended purely to build goodwill. As people conduct business, they establish professional relationships with customers, suppliers, **vendors**, and other associates. Business relationships are, in effect, business friendships. Just as you would write congratulatory, thank-you, and similar messages to friends, these types of messages are written to business "friends." This chapter focuses on strategies for writing goodwill messages.

The key elements of this chapter include:

* Types of goodwill messages.
* Writing style.
* Planning goodwill messages.
* Strategies for writing goodwill messages.

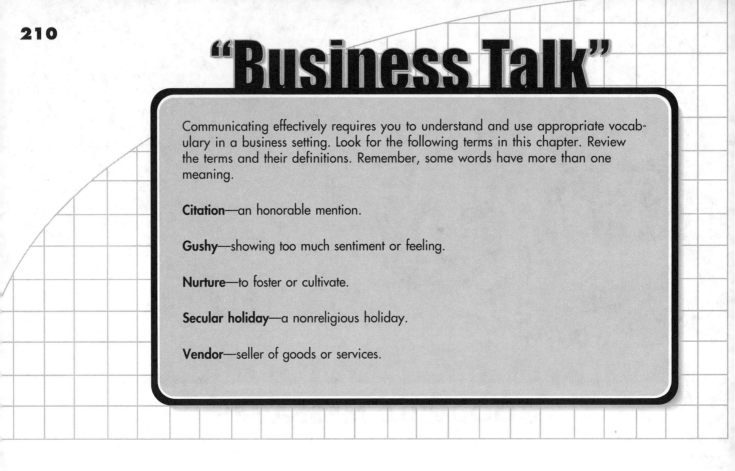

210

"Business Talk"

Communicating effectively requires you to understand and use appropriate vocabulary in a business setting. Look for the following terms in this chapter. Review the terms and their definitions. Remember, some words have more than one meaning.

Citation—an honorable mention.

Gushy—showing too much sentiment or feeling.

Nurture—to foster or cultivate.

Secular holiday—a nonreligious holiday.

Vendor—seller of goods or services.

TYPES OF GOODWILL MESSAGES

Goodwill messages are often referred to as personal business messages because they focus on fostering good relationships with specific persons in businesses. The message may be of a personal nature, such as sending a birthday wish or a congratulatory note to an individual. Writing goodwill messages is a good business strategy because they **nurture** relationships both with organizations and with individuals. Goodwill messages show that you have good manners and that you care about the business relationship.

Frequently written types of goodwill messages include the following:

- Thank-you messages.
- Congratulatory messages.
- Special occasion messages.
- Sympathy messages.

Thank-You Messages

Thank-you notes are the most frequently written goodwill messages. A thank-you note is simply a product of good manners. Remember that saying thank you is appropriate after someone does something that merits thanks, not at the time you request someone to do something for you. Thank-you cards with a short, personal message may also be used for some situations.

Many business situations provide an opportunity to build goodwill by writing a thank-you note. These include situations when you have been:

- Taken out for a meal.
- Given a gift, service, or large amount of business.
- Assisted in making a business contact.
- Provided with a reference.
- Granted an interview (covered in Chapter 9).

Congratulatory Messages

Congratulatory messages are written to acknowledge both business and individual successes. The following are examples of business situations in which you may want to write a congratulatory message:

- A company receives a special award or **citation**.
- An individual receives an award or a promotion.
- A company, team, or individual wins a competition.
- A company expands its business.

Special Occasion Messages

Special occasion messages are similar to congratulatory messages. They are sent to both businesses and individuals to recognize significant events. Examples of special occasions for which you may want to write a greeting or send your best wishes include the following:

- Holidays.
- Anniversaries.
- Company events, such as a merger or acquisition.
- Special days, such as Administrative Professionals Day (formerly Professional Secretaries Day).

Sympathy Messages

Sympathy messages are the most difficult type of message to write. Unless the business relationship is extremely close, most businesses purchase sympathy cards or have their own printed rather than trying to write sympathy messages. If the relationship is close, a short handwritten note is added to the card. Sympathy messages are typically sent when a company loses an employee or when a business associate loses a family member.

WRITING STYLE

Personal writing style, rather than objective writing style, should be used for goodwill messages. How personal a goodwill message should be depends on the relationship of the people involved. If they have a very close relationship, the message is often quite personal. If they have a cordial, professional relationship, the message is usually warm and friendly but not overly personal or **gushy**.

Many people debate whether personal messages should be handwritten or keyed. In most cases, it is a matter of personal preference. Busy executives usually send typewritten messages and often include a short handwritten note when they sign or initial the message. They save handwritten messages for individuals who deserve very special thanks or recognition. If a message is handwritten, the letter address is omitted.

Typically, letter format is used for goodwill messages even if they are internal messages. Memos or e-mail may be used if the message is sent to several people, such as a team, department, or group of employees.

PLANNING GOODWILL MESSAGES

Note that three of the four types of goodwill messages are easily identified as good-news messages. Although sympathy messages are not thought of as good-news messages, the reader is likely to receive them in the same way as a good-news

Global Connections

Formality of Communications

Americans tend to be more casual about communications than their customers in other countries are. Always carefully note the level of formality in the messages you receive from international customers. Then use the same level of formality when you write back to them. If you have no previous correspondence, use a conservative, formal approach. Be especially careful about including proper titles. In many cases, using a person's first name or leaving a title off is considered inappropriate and rude.

message. You are not delivering good news, but you are showing that you cared enough to write to a person who has lost someone close to them.

You can use the same basic planning steps for goodwill messages that you would use for any good-news message:

Determine objectives. The primary objective of goodwill messages is to nurture business relationships. Therefore, the message should show interest in or concern for the person or business.

Analyze the reader. You typically send goodwill messages to readers whom you know and who are likely to respond well to them. Your challenge is to make sure that the message is tailored to the reader and is sincere.

Make decisions and collect information. The only decision needed is the decision to write the message in the first place. You may need to collect information about the occasion for the message.

Develop a writing plan. The writing plan is usually a mental one because the message is short and easy to write.

STRATEGIES FOR WRITING GOODWILL MESSAGES

Use the same basic strategy for goodwill messages that you learned for good-news messages:

1. Present the good news.
2. Provide specific information.
3. Close on a warm, friendly note.

The good-news strategy can be modified slightly for the various types of goodwill messages.

Thank-You Messages

Thank-you messages should be short, warm, and friendly. They should be very specific about the reason for which they are written. Thank-you messages should not be excessive or gushy. An example of a thank-you message to an individual is shown in Figure 8-1 on page 214.

Time spent writing goodwill messages is a wise investment.

Success Tip

Technology Connections

Who Gets Copies of E-Mail

Just because it is easy to send an e-mail to a large group does not mean that it is effective to do so. Businesspeople spend a lot of time reading e-mails that contain information they do not need. Before you copy someone on e-mail, think about why the person needs the information. If you cannot come up with a reason other than that it might be nice to have, do not copy the person.

Congratulatory Messages

Congratulatory messages should be short, specific, and sincere. An example of a congratulatory message written when a company received an award appears in Figure 8-2 on page 215.

Special Occasion Messages

Special occasion messages are written in the same way as congratulatory messages. A special caution applies to holiday messages. Many holidays are religious rather than **secular holidays**. It is important not to risk offending business associates by assuming they celebrate the same holidays that you do. For example, businesses usually use a "Season's Greetings" message for the Christmas holidays. This type of message is appropriate because almost everyone celebrates the season, but not everyone celebrates Christmas. Many businesses use greeting cards rather than personal messages for holiday greetings. Some companies thank customers for their business over the past year.

Sympathy Messages

Choose sympathy cards carefully. Make sure they are secular unless you know a person's religious preference. Avoid cards with long messages unless you know the reader well and are certain that this style meets the reader's needs. If you include a handwritten message, keep it short. The reader is likely to respond favorably to a brief personal note.

Figure 8-1: Thank-You Letter

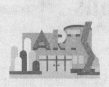

The Midlands Arts Council
1208 S. Capitol Avenue
Indianapolis, IN 46225-1508
(317) 555-0194

February 24, 200_

Ms. Gabriella Devarez, President
Devarez Industries, Inc.
2468 S. State Avenue
Indianapolis, IN 46203-4462

Dear Ms. Devarez

Thank you for sponsoring the Miguel Exhibit for the National Arts Convention
here in Indianapolis this past week. The Miguel Exhibit was one of our most
popular exhibits during the entire convention.

We opened all the exhibits to the general public from 9:15 a.m. to 6:30 p.m. last
Thursday. People were lined up to see the Miguel Exhibit during the entire time
that the facilities were open. Over the week, several thousand people had the
opportunity to view this magnificent show.

We sincerely appreciate your generosity in making this opportunity available to
our own citizens as well as to our national guests. It was truly enjoyed by all who
visited the exhibit.

Very sincerely yours

Carroll W. Showman, Chair
Midlands Art Council Board of Directors

pr

Figure 8-2: Congratulatory Letter

The Yankee Seafood Pot
157 Ocean Avenue ☺ Kennebunkport, ME 04046-6309
(207) 555-0135   ☺   www.yankeeseafoodpot.com

January 24, 200_

Mr. and Mrs. Robert C. Timmerman
The Glover Cove Bed and Breakfast
181 Ocean Avenue
Kennebunkport, ME 04046-6310

Dear Nancy and Bob

Congratulations on winning the Maine Bed and Breakfast of the Year Award! The
Glover Cove Bed and Breakfast is a historic and charming inn nestled in a
beautiful setting on the rocky coast of Maine. As you know, many of our
customers stay at the Glover Cove when they visit Kennebunkport. They tell us
that they love to relax in your stately suites with a cozy fire and awaken to the
sumptuous breakfast you always prepare.

Combine those elements with the wonderful customer service you provide, and
you have the elements of a winning bed and breakfast. The award you have just
won is simply recognition of what your friends in Kennebunkport have always
known—the Glover Cove Bed and Breakfast is a great place to stay.

We are proud that we refer customers to each other, and we wish you many more
years of success. Again, congratulations on winning a much deserved award.

Sincerely

Lynn Stafford

sv

! Points to Remember

About Goodwill Messages

- ☑ All business correspondence should be designed to build goodwill, as well as to accomplish the specific purpose of the message. In addition, some messages are intended purely to build goodwill.

- ☑ Goodwill messages should nurture relationships both with organizations and with individuals.

- ☑ Thank-you notes are the most frequently written goodwill messages. A thank-you note is simply a product of good manners.

- ☑ Congratulatory messages acknowledge awards, citations, prizes, and other successes.

- ☑ Special occasion messages recognize significant events, such as holidays, anniversaries, or mergers.

- ☑ Unless a business relationship is extremely close, most businesses purchase sympathy cards or have their own printed rather than trying to write sympathy messages. If a relationship is close, a short handwritten note is added to the card.

- ☑ Personal writing style, rather than objective writing style, should be used for goodwill messages.

- ☑ Typically, letter format is used for goodwill messages even if they are internal messages.

- ☑ You can use the same basic planning steps and strategy for writing goodwill messages that you would use for any good-news message.

Review Guide 6—Use an Efficient, Action-Oriented Style

Review Guide 6 of Chapter 2 on pages 35–38. Then revise each of the following sentences or paragraphs so that it will be written in an efficient, action-oriented writing style.

1. The nomination form for the award was reviewed and studied carefully by the Selection Committee. The Committee will make a decision on the person who will receive the award the next time that it meets, on the date of November 4.

2. The receptionist has scheduled your next appointment for October 30.

3. Congratulations were extended by the company president, John C. Johnson, to the employee, Shannon Rabune, who was selected to be our Employee of the Year.

4. A check in the amount of $100,000 was sent to Shirley Sinclair, the mayor of the city of Gilbert in the state of South Carolina, to assist with the project for the beautification of the city.

5. Sales representatives were encouraged by our marketing vice president, Lynn Sharpe, to add personal information about customer contacts, such as birthdays, company anniversaries, or colleges that they attended, to the company database.

Editing and Language Arts Checkpoint

1. Carefully read the document that follows; it is packed with errors. Use proofreaders' marks to mark all errors in grammar, spelling, usage, word choice, capitalization, punctuation, and keying. If you need help with proofreaders' marks, refer to the table on page 53. Do not revise sentence or paragraph structure unless you find an error.

2. Access *File 8B* in the Chapter 8 folder on your student data disk and make the corrections. If you are not working with the data disk, key the document, making the corrections as you key. You may use online reference tools just as you would on the job.

3. Format the document as a report with a memo heading. The report will be sent to the sales staff from you. Use the current date, and supply an appropriate subject line. Save as *8Bsi*.

The first quarter revenue figures for region IV was released today

and you will be pleased to learn that once again the team exceded

it's first quarter revenue budget. Congradulations! Each member

of the team exceeded their budget for the first quarter. We have

consistently met both team goals for the passed three years; but

rarely has every member off the team exceeded the budget plan.

Let me complement you on a job well done.

Its important that you review carefully the enclosed report, that

itemizes the revenue generated for all targeted software products.

Of the 6 application software packages, the one that that concerns

me more is the project management software. Our project

management software sales is 1/3 of the national average for the first quarter. In fact, not a single sales representative on our team met teh budget for project mangement software.

Would each of you analyze their territory carefully and give me an account by account projection of theproject management sales for the next quarter. I have asked Liz Jordan our technical support manager for the midwest to come to our next regular scheduled team meeting and talk at us about ways we can increase our sales in this deficient area. Liz worked with the region III team when it begun increasing it's sales of project management software. I am sure she can give us some good advise that will hep us improve our sales in this area.

During the next team meeting we will also view a new product release, and begin planning for launching the sale of this product in our territory. You will recieve a product release package be fore the meeting. Please review them carefully so that we can use the meeting time effectively. If you have any questions or comments which should be addressed before the meeting, please contact John or I.

Enclosure

Writing Goodwill Messages

In this application, you will write various types of goodwill messages. Letterhead for some activities is available in the chapter folder on the student data disk. If you are not using the data disk or if letterhead is not provided, key the documents on plain paper.

Format your documents as shown on pages 47–49. Consult the database in Appendix A or on the student data disk (*Address Directory*) for addresses and contact information. Use the current date. For letters, supply an appropriate salutation and complimentary close. For memos, add an appropriate heading. All documents are from you unless you are directed otherwise.

Your instructor may ask you to use the guide on page 224 for evaluating your documents. Your instructor may also use this form to evaluate your work.

1. You are a student at Prospect Business College. Your Entrepreneurship class recently completed a major unit on "Furnishing and Equipping Your Business Effectively." Mr. Ralph E. Marino, president of Marino Office Systems, invited your class to visit his showrooms and manufacturing plant. The company hosted your class for the following activities:

- A tour of the showrooms.
- A tour of the manufacturing plant.
- A presentation by one of the major designers, Ms. Rae LaFleur.
- Lunch with employees in the company dining room.

On the tours, you saw the latest in office furniture and systems and gained an understanding of how modular systems are manufactured. In addition, Ms. LaFleur's presentation gave you many ideas for a plan you must prepare for class for furnishing and equipping a business.

Write Mr. Marino a thank-you letter on behalf of your class. Save as *8C1si*.

2. Your company, Peerman Industries, Inc., is a major supplier for SteelGate Manufacturing. SteelGate just received the National Manufacturing Quality Award as an outstanding manufacturing company. The award is given each year to five manufacturing companies nationally. It is a major award coveted by many manufacturing companies. As a supplier, you submitted information about SteelGate as part of the award process. Write a congratulatory letter to Ms. Vivian Naufield, chief executive officer of SteelGate Manufacturing. Save as *8C2si*.

3. Crystal Owens, an accountant in the Administration Division of Nauman Publishing Company, just received the Community Volunteer Award. This award is given each year by your community to the citizen who has made the most outstanding contribution. Crystal is active in Junior Achievement, the Better Business Bureau, the Chamber of Commerce, and United Way, as well as several other charitable groups.

   Nauman encourages employees to get involved in community activities. Therefore, you want to acknowledge her award to the entire company. Prepare an e-mail message to all employees of Nauman Publishing, asking them to join you in congratulating your colleague on winning this award. Use the e-mail address employees@naumanpublishing.com. Save as *8C3si*.

4. Roger W. Kelly, maintenance supervisor with Peerman Industries, celebrates his twenty-fifth year with the company next Monday. Write a letter to Roger to acknowledge this special occasion. He will be formally recognized with all employees celebrating anniversaries at the annual end-of-the-year meeting. However, you have worked with him for many years and want to write him on his anniversary date. Your title is manager of human resources. Save as *8C4si*.

5. Write a memo to the members of the Productivity Enhancement Team thanking them for the excellent report they prepared on enhancing productivity at Brookfield Associates. The Executive Committee has reviewed the report, has indicated that it was outstanding, and plans to implement the recommendations made. Save as *8C5si*.

6. Six executives from different industries in your community or a nearby city recently visited your school and talked about careers in their companies. The sessions were very informative. They provided information about qualifications required for jobs in those industries. The executives also discussed the expectations they have of employees, salaries, and advancement opportunities.

Form a team with two classmates to write thank-you notes to these executives on behalf of your class. Use the Internet or telephone to find six local business executives in different industries and their address information. Write the thank-you notes. Make the notes specific to the industry each executive represents. Decide how best to accomplish this team project. Save as *8C6tp-si.*

Team Activity

Internet Activity

Application 8C: Guide for Evaluating Your Goodwill Messages

Name: _____

Factors to Consider	Points	8C1		8C2		8C3		8C4		8C5		8C6	
		SE	IE	SE	IE	SE	IE	SE	IE	SE	IE	SE	IE
Self-evaluation (SE), Instructor evaluation (IE)													
Strategy—uses an appropriate strategy for the message	2												
Writing style—uses personal writing style	2												
Writing style—message is warm, friendly, and sincere	2												
Writing Guide 1—evidence of good planning; organized	1												
Writing Guide 2—meets the reader's needs; courteous	1												
Writing Guide 3—uses positive language	1												
Writing Guide 4—uses a clear, easy-to-read style	1												
Writing Guide 5—complete; includes all needed information	1												
Writing Guide 6—uses an efficient, action-oriented style	1												
Writing Guide 7—uses specific, concrete language	1												
Writing Guide 8—uses effective sentence and paragraph structure	1												
Writing Guide 9—uses correct format and attractive placement	1												
Writing Guide 10—has been edited and proofread; no errors	1												
Overall assessment of document	4												
Totals	20												

Mastery Check for Chapter 8

1. Explain why it is important to write goodwill messages.

2. What advice would you give someone purchasing sympathy cards or having them printed for use with business associates?

3. Describe the writing style that is appropriate for goodwill messages.

4. Describe an appropriate strategy for writing goodwill messages.

5. Why do most businesses use a secular approach to sending special occasion messages even though the holiday being celebrated may be a religious one?

6. For each of the terms shown below, write a complete, correct sentence using the term.

Gushy

Nurture

Secular holiday

Shell Cove—Golf/Tennis Division

Shell Cove delegates all responsibilities for the Shell Cove Beach and Racquet Club, the Tidewater Golf Course, and the pro shops in these facilities to the Golf/Tennis Division, directed by Mr. Arlo Blackmon. For this rotation of your training program, you are assistant manager to Arlo.

Arlo is an alumnus and former tennis coach of Atlantic Coast University (ACU), and he still maintains close ties with the school. For the past several years, Arlo has arranged for Shell Cove to host the President's Invitational Golf Tournament at the Tidewater Golf Course. The event begins with a reception and auction on Sunday evening at the Beach and Racquet Club. The tournament is held on Monday—the day on which the course is used least by members. Shell Cove waives all fees and provides golf carts for participants. All proceeds of the auction and tournament go to providing academic scholarships for needy ACU students.

The ACU Advancement Department solicits donations of items to be auctioned and arranges for sponsors to pay for food and prizes. The department also handles all fundraising activities associated with this popular event. Participants pay $1,000 each to play in the tournament.

Although Shell Cove hosts the tournament to help raise scholarship money, the event has provided excellent public relations for the company. Shell Cove has gained a number of corporate and individual memberships for golf and tennis as a result, and additional reception business has also been generated.

For this project, Arlo has asked you to draft the goodwill messages that he always sends out after the tournament for his signature. The tournament was held this past Monday and raised $128,000 in net profits for scholarships.

Job 1: Congratulatory Letter to Dr. Donna I. Palms

Write a letter to Dr. Donna I. Palms, president of ACU, congratulating her on the most successful golf tournament ACU has ever had. Tell her how much Shell Cove enjoys hosting the event, that you (that is, Arlo) are pleased to be able to give back to ACU by helping needy students, and that you enjoyed working with her staff. Indicate that Shell Cove looks forward to working with her and ACU next year for an even more successful tournament. Save as *8E1si*.

Job 2: Thank-You Letter to Lead Sponsor

Greg's Custom Golf Equipment, a supplier for the golf course pro shop, was the lead sponsor for this year's tournament. Write to Mr. Lee Moore, general manager, thanking him for sponsoring the event. Emphasize how successful the tournament was and how much it will help needy students at ACU. Also mention how much you appreciate doing business with Greg's Custom Golf Equipment. Save as *8E2si*.

Job 3: Thank-You E-Mail to Golf/Tennis Division Employees

All employees of the Golf/Tennis Division put in extra time to ensure that this event was successful. Send an e-mail to these employees thanking them for the significant role they played. Refer to the benefits the event has for Shell Cove as well as for ACU students. Use the group address Employees.tennis.golf@ shellcove.com. Save as *8E3si*.

EMPLOYMENT COMMUNICATIONS

OBJECTIVES

After you complete Chapter 9, you should be able to:

- Develop an effective employment strategy.
- Understand strategies employers use to hire employees.
- Write effective messages seeking employment.
- Edit messages more effectively.

OVERVIEW

The jobs you hold in your career will affect your entire life. Therefore, developing an effective job-search strategy is essential. You will be more successful if you view the employment process from the employer's perspective as well as from your own point of view. In this chapter, you will learn to prepare résumés, write application letters designed to gain an interview, and prepare thank-you letters for interviews and other employment communications. The key elements of this chapter include:

- Employment strategies.
- Technology and employment.
- Communications for the job seeker.

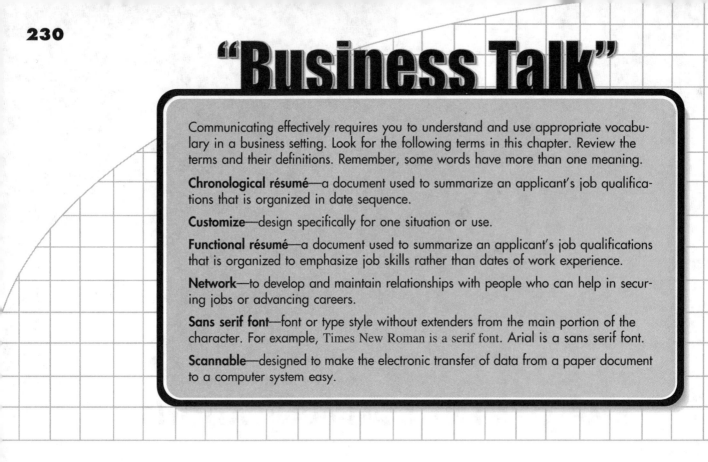

"Business Talk"

Communicating effectively requires you to understand and use appropriate vocabulary in a business setting. Look for the following terms in this chapter. Review the terms and their definitions. Remember, some words have more than one meaning.

Chronological résumé—a document used to summarize an applicant's job qualifications that is organized in date sequence.

Customize—design specifically for one situation or use.

Functional résumé—a document used to summarize an applicant's job qualifications that is organized to emphasize job skills rather than dates of work experience.

Network—to develop and maintain relationships with people who can help in securing jobs or advancing careers.

Sans serif font—font or type style without extenders from the main portion of the character. For example, Times New Roman is a serif font. Arial is a sans serif font.

Scannable—designed to make the electronic transfer of data from a paper document to a computer system easy.

EMPLOYMENT STRATEGIES

Having a good employment strategy is critical for both employers trying to hire the right employees and individuals seeking the right jobs. A successful strategy matches the right person to the right position. As a student and future employee, it is important that you understand the employment process from both perspectives.

Strategies for the Employer

Almost all companies believe that their most valuable asset is their employees. Hiring decisions are some of the most important decisions they make. Large businesses maintain departments or divisions (often called Human Resources) that specialize in developing and implementing strategies to ensure that:

- The right size workforce is maintained.
- Appropriate employees are hired for the positions available.
- Employees are oriented to the business.
- Employees are trained for the positions they will occupy.

Human resource professionals distinguish between a position and a job. A *position* is occupied by one person. A *job* is a collection of positions. For example, your position might be executive assistant to the president. Your friend's position may be executive assistant to the chief financial officer. The job is executive assistant, and a company may have 15 or 20 executive assistants. In this chapter, both terms—*job* and *position*—are used without making a distinction between them.

The employment process requires an employer to determine the following:

- What jobs are available and how many employees should be hired (*needs assessment*).
- Exactly what each job requires the employee to do (*job description*).

Success Tip

The key to success in the employment process for both the employer and the job seeker is matching the right person with the right position.

- What skills and qualifications the employee must have to do the job effectively (*job specifications*).

- Where and how to recruit employees (*job market analysis*).

The terms in parentheses and italics are the ones typically used in human resources management.

Strategies for the Job Seeker

The positions that you hold in your career will affect your entire life. You cannot afford to accept a job in which you are unlikely to be successful or likely to be dissatisfied. A well-planned, thorough job search is much more likely to produce good results than a disorganized, half-hearted effort. Therefore, developing an effective strategy for finding a job may have a very positive outcome for your future.

<table><tr><td>**Success Tip**
Strategic thinking and persistent effort are needed to find the right job.</td></tr></table>

An effective strategy for finding a job consists of the following steps:

1. Determine what kind of work you would like to do (*self-analysis*).
2. Find out what types of jobs would be most appropriate for you (*job analysis*).
3. Decide where and how you will find a job (*job market analysis*).
4. Conduct your search.
5. Prepare and submit application materials.
6. Participate in interviews.
7. Follow up interviews with the appropriate communications, including letters accepting or declining job offers.

Self-analysis. Self-analysis begins with determining your interests, strengths (including skills), and weaknesses. In a self-analysis, you think carefully about what you really want to do. You also consider the kind of environment that you prefer for work. Ideally, self-analysis should begin early in your education so that you can make wise decisions and select appropriate courses of study.

Job analysis. Job analysis consists of identifying types of jobs that would be best for you. An ideal match is a job in which your interests and strengths are the major requirements of the job and your weaknesses are not important in the job. Finding the perfect match may not be possible, but you should strive to get as close a match as you can.

Resources for a job analysis include teachers, guidance counselors, people who work in that job or a similar job, libraries, and the Internet. An excellent source of detailed, up-to-date information about all kinds of jobs is the *Occupational Outlook Handbook*, produced each year by the federal government. This book is available in many libraries and school guidance offices, as well as online.

Job market analysis and search. A job market analysis involves a number of decisions. For example, you will have to choose whether to search for a job locally or in other geographic areas. You must also decide whether you prefer to work in a small or a large business. Each type has advantages and disadvantages. This decision is important because different markets have to be tapped depending on company size.

Finding a suitable job requires careful planning and hard work. Some jobs are advertised in the open market. Notices may be placed in the classified ads of newspapers or listed with school placement departments, employment agencies, or governmental agencies. Job listings on the Internet are discussed in the next section.

These are not the only sources of jobs, however. In fact, employment specialists estimate that only about one-third of all jobs are advertised in the newspaper or posted with agencies. Two-thirds of jobs may be in what is often called the hidden job market. The higher the level and pay for a job, the more likely it is to be part of the hidden job market.

Two of the best ways to find out about jobs in the hidden job market are to talk to knowledgeable individuals and to read specialized publications. Well-informed people in a field are most likely to know about jobs that are available in that field.

Success Tip

Networking to discover jobs in the hidden job market may be the best career skill to learn.

Many people have no idea how to go about **networking** for job information. You can start by listing people you know who might be able to provide you with information about jobs. The more names you list, the better your chances of getting a contact. Friends, relatives, parents' friends, instructors, business associates (such as bankers, lawyers, doctors, and association members), and any other contacts you can think of are all potential sources of job information. A friendly letter or telephone call letting these people know you are in the job market and telling them you value their advice may be all you need for someone to suggest that you contact a particular company.

Specialized publications are journals, brochures, newsletters, and other communications that are read by people in certain fields. For example, publications are designed for bankers, insurance agents, computer programmers, and other occupations. You can obtain these publications from a local library, the Internet, or local employees who work in those occupations.

If you search only advertised sources or agencies, you may miss out on the best opportunities. If you are willing to devote the time and energy necessary to search for the best possible job, you are much more likely to find it.

TECHNOLOGY AND EMPLOYMENT

Both employers and individuals seeking jobs can use technology to great advantage in the employment process. Job seekers must understand the technology that companies use to ensure that their applications are considered.

Technology Connections

Input Technologies

Many options exist today for entering text and data for messages. While the keyboard and mouse remain the dominant input technologies, other digital tools are also used. Tablet PCs, personal digital assistants (PDAs), wireless telephones, scanners, pagers, digital cameras, and speech recognition all provide ways to enter text and data. Regardless of the input tools, proofreading and editing are still critical skills needed to produce high-quality messages.

Applicant Tracking Systems

Many companies use an applicant tracking system to manage the employment process. Résumés are scanned into a computer system and maintained online. When a position becomes available, a keyword search is used to match the job requirements of the position with the résumés in the database. The computer system screens and ranks the résumés by the number of keywords matched.

Résumés that will be read by computers need to be prepared differently than traditional résumés. These differences are described in the section on preparing résumés.

The trend today is to have a computer do the initial screening. But regardless of whether applications are screened by computers or by company personnel, your résumé will eventually be carefully reviewed by the person responsible for the position you are applying for. Therefore, the ideal résumé is usually one that passes computer screening and still appeals to the person or persons doing the hiring.

Technology for Job Seekers

You can use technology effectively in your job search in a number of ways. Here are several examples:

- Design your own attractive letterhead.
- Create employment documents that can be **customized** and personalized to give the appearance of professionally prepared, original documents created exclusively for the company that receives them.
- Use résumé preparation software (specialized software that guides you through the process of creating and formatting a résumé).
- Print employment communications on a high-quality personal printer.
- Leave professional messages on voice mail.
- Record messages on your answering machine or message system that are appropriate for prospective employers. If you share this equipment with others, make sure the message presents you in a positive light.

Internet Resources

The Internet can be very helpful in a job search. Remember, though, that using the Internet is not a substitute for other things that you should be doing, like networking and regularly checking with potential employers. The following are some types of job-related information you can get from the Internet:

- Profiles of many jobs that include a description of the work, job requirements, job outlook, salaries, and opportunities for advancement.
- Information about careers from professional organizations and the federal government.
- Guides for networking.
- Online job listings at company, newspaper, community, college placement office, government, and employment Web sites. You may be able to apply for many of these jobs online.
- Information about the employment process from employment job sites, recruiters, and other employment specialists.
- Tips to prepare for interviews, including how to dress and lists of frequently asked questions.
- Help in writing résumés and application letters, including step-by-step instructions, samples, dos and don'ts, lists of action or power verbs, and suggested keywords.

- Information about companies from their Web sites, online newspapers and journals, financial Web sites, and the U.S. Securities and Exchange Commission Web site.

Always ensure that your sources are credible and current before using information from the Internet.

COMMUNICATIONS FOR THE JOB SEEKER

The employment process often involves many communications. When you seek a job, you are likely to prepare the following documents:

- Résumés.
- Letters of application.
- Thank-you letters.
- Requests for references.
- Requests for transcripts or other records.
- Letters to accept or decline jobs.

In the early stages, telephone calls, your résumé, and your application letter are the primary ways in which you communicate with prospective employers. The most important point to remember is that these communications are **not** designed to get you a job. Few, if any, companies would hire you on the basis of a letter, a telephone conversation, or a résumé. The purpose of these communications is to get you an interview.

RÉSUMÉ

The résumé is usually the first document you will prepare. It is an outgrowth of the self-analysis process. A résumé is a summary of facts about you. Mass-produced résumés are not effective. Résumés posted on a Web site for anyone to review fit into this same category, except for high-tech companies. You must create a basic résumé and then customize or personalize it for each company. The style and content of résumés vary widely because they are designed to present the strengths of each person in the most effective way.

Résumé Integrity

The information you present in your résumé must be honest and accurate. Some people overstate their qualifications in their efforts to be hired. If information on a résumé or job application form is determined to be false after a person has been hired, most companies will fire the person immediately. Always make sure that everything in your résumé is accurate. Carefully check the names of degrees, titles of positions, grade point averages, dates, and the amount of experience listed.

Design for the Reader

The design of a résumé varies depending on whether it will be read by computer software (**scannable** résumé) or solely by a person (traditional résumé). Therefore, the first step in preparing a customized résumé for a particular job is to determine, if possible, how the résumé will be reviewed. One way to find out is to call the company's human resources department and ask if it has guidelines to ensure that your résumé meets its scanning requirements. Another good approach is to assume that your résumé may be scanned and format it appropriately. Follow these guidelines for both kinds of résumés:

- Use a simple, elegant design.
- Choose a clear, easy-to-read font.
- Use white space to present your information attractively.
- Use bold and italics where appropriate.
- Avoid graphics.
- Use good-quality paper.
- Print your résumé on a laser printer. Avoid photocopies or faxing.
- Print on just one side of the paper.
- Do not fold or staple your résumé.

Scannable résumés. Follow these additional guidelines for preparing scannable résumés:

- Use white paper only.
- Use a single column.
- Use one font, a 12- or 14-point **sans serif font** (Arial, Courier, Optima, etc.).
- Make sure that characters do not touch each other.
- Do not include graphic lines that touch characters.
- Avoid symbols (such as % and &), foreign characters, and graphics.
- Use solid, round bullets if you use bullets.

Many companies that scan résumés also track them electronically. Therefore, scannable résumés should contain keywords that would be likely to turn up in a computer search for a particular job that might interest you. For example, software tracking a job for a team leader in a human resources department may search for résumés with the following keywords:

Examples of keywords

benchmarking	leadership
best practices	negotiation
consensus building	planning
creativity	problem solving
development	team leader
interpersonal skills	training

Note that keywords are typically nouns rather than verbs. The words used in a job description or announcement often give you clues about what keywords to use.

Traditional résumés. A traditional résumé is quite similar to a scannable résumé. The difference is that it frequently uses two columns, one for headings and one for body text, and two fonts, a sans serif font such as Arial for headings and a serif font such as Times Roman for body text. Headings might be set larger than body text to draw attention to them. Traditional résumés are also more likely to use a few graphic lines and bullets to organize information. They may be printed on white or off-white paper.

Types of Résumés

The type of résumé you choose should be determined by the amount and kind of experience that you have had. Two basic types of résumés are used: **chronological** and **functional résumés**.

Chronological résumés. If you have a record of successful work experience over a number of years, you should design a résumé that presents the results you have accomplished. As a manager, for example, you would illustrate your results by what you were able to get other people to achieve. As a sales representative, you would feature your sales results. Résumés that report results in date sequence are called chronological résumés. Generally, they start with the most recent information and move back in time.

Functional résumés. If you have little or no work experience or if you are changing your career, you should design a résumé that presents the skills you have developed and emphasizes your potential. Résumés that present skills and abilities are called functional résumés.

Figures 9-1, 9-2, and 9-3 on pages 237–239 illustrate chronological and functional résumés. The chronological résumé in Figure 9-1 is scannable and includes keywords for electronic tracking. This résumé emphasizes results and skills developed through experience. The functional résumé in Figure 9-2 emphasizes education and qualifications and also includes keywords. Figure 9-3 is an example of a chronological résumé in traditional format.

Writing Style for Résumés

For résumés that will be screened by a person, you should use action verbs. For résumés that will be screened by a tracking system, you should use keywords. If you do not know how your résumé will be screened, use a combination of action verbs and keywords that relate to the job you are applying for.

Examples of action verbs

achieved	coordinated	instructed	planned	sponsored
analyzed	created	integrated	prepared	started
assessed	headed	led	presented	supervised
built	initiated	managed	produced	trained
conducted	instituted	negotiated	reorganized	verified

Résumés should be concise. A general guide is to prepare a one-page résumé if you have fewer than five years of experience and two to three pages if you have more experience. Your résumé must be error-free and formatted attractively. Use telescoped statements (shortened phrases rather than complete sentences). Avoid the pronoun *I*. Saying *I* is not necessary because the entire résumé is about you.

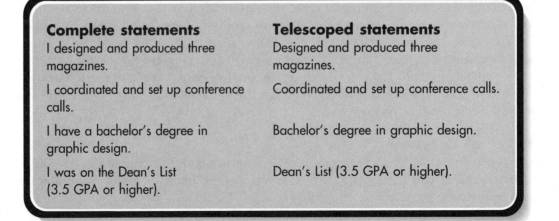

Complete statements	**Telescoped statements**
I designed and produced three magazines.	Designed and produced three magazines.
I coordinated and set up conference calls.	Coordinated and set up conference calls.
I have a bachelor's degree in graphic design.	Bachelor's degree in graphic design.
I was on the Dean's List (3.5 GPA or higher).	Dean's List (3.5 GPA or higher).

Figure 9-1: Chronological Résumé

Default or 1″

Jordan C. Turner
2498 South Boulevard   Charlotte, NC 28203-5010
(704) 555-0176   jordan.turner@nair.net

Career Objective

A sales management position with a state-of-the-art medical technology company, such as Tryon Medical Technology.

Work Experience

West Virginia Medical Equipment, Inc. Charleston, West Virginia.

Senior Account Manager. (2001–present) Manage ten large hospital accounts and sell medical equipment and integrated medical systems. Team leader and coordinate all sales activities of six account managers. Exceeded sales budget by at least 20 percent each quarter. Earned President's Club status.

Account Manager. (1998–2001) Sold medical equipment and systems to hospitals. Exceeded sales budget every quarter. Earned President's Club status.

Default or 1″

Sales Trainee. (1997–1998) Sold medical equipment and systems to physicians. Coordinated training for users.

Default or 1″

MEDMANAGE, Inc. Huntington, West Virginia.

Technical Assistant. (1995–1997; 20 hours per week) Installed medical office management software and provided technical assistance and training to customers.

Education

Virginia Medical Technology Institute, Roanoke, Virginia. Associate in Science degree, 1997, majored in medical technology.

MedTec Training Seminars, Columbia, Maryland. *Technical Selling Skills.* Earned Technical Medical Sales Certificate. May 1999.

Management Development for Technical Sales Representatives. Completed three-week program designed to prepare account managers for management positions. May 2001.

Community Service

Volunteer at Children's Hospital (10 hours per week)
Community Fund representative
Director of church outreach program

Default or 1″

Figure 9-2: Functional Résumé

Default or 1″

Rhonda M. Markland
1596 West Alameda Street
Santa Fe, NM 87501-1705
(505) 555-0143
Rhonda.Markland@rctm.com

Default
or 1″

Default
or 1″

Objective	A desktop publishing position with an opportunity to advance to positions involving graphic design with a leading publisher, such as Southwest Publishers, Inc.
Qualifications	Key accurately at 85 wpm. In-depth knowledge of and experience using PublishWrite and DesignArt desktop publishing software as well as all major word processing, graphics, and presentation software. General knowledge of and experience using spreadsheet, database, project management, and accounting software.
Strengths	Excellent interpersonal skills. Work effectively as a team member and team leader. Experience and training in making presentations supported by computer visuals. Superior writing, editing, and design layout skills. Creative. Excellent written and oral communication skills. Ability to manage projects and meet deadlines.
Education	Red Rock Junior College, Sedona, AZ, Associate in Arts degree, 2003. Majored in office systems and graphic design and earned a 3.5 grade point average on a 4.0 scale. Flagstaff Midtown High School, Flagstaff, AZ, diploma, 2001. Graduated in top 5 percent of class.
Leadership	President (2002–2003) and vice president (2001–2002) of the Office Systems Association. Editor of the *Red Rock News* (2002–2003); graphic designer and production manager (2001–2002). Flagstaff Midtown Honor Society and Cardinal Service Club (1999–2000). Editor of the *Midtown News* (2000–2001); production manager (1999–2000); reporter and regular column writer (1998–1999).
Experience	Production manager of the *Sedona Reporter* (2001–2003). Worked 20 hours per week. Responsible for layout and production of the *Sedona Reporter*, published three times per week. Met every deadline. Earned the Outstanding Designer Award (2002, 2003).

Default or 1″

Figure 9-3: Traditional Chronological Résumé

Default or 1"

Madison C. Littlefield
102 Ann Edwards Lane
Mt. Pleasant, SC 29464-5614
(843) 555-0148
mlittlefield@beachlink.net

Career Objective	An editorial position in a company specializing in business publications.
Work Experience	**Sand Dunes Publishing, Inc.**, Charleston, South Carolina (2000–2004)

- **Editor.** (2003–2004) *The Sand Dunes*, a weekly magazine Planned and selected materials for publication; managed a diverse team of editors; met all deadlines; increased circulation 15 percent.
- **Associate editor.** (2002–2003) Responsible for editing all and writing 60 percent of business articles; supervised production.
- **Production manager.** (2000–2002) Responsible for layout and production of *The Sand Dunes* and for several weekly real estate brochures. Received layout and design award. Team leader for production and sales associates.

Default or 1" Default or 1"

The Coastal Business News and Views, North Carolina Coastal University (1998–2000, 20 hours per week)

- **Production manager.** (1999–2000) Managed production and daily operations. Met all deadlines.
- **Production assistant.** (1998–1999) Assisted with all publications of the Business School.

Education	**North Carolina Coastal University**, Morehead City, North Carolina, Bachelor of Arts in Business Administration and English (2000). Graduated *magna cum laude*.

Myrtle Ocean View High School, Myrtle Beach, South Carolina, diploma (1997). Graduated in top 5 percent of class.

Leadership and Service	**North Carolina Coastal University**, student body president (1999–2000); treasurer (1998–1999). Outstanding student award.

Captain, golf varsity team (1998–2000); team leader for Community Care team (1998–2000). Accepted academic rather than golf scholarship.

Volunteer, elementary school reading team (1997–2002, 5 hours per week).

Default or 1"

The information in the different sections of a résumé should be parallel in structure. For example, all statements describing job activities should begin with an action verb.

Information to Include in a Résumé

Both chronological and functional résumés present basically the same information. They are simply organized and formatted differently to emphasize strengths. A combination of the two can also be used. In addition, the headings can be changed to suit your needs. As you read this section, refer to Figures 9-1 and 9-2 to see examples of the different résumé parts that are described.

Identifying information. Your name is the most important piece of information on the résumé and should be placed on the first line. Your contact information, including e-mail address if appropriate, should also be included in this section. Students often provide both temporary contact information at school and permanent home contact information.

Career objective. The career objective is a statement specifying the type of position you are seeking. The objective should be customized for the particular company or industry that will receive the résumé. Employment specialists often debate the value of including an objective.

Students who have not yet had any full-time job experience should include a career objective. A student's educational background could be applied in many different ways. Therefore, it is helpful to let a prospective employer know what type of career is desired.

Summary of qualifications. The summary of qualifications provides a brief statement of your most important qualifications. This section highlights what you believe are your key strengths that match the job. You may also present qualifications and strengths in separate sections, as in Figure 9-2. Some employment specialists suggest that the summary of qualifications offers a good alternative to the career objective because it tells the employer what you have to offer rather than what you want. You may include either or both of these sections.

The qualifications section is a good place to list nouns that could serve as keywords for résumés that will be tracked electronically. When the résumé is in response to an ad or job description, this section should be customized to show that your skills match the requirements of the job.

Education. List schools attended, diplomas and degrees earned, and the dates they were earned. The highest or most recent degree is listed first. Most employment specialists like to see information on academic performance, such as grade point averages, included for recent graduates with little work experience. When students omit this information, the reader may assume it was left out because the grades are not very good. You should also note certificates earned and classes and programs completed outside school that relate to your career area.

Experience. Describe jobs you have held, beginning with your most recent job. Include job titles, employer names and locations, dates, and brief information about each job that emphasizes results rather than activities. Include action verbs to show results and nouns to serve as keywords.

Honors and activities. Your résumé may contain a separate section for honors, hobbies, community service, special interests, or activities, or you may integrate this information into other sections. If you have limited work experience, use this part of the résumé to show your leadership potential.

Some employment specialists suggest including interests because this information can be used as an icebreaker in an interview. It gives the interviewer something easy to talk about that will put you at ease. If your résumé is long, you should save this space for more important information.

Special skills. Use this section to highlight special skills you have that relate to the job, such as computer skills, language skills, leadership skills, or highly specialized skills. You may also integrate your skills into other sections.

You should not include references or personal data on your résumé. References are not checked at this early stage, and most people do not consider personal data appropriate. However, you should bring a typed list of references to every job interview so that you can provide them if asked. You should also bring a copy of your résumé in case you must complete an application form. Having organized information will make completing the form much easier.

APPLICATION LETTER

The purpose of the application letter is to get an interview. As noted earlier, employers tend not to hire solely on the basis of a letter. Nor would you want to accept a job without meeting your prospective employer and learning more about the job. Therefore, in your application letter, you should focus on persuading the reader to give you the opportunity to show why you should be hired.

Planning
You have already completed most of the planning steps for writing an effective letter.

1. Your self-analysis determined your objective for the application letter.
2. Your job market analysis determined the reader's needs.
3. You decided to apply for the job, which is the only decision you need to make.
4. You collected and organized information about yourself when you prepared your résumé. The only information you need to collect is information about the company.
5. You also need to determine the best writing strategy.

Before you begin writing, research the company so that you can customize your letter. The more you know about the company, the better you can tailor your information to show how your qualifications meet the company's needs.

Always address the letter to an individual. If you do not have the name of a specific person, you can address your letter to the human resources manager. You can get this person's name by telephoning the company or looking on the Internet. Putting forth the effort to obtain information about the company makes a very positive statement about you. It implies that you do what it takes to be successful.

Writing Strategy
The strategy you use must be adapted to the company and must be based on the information you have about a particular job opportunity. The following examples illustrate different situations that would influence your letter:

- You are writing in response to a job announcement or ad. The company is asking qualified applicants to apply for a specific position. In this case, you know that the position is available, and you have specific information about it.

- You are writing because a networking contact who has information about the company has suggested that it has or may have positions available.

- You have researched a company, and you would like to be considered if a position is available. However, you do not know if a specific position is actually available.

The following writing strategy, with minor modifications, can be used for any of these situations:

1. Establish a point of contact.
2. Specify the type of job you are seeking.
3. Highlight your major qualifications and strengths.
4. Refer to the résumé that you will enclose.
5. Request an interview.

Note that the strategy for writing an application letter is similar to the strategy for writing persuasive messages that you learned in Chapter 5. The emphasis in this type of letter is on persuading the employer to give you an interview. You are, in effect, trying to sell yourself as a qualified prospective employee who can meet the employer's needs.

In Chapter 5, you learned that credibility, a logical appeal, and a psychological appeal can influence behavior. In your application letter, you should show that you are credible and use both logical and psychological appeals.

You can show that you are knowledgeable by presenting your qualifications effectively. The tone of your letter must be sincere. Demonstrating that your strengths match the requirements of the employer's job is the best logical appeal you can use. You can also use a psychological appeal by presenting your qualifi-

Global Connections

Learning a Second Language

A common joke in Europe is that a person who speaks three languages is called trilingual, a person who speaks two languages is called bilingual, and a person who speaks only one language is called an American. Is learning a second or third language important? Most people would answer yes, that it broadens your educational experience and is one of the best ways to learn more about another culture. It also makes a great impression on the people of that culture.

From a job perspective, if you deal with people from many different cultures, it would be difficult to learn the language of each culture. However, if you deal primarily with people from one culture, learning the language of that culture can be a great job asset. It says to people of that culture that you are interested in them and you care enough to spend time learning their language. Just because English is the primary language in which business is conducted does not mean that learning other languages is a waste of time. It may be one of the greatest investments of time that you could make.

cations in a unique or interesting manner, such as providing an account of something special or very successful that you did in your work or educational experience.

Establish a point of contact. Establishing a point of contact lets the reader know how you found out about the job or company. People tend to trust individuals they know more than they trust strangers. Therefore, you can gain credibility by referring to an individual whom the employer knows and respects. Networking goes further than just locating an opportunity; it helps to gain favorable attention. If you do not have a personal reference that you can mention, you can still establish a point of contact by demonstrating a knowledge of the company or its needs.

Applicants who make the effort to establish a reasonable point of contact demonstrate to employers that they have the initiative to do more than is required. That action builds credibility and appeals to employers. Review the following examples for establishing a point of contact:

Situation	Point of Contact
Letter responding to a job announcement	The job description posted on your Web site invites applicants with strong communication skills, computer skills, and a degree in business to apply for the position of director of the Call Center. I have those skills and would like to be considered for this position.
Letter based on a suggestion from a networking contact	Ms. Claire Wallace, my internship director at Wexford Industries, indicated you may have a position open for a sales representative. She suggested that I contact you about that position.
Letter based on company research	Your Chief Executive Officer, Ms. Paula Lipscomb, wrote in your annual report that Mayberry Medical Services was positioned for long-term success because of its quality products, outstanding employees, and commitment to excellence in customer service. I share those values and would like to be one of your outstanding employees.

Specify the type of job you seek. It is easy to specify the type of job you want when you are responding to a job announcement. It is more challenging if you are applying to an organization that has many jobs open or where you do not know if a job is available.

Specifying the type of job you want tells the reader that you have analyzed your qualifications, know what you can do well, and know what you like to do. A letter asking about "any job for which I may be qualified" makes a poor impression. It implies that you are desperate to get a job and will take anything. It also gives the impression that you do not know what you are qualified to do.

Highlight your major qualifications and strengths. Feature your greatest strengths and best selling points in this section. Show how they match the job requirements. Write in an action-oriented style. Most employers look for results-oriented employees. Therefore, use a style that conveys that you are accustomed to achieving excellent results. Make the point not just that you are qualified but that you are qualified for this specific job.

Refer to the résumé that you will enclose. The résumé provides, in a factual style, information that is more detailed than can be presented in a letter. A simple reference to the résumé is all that is necessary. An effective approach is to make a statement about the résumé or to refer to specific information in the résumé. Simply telling an employer that a résumé is enclosed is not as effective.

Request an interview. Obtaining an interview is the purpose of writing the letter. Therefore, request an interview in a positive, confident manner. Imply self-confidence by tactfully asking **when** the person would like to interview you, rather than **if** the person would like to interview you. Another option is to indicate that you will follow up with a telephone call to schedule an interview and to provide additional information that may be needed.

Guides for the Application Letter
- Use personal letterhead stationery. Never use company letterhead to apply for another job.
- Include all contact information in the letterhead to save space in your letter.
- Proofread your letter carefully. Errors may jeopardize your chance to obtain an interview.
- Use the letter to showcase your communication skills and your attention to details.
- Make your letter as nearly perfect as you can.
- Write the letter to transmit the résumé and set the tone for reading it.
- Use the same font and type of paper that you did for your résumé.
- Print your letter on a high-quality printer.

Figure 9-4 on page 246 illustrates an application letter.

FOLLOW-UP COMMUNICATIONS

The job application process includes several types of follow-up letters.

Thank-You Letters
Good manners dictate that you should write a thank-you letter very soon after an interview. Most people do not write thank-you letters after an interview, so if you do, you will create a good impression. The thank-you letter can be a powerful tool because you know more about the job once you have been interviewed. You can reinforce your strengths and show specifically how they match the job requirements. The guides you used in Chapter 8 for planning and writing thank-you letters work well for thank-you letters after interviews.

1. Begin with a warm, sincere thank-you.
2. Reaffirm your interest in the position.
3. Point out several specific things that were of interest or that matched your strengths.
4. Close with a confident and optimistic outlook.

Figure 9-5 on page 247 illustrates a thank-you letter.

Requests for References

Both good strategy and good manners dictate that you ask people if they are willing to provide you with a reference before you give their contact information to a prospective employer. Select individuals who you are confident will provide a strong, positive recommendation.

If you have a current relationship with the individual, either a telephone call or a visit may be the best medium. If you have not had contact with references such as former instructors or employers in some time, a letter may work best. Use this strategy to write letters requesting a reference:

1. Introduce yourself.
2. Make the request.
3. Tactfully present information about the classes or work you did for the person, if appropriate.
4. Suggest that you will call to confirm the individual's willingness to serve as a reference.

If your name has changed, make sure to provide the name you used when you were employed or were enrolled in classes. The person may wish to check your record before talking with you.

If the person hesitates to serve as a reference, leave him or her off your list. Most people will tell you directly if they are going to give you a good reference.

Requests for Transcripts or Work Records

Requests for transcripts or work records must be in writing. Many educational institutions charge for these documents. You can call or visit their Web sites to determine the cost. The guidelines you learned for writing neutral messages in Chapter 3 apply to these types of requests:

1. Make your request in the first sentence or paragraph.
2. Present details and less important information next.
3. Close with a positive, friendly paragraph designed to build goodwill.

Letters to Accept or Decline a Job Offer

Most companies require written acceptance of a job offer. To write a letter of acceptance, use the same basic good-news strategy that you learned in Chapter 3:

1. Express your delight in accepting the position.
2. Confirm the specific details, such as salary and the starting date for the job.
3. End on a friendly, optimistic note.

Writing to decline a job offer is more challenging. Always decline a position gracefully. In the future, the company that you are rejecting may become a customer or may offer you a different position that you would like to have. To write a letter declining a job offer, use the same basic bad-news strategy that you learned in Chapter 4:

1. Begin with a buffer to soften the bad news.
2. Present the reasons tactfully.
3. Decline gently.
4. End on a friendly note thanking the employer for considering you.

Success Tip

Even if you get rejection letters from 99 out of 100 employers, your search is 100 percent successful if you get one acceptance letter offering you a job that truly meets your career objective.

Figure 9-4: Application Letter

Jordan C. Turner
2498 South Boulevard   Charlotte, NC 28203-5010
(704) 555-0176   jordan.turner@nair.net

Current date

Ms. Rita M. Devarez
Manager, Human Resources
Tryon Medical Technology, Inc.
2974 W. Trade Street
Charlotte, NC 28208-3251

Dear Ms. Devarez

Your advertisement in the *Medical Management Monthly* specifies that only applicants with leadership ability, technical competence, and a proven track record in medical sales should apply for the position you have available for a sales manager. I can demonstrate that I possess those three qualities. Therefore, please consider me an applicant for the position.

Management development training and my experience as a senior account manager and team leader enabled me to develop the leadership skills you desire. I attribute my successful sales record to technical competence and to my ability to communicate technical information effectively to nontechnical decision makers and users. The enclosed résumé presents additional information showing you why I believe I am qualified to be a sales manager for Tryon Medical Technology.

May I come in and tell you about the plan I used to turn a sales territory that was below budget for three years into a territory that exceeded my sales budget and met President's Club (top 5 percent performers) requirements every single quarter? You will be convinced, I am confident, that I can be equally successful as a sales manager for Tryon Medical Technology, Inc. Please let me know the date and time that would be most convenient for an interview.

Sincerely

Jordan C. Turner

Enclosure

Establishes a point of contact.

Specifies the job sought.

Highlights major qualifications and strengths.

Refers to the enclosed résumé.

Requests an interview.

Figure 9-5: Thank-You Letter

Carolyn R. Sullivan
1728 Senate Street ▪ Columbia, SC 29201-3817 ▪ (803) 555-0186
Fax (803) 555-0149 ▪ crsullivan@roxlink.net

Current date

Ms. Kimberly H. McElwee
McElwee Communications
1297 Heyward Street
Columbia, SC 29201-4565

Dear Ms. McElwee

Extends a sincere thank-you.

Thank you very much for the opportunity to talk with you about a position as a marketing associate with McElwee Communications. You were extremely helpful in providing information about this exciting position, and I am now even more interested in it.

Confirms interest in the job.

Points out specific things of interest.

I especially enjoyed having lunch with several members of the sports marketing team. They were very complimentary of the organization, their colleagues, and the team environment. They also seem to enjoy working as a team. I would like to be a part of that team. My most enjoyable and successful projects at the University were team projects that encouraged creativity.

Shows how strengths match the job.

Please let me hear from you soon. I hope you will give me the opportunity to demonstrate that I can be an effective team member and marketer for McElwee Communications.

Closes with a confident and optimistic outlook.

Sincerely

Carolyn R. Sullivan

! Points to Remember

About Employment Communications

☑ Having a good employment strategy is essential. A well-planned, thorough job search is much more likely to produce good results than a disorganized, half-hearted effort.

☑ As a job seeker, you should determine your interests, strengths, and weaknesses; what you want to do; the types of jobs you are qualified for; the kind of work environment you prefer; and where and how you will find a job.

☑ Networking is one of the best ways to find out about jobs on the hidden job market.

☑ Understand and use technology effectively in your job search.

☑ The Internet has extensive information about the employment process. Use it especially to research companies before applying for a job.

☑ A résumé is a summary of your education, qualifications, and work experience.

☑ Many companies scan résumés. Therefore, you should learn how to prepare a scannable résumé.

☑ A chronological résumé works best for individuals who have a record of successful work experience over a number of years.

☑ A functional résumé works best for individuals who have limited work experience or who are changing careers.

☑ The information you choose to present in a résumé and the way you organize it should be designed to showcase your strengths.

☑ The goal of an application letter is to persuade the employer to interview you.

☑ A good strategy for writing an application letter is to establish a point of contact, specify the type of job you seek, highlight your major qualifications and strengths and show how they match job requirements, refer to your résumé, and request an interview.

☑ Always write a thank-you letter after an interview. Use it to reinforce your strengths and show how they match the job requirements.

☑ Select references who will give you a good recommendation, and request their permission before providing their names.

☑ Use the good-news strategy to accept job offers. Use the bad-news strategy to decline job offers, and do so gracefully.

Review Guide 7—Use Concrete Language

Review Guide 7 of Chapter 2 on pages 38–39. Then read the following sentences and paragraphs and interpret the general language from your perspective. Rewrite the sentences and paragraphs, substituting what you believe to be appropriate specific language.

1. I have a good educational background and a lot of experience as a sales representative.

2. Our research showed that preparing to be a doctor takes a long time, but most doctors make a lot of money.

3. John's résumé and application letter were very long, but his interview was very short.

4. I used the Internet to research a lot of companies and only found a few that provided long descriptions for job openings.

5. A number of my classmates and I drove a long distance to participate in a Career Day sponsored by several colleges. Lots of companies had information booths, and many students attended.

Editing and Language Arts Checkpoint

1. Carefully read the document that follows; it is packed with errors. Use proofreaders' marks to mark all errors in grammar, spelling, usage, word choice, capitalization, punctuation, and keying. If you need help with proofreaders' marks, refer to the table on page 53.

2. Access *File 9B* in the Chapter 9 folder on your student data disk and make the corrections. If you are not working with the data disk, key the document, making the corrections as you key. You may use online reference tools just as you would on the job.

3. Format the document as an application letter to Mr. David Lin. Use the date of June 2, 2004. Save as *9Bsi*.

Ms Gina Spivey head librarian at the Conimicut branch

indicated you may have a position open for an asistant Webmaster.

she suggested that i contact you about that position.

Maintaining and updating the fine Web sight of the Warwick

Free Libary will require a individual with creativity skills in

advanced Web page design and HTML codeing, and a strong

background in programing. As a senior at narragansett high

school I have competed classes in all them subjects with high

distinction. Through our career center I am enrolled in

Narragansett Technical Institute's Web Page Design certificate

program. In this program I interned for 4 months with the award

winning company Makeda Web design. Their, I utilized my skills to crate web sites for Real Estate, Consulting Restaurant, and Insurance businesses

Last year I worked with the principle and computer instructors to estabish the Narragansett High School Web cite, which I maintain as a part time job. The enclosed résumé describes my article about the sight, *Designing the Future: Developing You're School Web Site* which apeared on the november issue of the national magazine "Internet School." For the previous to years I worked as a part time Circulation Assistant at the Conimicut branch. I recieved excellent job evaluations and spent much off my time updateing the branch web page.

I will call next week to to provide any additional information which you may need and to see if I may schedule a interview.

Very truely yours/Karen Brown

Writing Employment Messages

In this application, you will write various types of employment messages. Format letters and résumés as shown on pages 47–48 and 237–238. For letters, use the personal letterhead that you created in Chapter 5, Application 5C10. Use the current date, and supply an appropriate salutation and complimentary close. All documents are from you. Use Activities 1–4 as part of a self-analysis before preparing your résumé in Activity 5.

Your instructor may ask you to use the guide on page 256 for evaluating your documents. Your instructor may also use this form to evaluate your work.

1. Think about your qualifications and the type of job you are preparing for and would like to have. Write a paragraph listing and describing your strengths.

2. Write a paragraph listing and describing your weaknesses.

3. Think about the type of work environment you would like. Consider factors such as small company versus a large company, outdoor job versus a desk job, working alone or being part of a team, and geographical area. Then write a paragraph describing the type of work environment you prefer.

4. Use the information from the previous three activities to write a paragraph describing a type of job you would like to have and for which you are qualified.

5. Prepare a scannable résumé for the job you just described in Activity 4 above. Use your own factual information and the information you gleaned from your self-analysis. Include a summary of qualifications. Save as *9C5si*.

6. Read the following job announcements. Select the job that you are best qualified for and in which you are most interested. Customize your résumé for this position. Save as *9C6si*.

Office Assistant

Great opportunity for person with excellent computer and communication skills. Knowledge of word processing and spreadsheet software required; knowledge of other software applications desired. Need initiative, good organizational skills, and ability to work without close supervision. Send letter and résumé to Elaine C. Anderson, General Manager, Charpentier Construction Company, P.O. Box 1258, your city, state, and ZIP Code.

Management Trainee

Excellent opportunity for a bright person with limited experience. Six-month training program leading to a management position. Opportunity for future advancement in different functional areas including management, marketing, finance, operations, customer service, computer services, and production. Must have leadership skills, interpersonal skills, communication skills, and a good work ethic. Business background preferred but not required. Send letter and résumé to Theresa A. Hartwell, Manager, Human Resources, Hartwell Enterprises, P.O. Box 4296, your city, state, and ZIP Code.

Sales Representative

Leading technology firm looking for confident, aggressive sales representatives who have excellent communication and interpersonal skills. Positions available for both individuals with sales experience and individuals who do not have experience but are fast learners. Excellent training programs provided for all employees. Business background preferred but not required. Salary plus commission. Great opportunity for high earnings for successful sales representatives. Some travel required. Send letter and résumé to Joseph C. Markswell, Markswell Pharmaceuticals, P.O. Box 4857, your city, state, and ZIP Code.

7. Write an application letter for the position you selected in Activity 6. Save as *9C7si*.

8. You want to prepare a list of references to take to an interview. Select a former instructor or employer and write a letter asking that person for permission to use him or her as a reference in your job search. Save as *9C8si*.

9. You were granted an interview for the job you applied for in Activity 6. You interviewed with the person listed in the job announcement and with Ms. Charlene Martin, the person to whom this position reports. Both individuals were very nice and provided extensive information about the position, the work expectations, and the benefits. Other employees in similar positions took you to lunch. You were very impressed with the position, the company, and the employees. You would like to have this job. Write a thank-you letter to the person listed in the announcement. Save as *9C9si*.

10. You received a letter from Ms. Charlene Martin offering you the position. You will report to work one month from today. You will spend the first week getting oriented to the company, and then you will participate in a training program. The salary was specified, and it was acceptable. Write a letter accepting the job. Confirm the salary and the beginning date. Use a salary that you believe is appropriate for the job and for your qualifications. You are pleased with the job offer and are very excited about getting started. Save as *9C10si*.

11. Work with two classmates on the following team project: Select a career or industry (such as banking or sales) in which all members of the team would enjoy working. Have each member of the team use the Internet to research a different company in the industry. Compare the types of information that each of you found. Make a team presentation to your class on using the Internet in a job search to gather company information.

Team Activity

Internet Activity

Application 9C: Guide for Evaluating Your Résumés and Letters

Name: _____

Factors to Consider	Points	9C5		9C6		9C7		9C8		9C9		9C10	
		SE	IE	SE	IE	SE	IE	SE	IE	SE	IE	SE	IE
Self-evaluation (SE), Instructor evaluation (IE)													
Strategy—uses an appropriate style for résumés and letters	2												
Strategy—uses an appropriate organizational approach	2												
Strategy—scannable and uses keywords and action-oriented words when appropriate	2												
Writing Guide 1—evidence of good planning; organized	1												
Writing Guide 2—meets the reader's needs; courteous	1												
Writing Guide 3—uses positive language	1												
Writing Guide 4—uses a clear, easy-to-read style	1												
Writing Guide 5—complete; includes all needed information	1												
Writing Guide 6—uses an efficient, action-oriented style	1												
Writing Guide 7—uses specific, concrete language	1												
Writing Guide 8—uses effective sentence and paragraph structure	1												
Writing Guide 9—uses correct format and attractive placement	1												
Writing Guide 10—has been edited and proofread; no errors	1												
Overall assessment of document	4												
Totals	20												

Mastery Check for Chapter 9

1. Describe ways to find out about jobs on the hidden job market.

2. What is an applicant tracking system?

3. How does a chronological résumé differ from a functional résumé, and how should you decide which to use?

4. Describe the writing strategy that should be used for a job application letter.

5. Write complete sentences using the following terms.

Scannable

Customize

Sans serif

Case Study

Shell Cove—Corporate Headquarters

You began your Management Training Program in corporate headquarters as an assistant to Ms. Jane Cargile, senior vice president of human resources. You successfully completed your rotation through all seven divisions and have now returned to corporate headquarters. You are ready for a permanent position at Shell Cove.

Shell Cove has created a new position in each division. The position is titled director of communications and reports to the director of the division. You and the six other participants in your training program are assured one of these positions if you apply for it. You would be responsible for all promotional materials developed by the division. Customer service for the division would also report to you.

The seven directors will be assigned to a special team known as the Corporate Communications Team for Shell Cove. This team will be responsible for maintaining and enhancing the Shell Cove brand within all divisions. One of the seven directors will be named the team leader.

You are excited about this opportunity and would like to be named team leader as well. You know that it is not appropriate to bring up the team leader position before you are named as director of communications in one of the divisions. However, you are determined to showcase your written communications skills and your leadership ability in the application process. You will put together a portfolio of communications that you have prepared at Shell Cove to submit with your application.

Job 1: Update Your Résumé for Shell Cove

Using the résumé you prepared in Application 9C5, create a customized résumé for Shell Cove. The résumé should reflect your experience in each of Shell Cove's divisions. Save as *9E1si*.

Job 2: Write an Application Letter

Write Jane Cargile applying for the position of director of communications in the division of your choice. Jane will solicit input from each division director about all trainees. Then she and a team of two other corporate officers will make the final assignments. Showcase your communication skills, creativity, leadership ability, and other strengths. Refer to both your résumé and the portfolio you are enclosing (see Job 3). Save as *9E2si*.

Job 3: Prepare a Portfolio and Portfolio Analysis

Select five communications that you prepared during your training program, each from a different division. Choose documents that focus on the strengths you wish to highlight. Include at least two documents that you completed in a team to showcase your leadership abilities. Determine an attractive and professional way to present this portfolio of communications; in a folder, for example.

259

Prepare a document to accompany your portfolio entitled *Portfolio Analysis.* Use standard report format. Write a paragraph indicating that you have analyzed the documents you prepared during your training program and that this portfolio contains five of them that you believe are examples of your best work. List each document and the division in which it was prepared. Explain why you selected it and what it accomplished. Save as *9E3si.*

APPENDIX A

ADDRESS DIRECTORY

Title	First Name	MI	Last Name	Professional Title	Organization Name	Address	City	State	Postal Code
					Best Grills, Inc.	500 South Front Street	Memphis	TN	38103-4433
Ms.	Karen		Brown			278 Post Road	Warwick	RI	02888-1518
Dr.	Alex		Bryant	Athletics Director	Westfield University	6752 Bradley Avenue	St. Louis	MO	63139-2235
					Central Technical College	775 Harmon Road	Hopkins	SC	29061-8624
Dr.	Peter		Chang	MBA Program	Meetze School of Business	Kerry University	Schaumburg	IL	60173-3827
Ms.	Emma		Garrison			514 Smith Street	Providence	RI	02908-4308
					The Hess Center	1493 Stemmons Avenue	Dallas	TX	75208-2301
Mr.	Roger		Johns			5239 S. Lawton Avenue	Tulsa	OK	74107-9404
Mr.	Bradley	E.	Jones			Two Calvert Street	Baltimore	MD	21225-1747
Mr.	David		Lin	Director	Warwick Free Library	26 Kilvert Street	Warwick	RI	02888-1518
Mr.	Jonathan		Logan		Logan Containers, Inc.	400 N. Lamar Boulevard	Oxford	MS	38655-3204
Mr.	Ralph	E.	Marino	President	Marino Office Systems	954 N. Jackson Street	Magnolia	AR	71753-2446
Mr.	Roger		Meekins		Meekins and Meekins	1537 Toms Creek Road	Hopkins	SC	29601-8556
	Jose		Mendoza	M.D.	Canyon Medical Associates, PA	5842 W. Overland Road	Boise	ID	83705-3009
					Midlands Appliance, Inc.	78 Piedmont Street	Providence	RI	02909-1042
Ms.	Vivian		Naufield	Chief Executive Officer	SteelGate Manufacturing	842 Washington Road	Pittsburgh	PA	15228-2007
Mr.	Taku		Patel		Custom Construction Software	1328 Washington Avenue	St. Louis	MO	63103-1919
					Pathmark Construction	5498 Western Avenue	Little Rock	AR	72209-1956
					Peerman Industries, Inc.	1464 Perri Drive	Pittsburgh	PA	15226-2519
					Prospect Business College	621 E. Main Street	Magnolia	AR	71753-3728
Ms.	Theresa		Ramos	Benefits Manager	Inner Harbor Investments	101 W. Fayette Street	Baltimore	MD	21201-3703
					Rosselot Fitness Solutions	105 S. Calvert Street	Baltimore	MD	21202-3200
					Southwestern State University	1836 Highland Road	Dallas	TX	75228-6234
Mr.	Ryan		Sparks	Marketing Manager	Palm Atlantic Airlines	1720 East Higgins Road	Schaumburg	IL	60173-5114
					Sterling Technical College	416 W. First Street	Duluth	MN	55802-1516
Ms.	Mary		Turnquist	President	Turnquist and Associates	3206 Midway Road	Duluth	MN	55810-9549
					USA Youth Soccer	900 S. Washington Avenue	Columbus	OH	43206-2350
					VanHuss Associates, Inc.	6974 Garners Ferry Road	Columbia	SC	29209-2101
Mr.	J.	T.	Wang			9156 W. Fairview Avenue	Boise	ID	83704-8220

APPENDIX B

SHELL COVE ADDRESS DIRECTORY

Title	First Name	MI	Last Name	Professional Title	Organization Name	Address	City	State	Postal Code
Ms.	Isabella		Cabrera	President	Marbex Corporation	1798 Olive Drive	Aberdeen	SC	57401-1138
Mr.	Robert	L.	Cash		Ocean City Resort Investors, Inc.	9935 Stephen Decatur Highway	Ocean City	MD	21842-9579
Ms.	Marissa		Layden		Layden Properties	258 Walnut Street	Philadelphia	PA	19106-3943
Mr.	Lee		Moore	General Manager	Greg's Custom Golf Equipment	3159 N. Calvert Street	Baltimore	MD	21218-3807
Dr.	Donna	I.	Palms	President	Atlantic Coast University	12800 Coastal Highway	Ocean City	MD	21842-4717
Mr.	James	S.	Wilson			2598 Monument Avenue	Richmond	VA	23220-2619

EDITING AND LANGUAGE ARTS CHECKPOINT GUIDES

CAPITALIZATION	
Item	**Description**
C.1	Capitalize proper nouns (the names of particular persons, places, or things) and the pronoun *I*. Do not capitalize common nouns (nouns that do not refer to particular persons, places, or things).
C.2	Capitalize the first word of a sentence. Also capitalize the first word of a complete sentence in quotation marks.
C.3	Capitalize days of the week, months of the year, holidays, periods of history, and historic events (*World War II, the Middle Ages*).
C.4	Capitalize titles before a name (*Deputy Director Smith*). Do not capitalize job titles that stand alone or that follow a name unless the organization does so or they are titles of high distinction.
C.5	Capitalize common names of departments, boards, committees, or divisions within the writer's organization (*Sales Department, Board of Directors*). Do not capitalize them when they refer to another organization.
C.6	Capitalize specific geographic areas; do not capitalize compass directions or general locations (*Midwest, the South, northwest of town*).
C.7	Capitalize the first and main words in titles of literary and artistic works, such as books, magazines, movies, and plays. Do not capitalize words of fewer than four letters that are conjunctions, prepositions, or articles.
C.8	Capitalize nouns that precede numbers and letters except page, paragraph, and line references (*Room A, Section 2, page 2, paragraph 3, line 2*).

GRAMMAR

Subjects/Verbs	
Item	**Description**
G.1-1	Use complete sentences: sentences with both a subject and a verb that express a complete thought.
G.1-2	Ensure that subjects and verbs agree in person and number.
G.1-3	Use the appropriate tense of a verb to express time.
G.1-4	Correct dangling modifiers (words, phrases, or clauses that describe, limit, or qualify) that are supposed to modify the subject of a sentence but do not.

Pronouns	
G.2-1	Ensure that a pronoun agrees with its antecedent (the word or words for which the pronoun stands) in person, number, and gender.
G.2-2	• Use the **nominative case** (*I, we, you, he, she, it, they*) when the pronoun serves as the subject of the sentence or as a predicate pronoun (a pronoun used after a verb that refers to the same person or thing as the subject of the verb—*The doctor is she*). • Use the **objective case** (*me, us, you, him, her, it, them*) when the pronoun serves as a direct or indirect object. • Use the **possessive case** (*my, mine, your, yours, his, her, hers, our, ours, their, theirs*) when the pronoun shows possession, or ownership.
G.2-3	*Who* and *whom* are often confused. *Who* is used as the subject of a verb or as a predicate pronoun. *Whom* is used as the object of a verb or preposition. If you can substitute *I, he, she, we,* or *they, who* is correct. If you can substitute *me, her, him, us,* or *them, whom* is correct (*Who* is going? *I* am going. To *whom* did you speak? I spoke to *her.*)

Adjectives and Adverbs	
G.3-1	Use the comparative degree of an adjective (*taller, smarter, stronger*) when comparing two items. Use the superlative degree (*tallest, smartest, strongest*) when comparing three or more items.
G.3-2	Use adverbs to modify verbs, adjectives, and other adverbs.
G.3-3	Use the comparative degree of an adverb (*more, less*) when comparing two items. Use the superlative degree (*most, least*) when comparing three or more items.

Conjunctions and Prepositions	
G.4-1	Use coordinating conjunctions (*and, but, or, nor,* and *yet*) to link sentence parts of equal rank. Use correlative conjunctions (*either/or, both/and, neither/nor, not only/but* or *but also, whether/or*) in pairs.
G.4-2	Choose the correct preposition to show the relationship between a noun or pronoun and other words in a sentence. Do not leave out a preposition when it is needed.

NUMBER USAGE	
General	
Item	**Description**
N.1-1	Use words for numbers one through ten unless the numbers are in a related category with numbers above ten (*The 2 doctors and 9 nurses saw 18 patients in four hours*). Use numerals for numbers larger than ten.
N.1-2	Spell out numbers that begin sentences.
N.1-3	Use words for approximate numbers or large round numbers that can be expressed in one or two words. Use numerals for round numbers in millions or higher with their word modifier (*$5 million*).
N.1-4	When two numbers are adjacent, use figures for the larger number (*We mailed four 5-pound boxes*).
Times and Dates	
N.2-1	Use figures with *a.m.* and *p.m.*; use words with *o'clock*.
N.2-2	Use figures for days when they follow the month; use ordinals (*5th, 2nd, 1st*) only when the day precedes the month or is used alone (8th *of May; the 22d*).
Percentages, Fractions, Money, and Measurements	
N.3-1	Use figures with percentages, and spell out the word *percent*, except in statistical copy.
N.3-2	Use figures for money amounts, except for approximate amounts (but see N.1-3) and amounts under a dollar (*79 cents*). In ranges of numbers, include a dollar sign and a word, if appropriate, with each figure (*$5 billion to $10 billion*, not *$5 to 10 billion*).
N.3-3	Do not add zeros to even sums of money, like $25.
N.3-4	Spell out fractions, except when they appear in combination with whole numbers (*two-thirds; $5\frac{1}{2}$*).
N.3-5	Use figures for units of measure and with symbols (*5 cm; 71°F*), except for occasional uses where the exact number is not important (*I must have walked five miles*).
Addresses	
N.4-1	Use words for street names *First* through *Tenth* and figures for street names above *Tenth* (*Second Avenue; 14th Street*).
N.4-2	Use figures for highways.
N.4-3	Use figures for house numbers and post office boxes except for the number *one* (*One Lytle Place; 16 Overlook Avenue*).

PUNCTUATION AND ITALICS	
Comma	
Item	**Description**
P.1-1	Use a comma to set off introductory words, long introductory phrases, and introductory dependent clauses.
P.1-2	Use a comma to set off independent clauses joined by a coordinating conjunction (*and, but, or, nor, yet*). You may omit the comma in very short sentences. Do not use a comma to separate the parts of a compound verb.
P.1-3	Use commas to separate three or more items in a series (the comma before the conjunction is optional).
P.1-4	Use a comma to set off interrupting or nonessential elements—words, phrases, and clauses that can be removed from a sentence without affecting its structure or meaning. Do not use a comma with essential elements.
P.1-5	*Which* is used to introduce nonessential phrases and clauses and is preceded by a comma. *That* is used to introduce essential phrases and clauses and is not preceded by a comma.
P.1-6	Use commas to set off appositives and words of direct address (*Jerry, our district representative, will call shortly; Petra, this order is very important*).
P.1-7	Use a comma to separate a day from a date, a date from a year, and a city from a state (*Tuesday, June 6, 1944; Birmingham, Alabama*).
P.1-8	Use a comma to set off a quotation from the rest of the sentence (*Cora said, "Meet me at school." "I'll drive," Thomas replied*). Do not use a comma if the sentence flows smoothly without it (*Every car "will be sold at a discount of at least 20 percent"*).
P.1-9	Use a comma to set off contrasting and transitional expressions (*I might buy it, but not at that price; As a result, we got the contract*).
P.1-10	Use a comma to set off two or more parallel adjectives (adjectives that could be separated by *and* instead of a comma).
Colon and Semicolon	
P.2-1	Use a colon to introduce enumerations and lists.
P.2-2	Use a semicolon (not a comma) to separate independent clauses that are not linked by a coordinating conjunction (*and, but, or, nor,* or *yet*).
P.2-3	Use a semicolon to separate independent clauses that are linked by a conjunctive adverb or transitional expression (such as *however, therefore,* or *on the contrary*).
P.2-4	Use semicolons to separate items in a series when the items contain commas, unless the meaning is clear without the semicolons.

PUNCTUATION AND ITALICS *(continued)*	
Period and Question Mark	
Item	**Description**
P.3-1	Use a period after a declarative sentence (a statement of fact), an imperative sentence (a command), an indirect question, or a courteous request.
P.3-2	Use a period after an initial and after most abbreviations (*K. C. Smith, Mrs., p.m.*). Many acronyms (*CEO, SEC*) do not use periods.
P.3-3	Use a question mark after a direct question or a series of questions.
Apostrophe and Hyphen	
P.4-1	Use *apostrophe + s* to form the possessive of singular nouns and plural nouns not ending in *s* (*dog's, Terry's, women's, daughter-in-law's*).
P.4-2	To form the possessive of plural nouns ending in *s*, add just an apostrophe (*builders', Smiths'*).
P.4-3	Do not use an apostrophe to form the plural of capital letters, acronyms, or numbers (*Cs, SUVs, 1990s*), but do use it to form the plural of lowercase letters and abbreviations (*abc's, c.o.d.'s*) or to avoid confusion (*A's, I's*).
P.4-4	Use an apostrophe in the last item in a series to show joint ownership. Add it to each individual item to show individual ownership.
P.4-5	Use an apostrophe in contractions to indicate omitted letters.
P.4-6	Use a hyphen in most compound adjectives when they come before a noun (*high-octane fuel, 30-minute, well-known fact, case-by-case analysis*). Do not use a hyphen with adverbs ending in *ly* (*extremely fast decision*).
Quotation Marks and Italics	
P.5-1	Use quotation marks to enclose the exact words of a person (a direct quotation). Do not use quotation marks for quotations of four lines or more that are set off in a separate, indented block of text.
P.5-2	Use quotation marks to set off titles that represent only part of a published work, such as chapters of a book or magazine or newspaper articles.
P.5-3	Use italics for the titles of complete works, such as books, newspapers, magazines, movies, and television series.

WORD CHOICE		
Item	**Description**	
W.1	a an	Use *a* before words beginning with a consonant sound. Use *an* before words beginning with a vowel sound.
W.2	accept except	(v.) to receive or take; to agree to (prep.) not including; (v.) to omit or exclude
W.3	advice advise	(n.) recommendation (v.) to give counsel
W.4	affect effect	(v.) to change or influence (n.) outcome or result; (v.) to cause or bring about
W.5	among between	(prep.) refers to more than two people, groups, or things (prep.) refers to two people, groups, or things
W.6	appraise apprise	(v.) to establish the value of (v.) to notify or inform
W.7	as like	(conj.) introduces a clause (prep.) followed by noun or pronoun in the objective case
W.8	assure ensure insure	(v.) to make confident; guarantee (v.) to make certain (v.) to protect against loss
W.9	cite sight site	(v.) to quote or summon (n.) vision; something worth seeing (n.) location or place, including *Web site*
W.10	complement compliment	(v.) to complete or fill (n.) a flattering comment; (v.) to praise
W.11	eminent imminent	(adj.) distinguished; famous (adj.) threatening; about to happen
W.12	good well	(adj.) skillful; admirable; having the right qualities (adv.) properly; with skill; in a kindly way
W.13	it's its	contraction of *it is* (adj.) shows ownership or possession
W.14	loose lose	(adj.) not restrained or secured (v.) to be unable to find something that one had previously
W.15	personal personnel	(adj.) private; individual (n.) staff; employees
W.16	perspective prospective	(n.) point of view (adj.) upcoming; likely to happen
W.17	precede proceed	(v.) to come before (v.) to continue; to go forward

WORD CHOICE *(continued)*		
Item	Description	
W.18	principal principle	(n.) head of school; sum of money; (adj.) main, chief (n.) basic truth; rule of conduct
W.19	stationary stationery	(adj.) fixed; not moving (n.) writing paper
W.20	than then	(conj.) shows a comparison of two items (adv.) at that time
W.21	there their they're	(usually adv.) in that place (adj.) belonging to them contraction of *they are*
W.22	to too two	(prep.) toward (adv.) also; besides (n.) a number
W.23	who's whose	contraction of *who is* (adj.) shows ownership or possession
W.24	you're your	contraction of *you are* (adj.) belonging to you

KEYING AND SPELLING ERRORS		
Item	Description	
K.1	keying errors	Letters mistakenly keyed in the wrong order (*teh* instead of *the*, for example); one word mistakenly keyed for another (*mangers* instead of *managers*); repeated words; symbols mistakenly not keyed (*10.25* instead of *$10.25*); etc.
K.2	spelling errors	Misspelled words

INDEX

271